The New American Exceptionalism

Critical American Studies Series

George Lipsitz
University of California–Santa Barbara
Series Editor

The New American Exceptionalism

Donald E. Pease

Critical American Studies Series

University of Minnesota Press
Minneapolis
London

An earlier version of chapter 1 was published as "Hiroshima, the Vietnam Veterans Memorial, and the Gulf War: A Postnational Spectacle," in *Cultures of U.S. Imperialism*, ed. Amy Kaplan and Donald E. Pease (Durham: Duke University Press, 1992). Earlier versions of chapters 3, 4, and 5 were published in issues 26, no. 3, 29, no. 2, and 30, no. 3 of the journal *boundary 2*, published by Duke University Press. Chapter 5 includes a revision of the Afterword to *Dissent from the Homeland: Essays after September 11*, ed. Stanley Hauerwas and Frank Lentricchia (Durham: Duke University Press, 2003).

Published by the University of Minnesota Press
111 Third Avenue South, Suite 290
Minneapolis, MN 55401-2520
http://www.upress.umn.edu

Library of Congress Cataloging-in-Publication Data

Pease, Donald E.
    The new American exceptionalism / Donald E. Pease.
        p.   cm. — (Critical American studies series)
    Includes bibliographical references and index.
    ISBN 978-0-8166-2782-0 (hc : alk. paper) — ISBN 978-0-8166-2783-7 (pb : alk. paper)
    1. National characteristics, American. 2. United States—Politics and government—1989– 3. United States—Foreign relations—1989–
4. United States—Civilization. I. Title.
    E169.1.P38   2009
    973—dc22   2009028990

Printed in the United States of America on acid-free paper

The University of Minnesota is an equal-opportunity educator and employer.

20 19 18 17 16 15 14 13 12 11 10   10 9 8 7 6 5 4 3 2

For Patricia McKee

Contents

Acknowledgments

Edward Said wrote that "the starting point of critical elaboration is the consciousness of what one really is, and is 'knowing thyself' as a product of the historical process to date, which has deposited in you an infinity of traces without leaving an inventory." In a seminar at Dartmouth in 1986, Said explained that these traces would continue to overshadow the present as long as we did not find the imaginative means to come to terms with them. Since everything inside us actively works against arriving at such knowledge, he added, it requires our active collaboration with fellow scholars in seminars and private conversations and public debates to discover it.

This book originated from my desire to find the terms to understand the unacknowledgeable inventory of traces that oversaw the long transition from the termination of the cold war in 1989 to the election of Barack Obama in 2008. The elaboration of that desire into this book required the imaginative insights, criticism, countermemories, and revisionist explanations of numerous friends, colleagues, and students.

Earlier versions of chapters 3, 4, and 5 first appeared in the journal *boundary 2*. Before they found their way into print, these essays passed through the ordeal of critical conversation among the members of the journal's editorial collective—Paul Bove, Bill Spanos, Daniel T. O'Hara,

Jonathan Arac, and more recently Rob Wilson. The essays I have published since 1996 ("The Tocqueville Revival," "The Patriot Acts," and "Bush's Biopolitical Settlement") were first delivered as plenary lectures at the Dartmouth Futures of American Studies Institute. The incisive public responses of the participants at those plenary sessions resulted in crucial revisions. My codirectors of the institute (Robyn Wiegman, Elizabeth Dillon, Eric Lott, and Winfried Fluck) were generous in their willingness to become interlocutors. Their reactions proved indispensable to the essays' completion.

Over the past twenty years, several of my Dartmouth colleagues took the time to read and challenge my vision. Louis Renza, Colleen Boggs, Marty Favor, Michael Chaney, Soyica Diggs Colbert, Shalene Vasquez, Ron Edsforth, and Klaus Mladek have been particularly generous with their timely attention. Dean of the Humanities Kate Conley, Dean of the Faculty Carol Folt, and Dartmouth's Provost Barry Scherr were always supportive of my scholarly ventures.

My discovery of the importance of American exceptionalism as a form of the work of state fantasy emerged from a 2006 Summer Symposium at the Master of Arts in Liberal Studies program at Dartmouth, "The Challenges of American Exceptionalism." Lauren Clarke, executive director of the program, and Ron Edsforth, chair of its globalization studies concentration, made certain that none of my assertions went uncriticized. Wole Ojurongbe, the MALS administrator, compiled a bibliography of essays for MALS students that turned every meeting into a memorable event.

Donatella Izzo, Giorgio Mariani, and Mario Corona kindly invited me to discuss my view of American exceptionalism at a workshop in Bergamo, Italy, in 2006. The book's Introduction was inspired by a seminar on American exceptionalism that I had the pleasure of codirecting with Winfried Fluck in Berlin in the fall term of 2007. The members of that seminar (Martina Benz, James Dorson, Juliane Graf, Silke Hackenesch, Markus Kienscherf, Fabian Lindner, Susann Park, Hannes Schaser, Britta Schumacher, Jasper Trautsch, and Frank Wilker) clarified my understanding of American exceptionalism immeasurably.

In July 2008, Liam Kennedy invited me to Dublin to teach portions of my completed work at a Clinton Institute in American Studies seminar. I am grateful to him and to Catherine Carey for their supportive insights.

This book would not have been possible without the support and encouragement of George Lipsitz, series editor of Critical American Studies; the infinite patience of Richard Morrison; and the painstaking critical scrutiny of Adam Brunner.

Finally, I thank Patricia McKee, who read or had read to her and who responded to every iteration of this book. Since she bears the near infinite traces of an inventory that remains unacknowledgeable in the pages that follow, she remains an infinite inspiration.

June 10, 2009
Truro, Massachusetts, and Canaan, New Hampshire

Introduction
The United States of Fantasy

The institutors of laws and the founders of civil society... Poets are
the unacknowledged legislators of the world.

—Percy Bysshe Shelley, *A Defense of Poetry*

This book is primarily concerned with the irreconcilable rifts within
U.S. political culture that opened up during the lengthy period of transition from the termination of the cold war to the inauguration of the
Global War on Terror, and with the disparate state fantasies that emerged
to organize U.S. citizens' relations to these antagonisms. While they
differ in the relations they adduce between the state and U.S. citizens,
all of these fantasies emerged at the site of the breakdown of the encompassing state of fantasy called American exceptionalism that had regulated U.S. citizens' relationship to the political order for the preceding
half century.

As I am using the term, state fantasy does not refer to a mystification
but to the dominant structure of desire out of which U.S. citizens imagined their national identity. Rather than associating fantasy with a delu-
sion that requires critique, I align my discussion of state fantasy with
Jacqueline Rose's insight "that fantasy—far from being the antagonist

of public, social, being—plays a central, constitutive role in the modern world of states and nations."[1] Jacqueline Rose began her meditation on the relationship between fantasy and the state with the observation that theories of political culture were usually constituted out of the exclusion of fantasy. One of the reasons that political theorists were (and remain) reluctant to acknowledge fantasy as a crucial dimension of political reality has to do with the belief that fantasies threaten the state of things with psychic dissolution. Political theorists excluded fantasy as an analytical category because the traits they defined fantasy as lacking—seriousness, grounding in fact, foundation in established political theory—were considered prerequisite to the theorization of political culture. But in *States of Fantasy*, Jacqueline Rose has transposed all of these disqualifying criteria into proof of the inextricable correlations between states and fantasy.

Remarking that the anomalies inherent to the modern state could be illuminated by putting them into dialogue with Freud, Rose turned to psychoanalytic theory to explain that, despite the efforts of political theorists to suppress them, the state depended upon its subjects' affective investments in fantasy for its legitimation. Rose then proposed that psychoanalytic theory supplied especially useful analytic concepts for explicating what she described as the "symptom" of modern statehood, the fact that there was something inside the very processes upholding the modern state that threatened and exceeded it.

Rose illuminated the basis for the state's dependence on fantasy with the following questions: "When and why do men obey? Upon what inner justifications and upon what external means does this domination rest?"[2] This is where fantasy comes in. The state cannot get into rationally purposive action that the individual citizen can logically explain—it can only do so in terms of the inner meaning it holds for citizens or the subjective beliefs they attach to it. A modern state may represent itself as sovereign, but in the absence of any metaphysical guarantees, this self-representation only intensified the state's need to make itself appear sovereign. Over and above its monopoly of legitimate violence, the modern state relied on fantasy for the authority that it could neither secure nor ultimately justify.

Refusing to position the concepts of state and fantasy as facing toward public and private worlds, Rose displaced the word state from its settled meaning within political discourse—as the authorized regulatory agency of a polity—and restored an alternative meaning of "state" as a psychic condition that was accompanied by a loss of authority.[3] After the "state" was reassigned these forgotten significations, Rose explained, its private and public aspects ceased to remain opposites and instead became the outer and inner faces of the state of fantasy:

> If the expression "states of fantasy" does not appear to yoke opposites together, it is because state—in thrall to fantasy—one might say, has gone over to the private side of its semantic history and shed its public face. In fact the word "state" has a psychological meaning long before its modern day sense of polity. . . . To take a relatively modern instance . . . he was *fully conscious of his state* and had high hopes of being cured in an asylum. Here "state" is almost a synonym for "insanity." Think of the expression "in a state"; it has the same feel—you never have to spell out, especially if you are the sufferer, what exactly it means. As if to be "in a state" is precisely to lose the capacity to travel with any clarity through the world of words. "States of confusion," "states of panic," "state of dissociation" . . . were "states of mind" distinguished by their passivity from other mental acts and operations in which the mind was assumed to retain a grip on itself.[4]

The decisive shift in the political fortunes of the modern state took place at the historical moment when the ruler, instead of embodying the state, served a separate constitutional and legal state that it was his duty to maintain. Once real authority was no longer vested in the person of the ruler, it disembodied itself. It was this disembodiment, Rose concluded, that rendered the state itself a fantasy. The state thereafter relied on a ghostly, fantasmatical power no reason could fully account for to enact its authority.[5]

But according to Rose, it would be wrong to deduce from this change in its historical status that the modern state is any the less real for the fact that it relies on fantasy for an authority it can neither secure nor ultimately justify. Shelley called poets "unacknowledged legislators" because he believed that only poetry could resolve the legitimation crises that resulted after the Enlightenment stripped the state of its metaphysical guarantees. Poets accomplished this resolution by exercising the sovereign power of the poetic imagination, which Shelley considered the counterpart to the sovereign will of the state.

According to Jacqueline Rose, state fantasies continue to accomplish the feats Shelley restricted to poets. If citizens are subjected to the state through their belief in the state's authority, it is state fantasy that supplies this belief. State fantasies incite an operative imagination endowed with the power to solicit the citizens' desire to believe in the reality of its productions. The state's policies get internalized through state fantasy work. State fantasies lay down the scenarios through which the state's rules and norms can be experienced as internal to the citizens' desire. Fantasy endows the state's rules and laws with the authority of the people's desire for them. Fantasy does so by investing the state's rules with the desire through which the state's subjects imagine themselves to be the authors of these rules and laws as well as their recipients. The state's subjects' capacity to recognize a series of events as belonging to the same symbolic order also requires the guidance and supervision of state fantasies. These fantasies align the people's beliefs with the regulative discourse through which the state is empowered to bring the chaos of political events into order.

State fantasies have played these constitutive roles within U.S. political culture, I would add, by inciting within the citizens who take them up the desire to organize their identities out of the political antagonisms within U.S. national culture. To accomplish this cultural work, the core elements of these state fantasies must find empirical validation in everyday life. But the chief test of a state fantasy concerns its ability to supply the relationship with the national order that U.S. citizens want to have. Successfully produced state fantasies effect that relationship by inducing citizens to want the national order they already have. The legislative dimension of these fantasies does not refer to their capacity to entice U.S. citizens to establish imaginary relations to the real state of things. This operative component of state fantasy involves obtaining U.S. citizens' acquiescence to the processes whereby the state superimposes the legal identities through which it seeks to manage the everyday practices and the self-representations of its citizens.

Following the termination of the cold war in 1989, U.S. presidents and legislators have introduced four separate compacts with U.S. citizens—President George Herbert Walker Bush's "New World Order," President William Jefferson Clinton's "New Covenant with America," Newt Gingrich's "Contract with America," and President George W. Bush's "Homeland Security State"—to replace the cold war settlement. These legislators either inaugurated or consolidated their compacts as a response to traumatic events—the Persian Gulf War, the conflagration of the Branch Davidian Compound in Waco, the destruction of the Alfred P. Murrah Federal Building in Oklahoma City, the attacks on the World Trade Center and the Pentagon on September 11, 2001—where a radical discontinuity distinguished between what came before these catastrophes happened and what would follow in their wake. While the state was directly responsible for the production of the first two events, the state exploited the Oklahoma City bombing and September 11, 2001, for state fantasy-work.

As events that could not be incorporated within the normal order of things, these national traumas demarcated the sites at which alternatives to it became at once imaginable and desirable. A state fantasy successfully takes hold when it transposes these sites of trauma into the inaugural spaces within a newly configured order. While the fantasy is not reducible to the explicit terms laid out in a national compact, the fantasy nonetheless supplies the scenarios that are prerequisite to U.S. citizens' interiorizing the state's rules and norms. It was the state mode of staging the fantasy of a liberal multiculture rather than say Bill Clinton's inauguration of what he called a New Covenant with America that produced the desire within U.S. citizens to take up positions within the reconfigured state of things, and it was this fantasy as well that made that alternative order at once imaginable and desirable. The framing discourse that regulated the interpretive orientation of the newly configured order was part of the fantasy.

Myths normally do the work of incorporating events into recognizable national narratives. But traumatic events precipitate states of emergency that become the inaugural moments in a different symbolic order and take place on a scale that exceeds the grasp of the available representations from the national mythology. Before a national myth can narrate events of this magnitude, the state fantasy that supplies the horizon of expectations orienting their significance must have already become symbolically effective. At moments of decisive historical transition, like the one that emerged at the conclusion to the cold war, the official national mythology could no longer incorporate these traumatic events into the narrative logic of an unfolding teleology. That teleology had come to an end and the mythology for a newly configured order had not yet been invented.

I have described state fantasies as *legislators* because they occupy the site in between the supplanted and the emergent state of things and enable the citizens who take these fantasies up to interiorize the state's newly forged contractual terms. I have described these fantasies as *unacknowledged* legislators for two intertwined reasons. These fantasies assume the legislating power of legitimation and they take the place of an explicit contractual negotiation between the state and the people. Moreover, the legislation—in the sense of the reconfigured social arrangements that they put into place—is founded upon norms and rationalities that these fantasies deny explicit recognition. As *unacknowledged legislators*, these state fantasies produce the national subjects who want the state to govern them.[6]

It is only after they get linked to the legal fictions of the newly forged administrative rationalities that these state fantasies actually perform the work of unacknowledged legislators. Rather than explaining the significance of these legal fictions or defending the reconfigured order of things, these fantasies enable the citizens who take them up to structure their desires within the terms of the fantasy. A state fantasy should not be construed as a specific, restricted instrument of governance. It sustains the continued symbolic efficacy of the entire order it legislates. A state fantasy becomes symbolically effective when it produces a relation with the order it legislates that makes it seem an enactment of the will of the individual national subject rather than an imposition of the state.

Legislation in the dual sense of the legitimation and the naturalization of the order of things is an ongoing outcome of state fantasy. States depend upon the symbolic efficacy of state fantasy for these dual processes of legislation to achieve their effects. Unlike laws, state fantasies regulate the symbolic order by organizing U.S. citizens' relationship to its inherent rifts and contradictions as if they were sources of personal enjoyment rather than pain or resentment.

When a state fantasy's structures of disavowal are either suspended or, in the case of the cold war, discontinued, what remained unacknowledged under the aegis of the state fantasy demands acknowledgment. When the social substance of what these state fantasies had disavowed suddenly emerged into the post–cold war political field, it assumed the form of adjudicable social wrongs that demanded legal and political redress. For example, after the structures of disavowal through which the state fantasy of exceptionalism had justified Jim Crow, the Indian

Removal Act, Operation Wetback, and Japanese internment camps (to
name but four examples of the legislation that the cold war state fantasy had disallowed adequate juridical recognition) were suspended,
disparate groups within academic and political culture represented these
historical facts as national "wrongs" that demanded redress.[7]
Since these shameful events were always part of the national history,
why did they become so vividly evident around the time of the termination of the cold war? What is more to the point of this discussion,
what was the nature of the state fantasy that managed to disavow the
injustice of these acts of legislation? How did this state fantasy manage
to keep these structures of disavowal in place for as long as it did? Given
its remarkable longevity, what brought about the termination of this
state of fantasy? And why should U.S. citizens' relationship with the
state be described as a state fantasy rather than a national fantasy?

In what follows, I shall attempt to address each of these questions in
an account that I hope will also explain my rationale for the selection
of the state fantasies at work in the chapters that follow. I'll begin this
account with an explanation of the role American exceptionalism played
as the encompassing fantasy of the cold war state.

A Brief Critical Genealogy of the Fantasy of American Exceptionalism

American exceptionalism is the name of the much-coveted form of
nationality that provided U.S. citizens with a representative form of self-
recognition across the history of the cold war. As a discourse, American
exceptionalism includes a complex assemblage of theological and secular assumptions out of which Americans have developed the lasting
belief in America as the fulfillment of the national ideal to which other
nations aspire. Although its specific attributes were conceptualized differently at different moments of the cold war, American exceptionalism was commonly believed to have originated in the sixteenth century
when North America's first white settlers brought a belief in America
as the fulfillment of European dreams for a fresh start along with them.

Throughout the cold war, American exceptionalism supplied a prerequisite horizon of intelligibility for the understanding of American
events. Despite its standing as an invariant belief, however, accounts of
the discourse's content have changed with historical circumstances. Some

have described America's exceptional historical role as the result of its
distinctive geopolitical positioning. The Atlantic and Pacific Oceans
and a middle class ethos separated America from what Thomas Jefferson called "the exterminating havoc" of the other three quarters of the
globe. Others have explained that the fact that America was spared the
cataclysmic disasters that plagued Europe over the last two centuries resulted from the nation-state's exemption from history.[8]

The *American* dimension of American exceptionalism has undergone
decisive shifts in its self-representation—from the City on the Hill in
the sixteenth century to the Conqueror of the World's Markets in the
twentieth century. But the conviction concerning America's exceptional
status nevertheless sustained the sense of continuity in the nation's geopolitical standing from 1945 to 1989. Over that period, the interpretive
assumptions embedded within this foundational term have supplied
American citizens with the images and beliefs that have regulated the
production, transmission, and maintenance of their understanding of
what it means to be an American.[9]

As a classificatory scheme, American exceptionalism has been said
to refer to clusters of absent (feudal hierarchies, class conflicts, socialist
labor party, trade unionism, and divisive ideological passions) and present
(a predominant middle class, tolerance for diversity, upward mobility,
hospitality toward immigrants, a shared constitutional faith, and liberal
individualism) elements that putatively set America apart from other
national cultures. While descriptions of these particulars may have differed, the more or less agreed upon archive concerned with what made
America exceptional would include the following phrases: America is a
moral exception (the "City on the Hill"); America is a nation with a
"Manifest Destiny"; America is the "Nation of Nations"; America is an
"Invincible Nation." These conceptual metaphors do not supply definitions of America, but they do give directions for finding the meanings
that are intended to corroborate the belief in American exceptionality.
All of which leads to the conclusion that American exceptionalism operates less like a collection of discrete, potentially falsifiable descriptions
of American society than as a fantasy through which U.S. citizens bring
these contradictory political and cultural descriptions into correlation
with one another through the desires that make them meaningful.

The fantasy dimension of the discourse is evidenced in the fact that
U.S. citizens could express their belief that America was exceptional

even though they harbored very different accounts of what that belief meant. American exceptionalism has been taken to mean that America is "distinctive" (meaning merely different), or "unique" (meaning anomalous), or "exemplary" (meaning a model for other nations to follow), or that it is "exempt" from the laws of historical progress (meaning that it is an "exception" to the laws and rules governing the development of other nations).

When one version of American exceptionalism no longer suited extant geopolitical demands, policymakers reconfigured its elements to address the change in geopolitical circumstances. Indeed American exceptionalism may have managed to survive as the dominant fantasy of cold war American political culture precisely because the incompatible elements out of which it was composed lacked any fixed relationship to a binding state of affairs. The determination as to which of its phrases would be symbolically efficacious was a function of the historical events to which the fantasy was linked. Harry Truman invoked the representation of America as the "Leader of the Free World" when he rebuked Moscow for the occupation of East Berlin. Ronald Reagan associated his demand that "Mr. Gorbachev tear down this wall!" with the renewal of the ideals of America as a City on the Hill.

At such moments of change *within* the cold war epoch, American exceptionalism operated by way of the double function of selecting a specific set of themes and elevating one or another of them into the position of the metaconcept empowered to represent the entire cluster. It was the semantic indeterminacy of American exceptionalism that allowed this paradoxical linkage interconnecting descriptions that appeared to be empirical and even positivistic with the conceptual metaphors through which U.S. citizens made imaginative as well as practicable sense of them. While they might seem to have done the work of straightforward description, these multifaceted frameworks and value-laden perspectives did not explain what American exceptionalism meant; they performed the overdetermining fantasy-work that regulated what it was supposed to mean, in what ways it should be analyzed, and how those meanings and modes of analysis were normalized.

But if the specific meaning of this conceptual terminology was a function of the historical events that American exceptionalism was supposed to explain, the primal event to which it was connected was the global catastrophe that was imagined as the inevitable result if the cold war between the United States and the Soviet Empire ever went nuclear. That event did not become imaginable until the 1950s, but the term's relation to that antagonist originated at its coinage.

American exceptionalism has been retroactively assigned to the distant origins of America. But the term did not in fact emerge into common usage until the late 1920s when Joseph Stalin invented it to accuse the Lovestoneite faction of the Americanist Communist Party of a heretical deviation from Party orthodoxies.[10] Stalin's usage of the term as a "heresy" is helpful in explaining why exceptionalism was reappropriated as the core tenet of belief within cold war orthodoxy.[11]

Since Stalin had excommunicated the Lovestoneite sect for having described the United States as exempt from the laws of historical motion to which Europe was subject, cold war ideologues transposed American exceptionalism into the revelation of the truth about its nature that explained *why* the United States was exempt not merely from Marxian incursions but from the historical laws that Marx had codified. As the placeholder of a communist heresy, American exceptionalism named the limit to the political provenance of the Soviet Empire. As the manifestation of economic and political processes that negated communism at its core, this "heresy" constituted the primary means whereby U.S. citizens could imagine the nullification of communism.

While the belief in American exceptionalism derived its authority from the account of the unique place of the United States in world history that it authorized, it drew its structure out of its difference from the social imaginaries that it attributed to the Soviet Union, to Europe, and to the so-called third world. Representations of the United States as an exception to norms of Europeanization also promoted an understanding of the United States as the standard for the future of democracy that Europe should emulate. As an exception to the rule of European normalization, American exceptionalism sustained an image of Europe as that which could not find reflection in the U.S. mirror. What the United States was lacking rendered it not merely different but also qualitatively better than the European nation-states whose social orders were described by exceptionalist historians as having been devastated by Marxian socialism. Exceptionalism imagined a Soviet Empire that threatened to overthrow the world order through the spread of revolutionary socialism, and it represented Europe as especially susceptible to this threat.[12]

Overall American exceptionalism was a political doctrine as well as a regulatory fantasy that enabled U.S. citizens to define, support, and defend the U.S. national identity. But the power of the doctrine to solicit the belief that the United States was unencumbered by Europe's historical traditions depended upon the recognition of European observers for its validation. In the transition from World War II to the cold war, U.S. consensus historians like Arthur Schlesinger Jr. and Henry Steele Commager cited Alexis de Tocqueville's nineteenth-century account of his travels through the United States as definitive verification of the doctrine of American exceptionalism.

Observing that Tocqueville had found U.S. political society exceptional in lacking the feudal traditions that had precipitated the violent confrontations in France's moment of transition, Daniel Bell grounded his "end of ideology" thesis upon this absence. As an addendum to Bell's argument, Louis Hartz advanced the claim in *The Liberal Tradition in America* that the absence of class conflict from a liberal capitalist order had rendered impossible the emergence of socialism within U.S. territorial borders. In thus eliminating from U.S. territory the socialist initiatives that Bell had excepted from its history, Hartz in effect deployed *Democracy in America* to secure the nation's borders against the negative exceptionalism of the imperial Soviet.[13]

Describing the national past as lacking the history of class antagonism that they posited as the precondition for world communism, the vast majority of the scholars working within the field of American studies cooperated with policymakers and the press in constructing a mythology of national uniqueness out of whose narrative themes U.S. citizens constructed imaginary relations to the cold war state. Events on a world scale were thereafter assimilated to this cultural typology that was made to translate them.

U.S. policymakers depended upon the fantasy of American exceptionalism to authorize their practices of governance, but historians and literary scholars turned the beliefs embedded within the fantasy into the principles of selection through which they decided what historical events they would allow representation within the historical record and which literary works they would include within the U.S. canon. Examining the past became for scholars who were steeped in exceptionalist convictions a romance quest whereby they would understand the meaning of their "American" identity through their uncovering of the special significance of the nation's institutions. In the early years of the cold war, the proponents of the Myth and Symbol school of American studies constructed an image of the United States out of exceptionalist assumptions. Then they propagated this image throughout Europe and the newly decolonized world as a prescriptive model for the construction of political communities that would, like the United States in whose image they were to be remodelled, be defended against the incursions of Marxian socialism.[14]

The fantasy of American exceptionalism also shaped the contours of the academic field of American studies out of the prolonged debate conducted therein over whether the nation was a variation upon or a deviation from European models. Whether and how it differed released a range of problems that delimited the scope of the field's inquiry. In restricting its understanding of U.S. culture to these standpoints, American studies has in turn provided an operational context determining how U.S. culture gets taught, administered, and pronounced upon.

But if the fantasy of American exceptionalism produced beliefs to which the state has regularly taken exception, the state nevertheless needed the fantasy to solicit its citizenry's assent to its monopoly over the legitimate use of violence. The state presupposed this belief when it declared that its power to make and preserve laws at times required it to create exceptions to the laws it enforced. In recasting Japanese internment camps, Operation Wetback, and the Vietnam War as "exceptions" to the norms of American exceptionalism, for example, state policymakers removed these troubling events from the orderly temporal succession organizing the nation's official history.

The fantasy of American exceptionalism was comprised of the assemblage of tenets and beliefs out of which the term's ever-changing significance could be deduced. But the political efficacy of the *fantasy* of American exceptionalism is discernible in its supplying its adherents with the psychosocial structures that permitted them to ignore the state's exceptions. These structures of disavowal were crucial to the production of the state's exceptions insofar as they sustained the attitude through which U.S. citizens willfully misrepresented their history as well as their place in the world. Since it was the state's exceptions that produced the contents of the exceptionalism that the fantasy rendered meaningful, the U.S. citizens' ongoing need for the fantasy depended upon the state's construction of these exceptions to its rules.

Official historians have fashioned their accounts of U.S. domestic policies out of their conviction that the United States was different from European imperial states in that it repudiated the acquisition of colonies. Disowning knowledge of the historical realities of imported slave labor, of overseas colonialism, and of the economic exploitation of refugees has entailed historians' differentiating the U.S. government's domestic policies from the Realpolitik of the international arena. But in their distribution of ethnic and "racialist" differences into hierarchical social rankings, U.S. immigration laws in particular have depended upon stereotypes developed out of a residual colonial discourse. Moreover, throughout much of the nation's history, U.S. foreign policy has worked in more or less open violation of democratic ideals. The historical struggles of Asian, Hispanic, and American Indian groups for recognition of their equal rights reveal linkages between domestic and foreign policies that American exceptionalism effaced.

American exceptionalism and the state's exceptions to it at once required one another's operations yet they were also set in opposition. The efficacy of the state's exceptions became evident in what the subjects of the fantasy of exceptionalism felt compelled to disavow. By way of its exceptions, the state in fact produced the absences—of trade unions, a feudal hierarchy, and ideological absolutes—that doctrinaire exceptionalists had described as missing from the national history. The *fantasy* occluded recognition of the fact that it was the state that produced the absences that the manifest content of the credo of American exceptionalism described as foundational to the nation-state.

William Appleman Williams has described the dissociative reasoning through which historians have recounted the exceptionalist narrative succinctly:

> One of the central themes of American historiography is that there is no American Empire. Most historians will admit, if pressed, that the United States once had an empire. They then promptly insist that it was given away. But they also speak persistently of America as a world power.[15]

In between U.S. historians' admission of a U.S. colonial empire and their insistence "that it was given away" an entire imperial history comes into visibility as what cannot become straightforwardly referential in American exceptionalism.

The Primal Scene of American Exceptionalism

But if the terms and tenets of the discourse of American exceptionalism were always falsifiable if assessed according to strictly empirical evidence, why did the fantasy of American uniqueness enjoy such a *longue durée*? My effort to answer this question requires an elaboration of one of the central claims in the foregoing account, namely that the "political efficacy of the *fantasy* of American exceptionalism is discernible in its supplying its adherents with the psychosocial structures that permitted them to ignore the state's exceptions." In order to better understand how those psychosocial structures accomplish their work, I need to return to some of the psychoanalytic concepts that previously supplied Jacqueline Rose with the understanding of the inextricable relationship between the state and fantasy.

In Rose's view, the state was able to reach into heretofore unacknowledged dimensions of social belonging because it was accompanied by a state fantasy that extended into the most intimate recesses of its subjects' psyches. The modern state became intertwined with its subjects' psychic fantasies in that part of the mind that Freud called the superego, and that he conceptualized as the dialectical contrary of the state's public law.[16] The Freudian superego did not merely accompany public law. As its dark underside, the superego supplied the public face of the law with an implacable authority that the superego acquired by acting upon all of the unruly impulses that the law prohibited. The superego at once insisted that the subject recognize the law's prohibitions even as it tied the subject to the superego's illicit enjoyment of what it prohibited. It was its subjects' positioning within this scenario wherein the superego's prohibitions were structured upon the superego's illicit enjoyment of things that it prohibited that constituted the psychological preconditions for the efficacy of the state's fantasies.

The superego binds its subject to a viciously circular logic: the more the subjects under its sway repress the desire to do what the superego has at once prohibited yet illicitly enjoyed doing, the greater they assume this desire to be. It is its subjects' ties to the superego's ineluctably illicit enjoyment that constitute the psychic grounds for the uptake of the state's fantasies. But if the state acquires the authority to regulate its subjects' desires through its binding them to the superego's vicious circularities, how can these subjects remain bound to this vertiginous process without experiencing abject subjection? Has not the state's law drawn the efficacy for the demands it makes on its subjects from the psychic energies that the superego would appear to have deprived them of in personifying the agency of prohibition? But how can the agency of symbolic law, which is responsible for guaranteeing order and stability, depend on this perverse figure, who enjoys its transgression, for its efficacy?

Freud's answers to these questions lead him to complicate the model of fantasy by redescribing the agency responsible for its achievement as comparably self-divided. If state fantasy names the agency whereby citizens take up symbolic law, which is preoccupied by the superego's double binds, it is necessarily doubled in itself. The fantasy simultaneously gives expression to the agency of the law and to the desire seeking to transgress that very law. Identification with this desire involves the state's subjects in an ambivalent process whereby they simultaneously identify with the authority of the state's law, as well as with the illicit desires that would transgress the law.

As we have seen, state fantasy produces the desire that binds the subject to authority and law. But the subject's desire to believe that the authority of the state's laws is identical with his or her will would appear to be impossible because of the obscenely duplicitous relationship to the state's laws enacted by the superego in giving expression to them. If the superego transgresses the laws in the very act through which the superego gives expression to the law, it obliges the state's subject to undergo a comparable doubling through the state fantasy whereby they take up the law. The fantasy positions the subject's desire in a relation to the bar separating the law from its transgression. Identification with this desire involves the subject in an ambivalent process whereby the subject simultaneously obeys yet transgresses the law.

State fantasy does not hold the national community together by fostering its subjects' identification with the public or symbolic law that regulates the community's everyday normal life. It is the function of fantasy to conceal the inherent impossibility of social cohesion precipitated by the law's transgression of itself. Fantasy accomplishes this outcome by covering over the inconsistency in the state superego's relation to the state's laws by constructing a vision of society that is not split by internal division, a society in which the relations among the parts appear organic and complementary. The concealment of the state's duplicitous relationship to the law requires that the subjects of the state fantasy identify with the state's power to declare itself an exception to its own rules. It was through their identification with the state's power to suspend its laws that the subjects of the U.S. state's fantasy of exceptionalism were able to disavow the flagrant transgressions of the state's law that took place throughout the cold war.

At the outset of the cold war, the external opposition between the state laws and their criminal transgression was transmuted into the opposition internal to the State of Exception, between particular transgressions—for example, Operation Wetback or the Hollywood blacklist—and the absolute transgression, which empowered the State of Exception to exempt itself from already constituted laws in order to protect and defend the entire constituted order. It was the cold war state's suspension of its own rules and laws that instantiated the ultimate transgression against the nation-state, but the state fantasy projected the responsibility for this violation onto the alien legality of the Soviet Empire. In doing so, it permitted the subjects who took up this fantasy to enjoy this antagonism that split the entire social order, as the subject's interiorization of the state's desire to annul the laws and rules that ordered the Soviet state in its entirety.

More specifically, what held the imagined national community together throughout the cold war was the attribution of the illicit enjoyment of the transgression of the state's laws to the Enemy of the State rather than the agency responsible for the inauguration of the State of Exception. The cold war state fantasy of American exceptionalism enabled U.S. citizens to experience their national community as coherently regulated through the disavowal of its inherent transgressions as exceptions required to counteract the Soviet threat. But U.S. citizens' relation to the unfathomable traumatic antagonism at the very heart of the symbolic order was correlated with a traumatic event through which the fantasy achieved its compelling force. American exceptionalism was imagined as the primary means of warding off not merely an enemy ideology but a scene of catastrophic violence that could include the entire planet within its sphere of destruction. Defined as a heresy none of whose tenets could become representable within the categorizations of the enemy's symbolic order, American exceptionalism positioned U.S. citizens who took up this fantasy within the fantasmatic space of catastrophic destruction. When they hallucinated themselves as positioned there, this sublime fantasy enabled U.S. citizens to enjoy the attainment of their exceptional American identity through this awe-inspiring image of its possible total loss. Freud understood the primal scene as a comparable scene of complete devastation. He described the events that took place there as elements within a scenario that his analysands constructed retroactively, through analysis, as the venue through which they came to comprehend what made them feel out of sorts. Since the fantasy of the primal scene underwrote the anxious desire of his patients, whether or not the events that took place there actually happened was of little importance. As the portal to a site that could not take up a place within the sortable places of the order it originated, the primal scene never actually did take place as raw fact. Definable as what could not take place except through the traumatizing displacement of all other representable spaces, the primal scene was itself an exception to the rules of placement.

The fantasy of the primal scene imagined an inaccessible place that could only be accessed retroactively. In his commentary on Freud's primal scene, Jacques Lacan condensed the excessive, traumatizing experiences that took place at this site into a nonphenomenal object he named the "Thing." This *je ne sais quoi* added properties of plenitude, intensity, and enjoyment to the primal experiences that happened there. Slavoj Žižek connected Freud's theory of the primal scene with Lacan's notion of the Thing to describe the individual citizen's primal encounter with the nation as that citizen underwent subjectivization within its fantasy. The nation is a Thing, according to Žižek, because the nation makes an individual's way of life seem to be "something more" than the sum of its specifics.[17]

According to Žižek, the national Thing is the object cause of a subject's desire in that it is the placeholder for that which the national subject desires and at the same time that which causes the subject's desire. If the national Thing causes the subject to exist as a desiring national subject, national subjects can only come into existence by desiring this fantasized relation to the national Thing. Although the national Thing solicits the desire of the national subject, it is constructed as that which will never satisfy this desire. For it to be a Thing, the national Thing must cause the subject to try to attain it, and yet it must also be unattainable. It is in this sense that the fantasy itself structures a space, since, in Lacanian theory, fantasy sets a scene into place that designates the subject's impossible relation to *objet a*, the object cause of its desire.

What the fantasy stages is not a scene in which our desire is fulfilled, fully satisfied, but on the contrary, a scene that realizes, stages the desire as such. The fundamental point of psychoanalysis is not the desire is something given in advance, but something that has to be constructed— and it is precisely the role of fantasy to give the coordinates of the subject's desire, to specify its object, to locate the position the subject assumes in it. It is also only through fantasy that the subject is constituted as desiring.[18]

If this fantasy space of the national Thing is to be imagined as possible, it requires something to explain its failure to come about. This require-ment led Žižek to explain the significance of the national Other. The national Thing may name what draws out national subjects' intensely felt yet impossible to gratify desire to attain fulfilled or ideal nationness, but it is the national Other in relation to which the national Thing is imagined to reside in intimate proximity that endows the Thing with the condition of unattainable desirability. As the force that threatens its way of being with total extinction, the Other to the national Thing is a constitutive aspect of its coming into being. The observation that nationals live under the constant fear that an enemy Other might at-tempt to destroy their entire way of life might seem obvious, and even commonsensical. But Slavoj Žižek took this commonplace to what might appear to be an illogical conclusion when he asserted it is the national Other that endows the national Thing with ontological consistency.

Žižek arrived at this conclusion by imagining the Other as occupy-ing a relation to the national Thing by way of a dual temporality. The enemy Other has always already completed the destruction of the national Thing that it has always not yet accomplished. The national Thing comes into being as an ideal that the national subject desires to attain because it is always about to emerge from an event, the nation's complete destruction at the hands of the national Other, that has always already happened but also always not yet taken place. The national Thing comes into being as a self-consistent "object," that is, whose complete theft or absolute annihilation has already taken place yet not yet happened. If the national Thing cannot emerge into being except through this threat of its complete dispossession, it is only by construct-ing an enemy Other as that which would attempt to steal or otherwise prevent the attainment of the national Thing that it can be imagined as coming into being by the national subjects who need to desire it.

What we conceal by imputing to the Other the theft of enjoyment is the traumatic fact that we never possessed what was allegedly stolen from us, the lack ("castration") is originary, enjoyment constitutes itself as "stolen," or to quote Hegel's precise formulation from his *Science of Logic*, it "only comes to be by being left behind."[19]

The national Other supplied Žižek with the theoretical fiction he needed to explain the ethnic tensions that had emerged in Yugoslavia following the breakup of the Soviet Empire. The Serbs, Slovenians, and Croats represented each other as placeholders for the national Other that would steal the impossible enjoyment of the national Thing from the rivals' national subjects. But in the United States, it was the presence of the Soviet Union as an Other Empire that performed this Other work. The Russian Empire's threat to absorb the national Thing within an alien imperial field constituted the distinguishing trait of the primal scene of American exceptionalism. The individuals who imagined themselves subjectivized within this primal scene were confronted with two incompatible processes of identification. Renata Salecl has described the procedures whereby an American identified with the image of a good citizen as an "ideal identification." And she differentiated this operation from what she called the citizen's "fantasmatic identification" with the enemy.[20]

Salecl brought these two processes of identification into a differential relationship with each other to explain why both were necessary before a national subject could emerge within an imperial field. When a Yugoslavian national subject emerged within an imaginary Russian imperial field, the disidentification from the fantasmatic imperial identity served as the necessary precondition for taking up the ideal national identification. Under Soviet rule, the only way a Yugoslavian subject could emerge as a Yugoslavian required the ongoing negation of the Russian identification that would subsume it within its imperial order.

But in the United States during the cold war, the procedure of identification was somewhat more complicated. Before U.S. citizens could become American, they had to take up identification with the desire for the national Thing and effect an ongoing disidentification with the fantasmatic Russian enemy. But the latter disidentification additionally required the American subject to disavow identification with the imperial Thing that the United States had itself become in its effort to destroy Russian imperialism. The primal scene of cold war America was comprised of the U.S. imperial Thing whose emergence into being was always already at once fully occluded yet never completely effaced by its proximity to the Russian imperial Other. In order to take up the position as a national citizen-subject within this uneven field, a U.S. citizen was obliged to negotiate the ideal identification with the national dimension of the imperial Thing by disidentifying with the fantasm of the Russian Empire and by disavowing the American imperial Thing that came into force through this disidentificatory disavowal. The fantasy that permitted U.S. citizens to achieve their national identity through the disavowal of U.S. imperialism was American exceptionalism.

American Exceptionalism as a State of Fantasy

I have elaborated this theoretical scenario to explain the complex psychosocial processes that constituted the preconditions for the symbolic efficacy of the fantasy of American exceptionalism. I have solicited the insights of Slavoj Žižek and Renata Salecl to articulate this explanation because they arrived at an understanding of the workings of state fantasy from within the precincts of the Soviet imperial formation onto whom the cold war state had projected the agency responsible for the construction of the U.S. State of Exception. As the subjects within a nation-state that had actually been subjected to the imperial formation that the U.S. state had described as its dialectical contrary, Žižek and Salecl are perhaps the theorists best suited by historical circumstances to explain the perverse logics of the U.S. State of Exception.

But the paradoxical logic at work in the primal scene of American exceptionalism discerned by two of its ego-ideals need not impede a more forthright description of the reality effects of this pervasive state of fantasy. After World War II, the U.S. government propagated the belief that America was the fulfillment of the world's aspiration for the "Nation of Nations" by constructing the threat to the attainment of that ideal in the image of the Soviet Empire. The construction of this national enemy in the image of an Evil Empire enabled the U.S. state to represent its imperial practices as preemptive measures that it was obliged to take to prevent the Soviet Empire from incorporating U.S. citizens within its imperial domain.

American exceptionalism produced the desire within U.S. citizens to construe U.S. imperialism as a nation-preserving measure that would prevent Soviet imperialism from destroying America's national ideals. American exceptionalism also enabled U.S. citizens to turn this nation-preserving measure into an exception to U.S. national identity that proved its rule. Rather than construing the occupation of South Korea and West Berlin as violations of the belief in American nationalism, the fantasy of American exceptionalism allowed U.S. citizens to derive enjoyment from these exceptions as necessary means to achieve the state's destruction of imperialism as a Russian way of life.

Exceptionalism became a state fantasy when it caused U.S. citizens to want to participate in the state's imperial will by changing the objective cause of their desire. The imperialism that the state in fact practiced intensified the need within U.S. citizens to disavow those practices. This need in its turn produced a counterloop of desire for the recovery of the ideal nation. But the latter desire could only be acted upon by renewing the practice of disavowal through which the U.S. national identity was produced. What was important in the practice of this desire was not whether or not the fantasy of American exceptionalism was "true." What mattered was the way that the *fantasy* of exceptionalism overwhelmed this question of the truth. Americans could not be deceived about American exceptionalism because, to paraphrase Renata Salecl, they articulated the truth of their nationalizing desire in and through this deception.

Throughout the cold war, U.S. citizens structured their position within the United States through the structuring disavowal of imperialism as an American way of life. But the vexed relationship between the ideal nation and the state's imperial practices did not lead U.S. citizens to abandon their national identity. On the contrary, this intimate transgressive relationship between the state's imperial practices and Americans' national ideals seemed to heighten and augment their desire for and identification with these imagined national ideals. American exceptionalism induced Americans to propagate the American national ideal domestically and globally so as to nullify the imperial enemy's desire for domestic and global dominance. Overall, the fantasy worked by enabling U.S. citizens to experience what was exceptional about their U.S. national identity as the disavowal of U.S. imperialism at home and abroad.

The United States differed from other nations in that its national fantasy was in fact a state fantasy. It became a state fantasy at the site where the national fantasy would otherwise take hold. Slavoj Žižek has described the site upon which the disparity between the national ideal that national citizens hoped for and the imperfect nations they could expect to produce as the place in which they took up the endless desire to achieve the ideal nation. But in the United States this national site was annulled through the state fantasy of American exceptionalism.

American exceptionalism defined America as having already achieved the condition of the ideal nation that normally incited national desire. After it defined America as the fulfillment of the world's dream of an ideal nation, the fantasy of American exceptionalism eradicated the difference between the national ideal U.S. citizens wanted and the faulty nation they had, by representing America as having already achieved all that a nation could be. American exceptionalism thereafter motivated U.S. citizens to displace their normal national desire—to achieve an ideal nation—with the abnormal desire to propagate the U.S. model of nationalism.

It was the cold war state that promoted the image of "America" as the fulfillment of the world's desire for an ideal nation into its rationale for imposing and defending the U.S. model of nationalism across the globe. After the state positioned the "Nation of Nations" as the keystone of its imperial foreign policy, America exceeded the conditions of normal nationness and became the imperial state's practicable model for nation-building. But the state practices that exceeded nationalism were not predicated on the state's desire to achieve the ideal nation but on its desire to become the sole imperial power.

In doing so, the imperial state formation had not merely surpassed the individual citizen's desire to achieve an ideal U.S. nation; it actively contradicted the U.S. citizens' belief that America was indeed an ideal nation. The identificatory mechanisms of American exceptionalism supplied U.S. citizens with the psychosocial structures through which they disallowed acknowledgment of these contradictions. At the level of what I earlier described as their ideal identifications, U.S. citizens wanted to believe that the United States was the perfection of a national ideal rather than a rapacious imperializing power. Moreover they could not articulate criticism of U.S. imperialism without feeling as if they had spoken on behalf of the imperial enemy with which they were also fantasmatically identified.

As we have seen, Freud named the figure who aroused such guilty identifications the superego. Jacques Lacan has called the dimension of the state fantasy that oversaw the processes of self-recognition that distinguished the ideal identification from the fantasmatic identification the Gaze. In the reconfigured cultural field that emerged after World War II, the fantasy of American exceptionalism assumed the vantage point of the superegoic Gaze. The fantasy performed its spectacular operation when it brought the visual field into line with the desires that individual U.S. citizens subjectivized when they identified with their appropriate positions in the symbolic order. When U.S. citizens identified with their mandated subject positions, the Gaze named the superegoic figure that made them feel good about their symbolic identifications.[21]

America's exceptional Gaze produced U.S. citizens' acquiescence to their cold war identities by facilitating their self-recognition within them. When it served as the superego, American exceptionalism also demanded that U.S. citizens perform the disavowal of American imperialism as the way to continue to feel good about their national identity. American exceptionalism may have explicitly represented the United States as an exception to the rule of nations, but it tacitly required that U.S. citizens continue to construe it as a nation so that they could practice the state's desire to proliferate the national model globally. U.S. citizens sustained their fantasies concerning how the nation should be by practicing the American exceptionalism that enabled them successfully to disavow the fact that it wasn't what it should be. The state fantasy of exceptionalism thereby introduced the disavowal of imperialism as the unacknowledged mediator in between the state's policies and the practicable life worlds of U.S. citizens. Exceptionalism activated a two-tiered process dividing the manifest organization of the U.S. role in the world with the latent fantasy whereby U.S. citizens imagined themselves as practicing nationalism through the disavowal of imperialism. It was at this site—where the U.S. imperial practices overran the condition of normal nationality—that U.S. citizens were taken up by a state fantasy of a different order.

The State of the Nation

In shifting the primary orientation of their everyday political practices from the nation to the State of Exception, U.S. citizens also underwent a shift in their way of inhabiting the nation. A nation normally enters a State of Exception when the state declares a war or deals with a national disaster. With the inauguration of the National Security State in 1950, the United States officially entered into a permanent state of war with the Soviet Union. The cold war state attenuated the reach of the subject's responsibility to loyalty to the state, and it demanded that other nations be construed as either friends or enemies of the state. But after the state declared itself in a permanent cold war, the Other to the nation was doubled as well—into the Enemy of the State and the emergency powers that the state itself must exercise to defend the people against the threat.[22]

The declaration through which the state inaugurated this war materialized a site whose surplus violence rendered it inassimilable to the terms of the national order. In conducting the cold war, the state was neither within the order nor outside the order. The state situated itself within the order that it protected but it occupied the position of internal externality of the exception. For in order to defend the order it also represented, the state was first required to declare itself an exception to the order it regulated. The State of Exception is marked by absolute independence from any juridical control and any reference to the normal political order. It is empowered to suspend the articles of the Constitution protective of personal liberty, freedom of speech and assembly, and the inviolability of the home and postal and telephone privacy. In taking up the site of the exception, the cold war state instituted a permanent alternative to the normative order that it called the National Security State.[23]

With the establishment of the National Security State in 1950, U.S. citizens underwent a profound alteration in the structure of their national desire. The fantasy of America exceptionalism empowered U.S. citizens to see themselves as exceptions to the rules that regulated the World of Nations and to identify their will with the will of the State of Exception that governed the international political order.

This complex dynamic may indeed explain the role that the state fantasy of American exceptionalism played in regulating U.S. citizens' attitude toward U.S. imperial dominance in the international sphere. But since U.S. citizens practiced the political dimension of their national identity within the territorial United States, what exactly promoted the desire within U.S. citizens to construe the ideal nation as already fulfilled within that sphere? If U.S. citizens believed that the United States had already realized its ideals why didn't this belief produce an unsurpassable obstacle to their participating in political life?

The abbreviated answer to these questions is that the state promoted U.S. citizens' desire to take part in national politics by transforming them into protectors of a political culture whose core political values had to be defended rather than altered. In obtaining the citizens' consent to this change in their orientation toward the nation, the state introduced a wholesale transformation in U.S. citizens' relationship to the state. After World War II, the National Security State did not merely change the rules of the game of American politics. The rules and constraints through which the National Security State regulated political discussion and debate in 1950 altered American politics even more drastically than would the Homeland Security State after September 11, 2001.

In 1950, the state's declaration of a global war against world communism authorized the partitioning of the globe into three worlds: the first world included member nations who embraced liberal democratic values, the second world gathered under its banner the countries committed to the propagation of communism globally, and the third world designated the newly decolonized populations of the so-called underdeveloped countries. This partitioning required political struggles that took place nationally and internationally to represent themselves within the discourse of the three worlds.

The political rationality that legitimated the rules of this new game did not merely occupy a place within an already existing political society. It instituted a political sphere as the terrain wherein political actors would normatively interiorize the rules and regularities upon which the new game of politics depended for its legitimation. This newly instituted political sphere was described as having been established by a rule of law that demanded as the precondition for its regulatory powers the autonomy of capital, owners, and the market.

Prior to the inauguration of the cold war, the political sphere was defined as a space that facilitated the noncoercive exchange of opinions and beliefs of every variety imaginable. But after the state defined the United States' role in the world in terms of its global opposition to communism, only political ideas that presupposed the values of the free market, private property, and the autonomous individual could be exchanged by subjects who had normatively internalized these values. The boundaries of the newly instituted political sphere were constituted out of the exclusion of political rationalities—revolutionary anticolonialism, trade union socialism, communism—that had formerly been permissible forms of political expressions. As representatives of the terrain over whose political disposition the U.S. imperial state struggled with the second world, U.S. citizens were obliged to extirpate processes of thinking and interaction that did not conform to these rules.

The National Security State described these illiberal measures as the sole way to protect and guarantee its citizens' liberal values. The Nazi jurist Carl Schmitt has supplied what may be the best way to understand the state's rationale in the critique he directed against the liberal state in *The Concept of the Political*.[24] According to Schmitt, a state must be based on some set of values that assured the substantive homogeneity of the people. The stability of the liberal state required the homogeneity of political society. But liberal political society could not achieve homogeneity because, in fostering a notion of politics as the noncoercive exchange of more or less equivalent political positions, political liberalism had to remain blind to the defining trait of the political sphere, which, according to Schmitt, was the irreconcilable antagonism between political friends and political enemies. Political liberalism could not permit a fundamental rift between friend and enemy to appear within the political sphere without losing its distinguishing trait, the recognition of the formal equivalence of all political positions. If the liberal state required the homogeneity of the political sphere for its stability, it could only achieve that stability by prohibiting what Carl Schmitt meant by politics.

These observations led Schmitt to the conclusion that if the liberal state did not represent at least one political disposition as an enemy to the field of liberal politics as such, that field would remain vulnerable to becoming violently disrupted by the appearance within it of political discourses that were predicated on the friend/enemy distinction that it had foreclosed. During the cold war the National Security State turned Schmitt's insight into the rationale for changing the rules of the entire political order. At its outset, the U.S. government replaced the liberal state with the National Security State by declaring the totalitarian truth claims of Marxian communism an exception to the rules of the liberal political order as such, and it founded a permanent State of Exception upon that exclusion.

In turning Russian communism into the rationale for entering the State of Exception, the state also shifted the terrain of political conflict from the internal domestic affairs of the nation-state to the international arena, where the conflict over fundamental political values was understood to be the matter of a conflict between utterly different state formations. The National Security State thereby enabled national political society to remain substantively homogeneous and yet open to a range of political positions and heterogeneous populations through this construction of an exception to its rules of democratic inclusiveness.

Under Truman, the National Security State took existing social relations, reconstituted them in terms of its geopolitical imperatives, and then gave them back to the U.S. citizens as if these imperatives were the enactments of their own will. U.S. citizens embraced the state's exceptions by taking up liberal anticommunism as a homogenizing political ethos. Indeed the energy for domestic politics was parasitic upon the state's projection of its irreconcilable internal political conflicts onto the arena of international conflict. Proponents of liberal (and conservative) anticommunism fostered a consensus about matters of political belief by actively soliciting the state to project fundamental antagonisms that emerged within the domestic political sphere onto the alien imperial state with whom the United States was engaged in an international war.

But how did the National Security State get the U.S. public's consent to this reconfiguration of the political order? Why didn't U.S. citizens object to the state's intervention in domestic political affairs? Why didn't they invoke the Constitution as grounds for retrieving their right to political rights?

Practicing American Exceptionalism in the State of Exception

The answer to the last two of these questions is that throughout the cold war era many U.S. citizens did in fact invoke the Constitution as grounds for retrieving their right to political rights. The leaders of several of these groups—the leaders of the Popular Front, the Hollywood 10, Martin Luther King Jr. in his opposition to the Jim Crow legislation, Cesar Chavez in his repudiation of Operation Wetback, Russell Means in his advocacy of the rights of native peoples, Betty Friedan in her agitation for equal rights for women, the participants of the Stonewall uprising, the Attica movement for prisoners rights (to name but a select few of a voluminous list of comparable examples)—did indeed redescribe the illegality of the state's "exceptions" to the nation's compact as the

legal bases for these social movements. Each of these extrastate social
movements resulted in legislation that changed the political standing
of the group's members. While the members of these groups harnessed
their petitions to the utopian demands organizing their national fantasies, however, none of the leaders of these groups inaugurated a state
fantasy to reconfigure the social order. In 1968, mounting opposition to
the War in Vietnam did result in the constellation of a range of social
movements whose members attempted to change the state fantasy. But
that oppositional movement failed.

To explain why it failed I need to return to the question that I have
not yet addressed, "But how did the National Security State get the
U.S. public's consent to this reconfiguration of the political order?" My
efforts to answer this question require the formulation of a distinction
between two different ways of belonging to the state of American exceptionalism that draws upon the work of Ghassan Hage.

Ghassan Hage is a sociologist whose fieldwork concerned the change
in the ethos of what he has named the "White Australian Nation" at
the moment when the Australian state officially declared its intention
to undergo a transformation from a monocultural to a multicultural
self-representation. Hage built a descriptive model of the effect of this
transition on white Australians that turned on his discovery that white
Australians and "multicultural" Australians practiced what he called
"national belonging" in two utterly different ways that he named "active" and "passive" modes of governmental belonging:

> The nationalist who believes him or herself to "belong to a nation," in
> the sense of being part of it, means that he or she expects the right to
> benefit from the nation's resources, to "fit into it," or to "feel at home
> within it."[25]

The white Australian national's mode of belonging was grounded in
the "belief in one's possession of the right to contribute (even if only by
having a legitimate opinion with regard to the internal and external
politics of the nation) to its management such that it remains 'one's
home.'"[26] To inhabit the nation at the level of what Hage called active
governmental belonging was to inhabit what he referred to as the
"state's will." This mode of governmental belonging led white Australians to perceive themselves as the enactors or the agents of the

state's will. Hage proceeded to contrast the active subjects of national belonging with those who belong passively to the nation. He describes the members of this latter category as populated by minoritized, "multicultural" Australians who do not feel as if they inhabit the nation at the level of identification with its will. Unlike white Australian nationals, these nonwhite Australians experienced their presence as object-like and subject to the managerial will of those who actively belonged to the nation.

The distinction Hage introduced between passive and active belonging became evident in the spatial field of everyday life as the distinction between an empowered national spatial manager and imagined national objects. White nationals were unlike nonwhites in that they construed themselves as spatial managers who exercised control over the ethnicized objects within their territory. According to Hage, white nationality "before being an explicit practice or a mode of classification is a state of body. It is a way of imagining one's position within the nation and what one can aspire to as a national."27

The white Australian fantasy positioned a white middle-class male in a position from within the national order in which he believed he produced an ideal national order by exercising governmental rule over ethnicized nationals who threatened to disrupt the order. Australian nationals gratified their yearning to bring about the national order in the very process of engaging in these managerial nationalist practices. What is more to the point, white nationals imagined themselves as bonded to the national order by securing nonnationals to their appropriately manageable positions as objects within the visual field.

Hage has described the way that Australian nationals inhabited, experienced, and conceived of their nation and of themselves as nationalists as a national fantasy. It was through this fantasy work that they managed to become the enactors/representatives/inhabitants of what he called the national will to realize the ideal Australian nation. He called that will a national will because it was continuous with the white national subject's desire to attain the ideal nation.

The difference between Hage's account of the fantasy of white Australian nationals and the cold war state fantasy of U.S. citizens might become discernible if we take the following description as the basis for the contrast:

It is also by inhabiting this will that the imaginary body of the nationalist assumes its gigantic size, for the latter is the size of omnipresence, the size of those whose gaze has to be constantly policing and governing the nation. It is also, by the same token, the inability to represent and inhabit such a will which makes the other a national object.[28]

Ghassan Hage's Australian nationals practiced citizenship as the aspiration to develop Australia into an ideal nation. In the passage I have just cited, he claims that they did so by participating in the state's governance, by seeing with the state's supervisory powers, and by inhabiting the state's gigantic omnipresence. *Pace* Hage, I would argue that the moment Australian nationals take up these positions they enact a state fantasy that enables them to acquiesce to the exceptions in the state's immigrant policies by imagining that they are enacting them. And it is at the site at which the Australian national's fantasy of national belonging gives way to the state fantasy of border policing that Australia's state of exception becomes discernible.

Cold war America differed from Hage's contemporary Australia in that the U.S. nation was structured in a relationship of permanent imagined warfare with an enemy empire. That structure transformed U.S. political practices into permanent exceptions to national political norms. Earlier I proposed that the National Security State had inaugurated a State of Exception. The nation entered a State of Exception at the outset of the cold war, when the National Security State declared itself as an exception to the rules of the legally constituted national order in order to protect and defend that order against Russian communism. The cold war State of Exception took hold through the National Security State's suspension of the nation's governing norms. When the National Security State emerged to guard and protect the nation against the permanent threat of enemy attack, the State of Exception became the spectral supplement to the nation-state. This spectral supplement transformed American exceptionalism into a quasi-permanent state of fantasy, rather than the contingent, merely provisional state fantasy.[29]

The cold war state obliged U.S. citizens to imagine their political enemies as intimately involved in the normal functioning of the political order. This image motivated U.S. citizens to transpose the state's construction of exceptions into its political norm. U.S. citizens practiced politics by way of a two-step operation: citizens first internalized the National Security State's exceptions to liberal inclusiveness into the basis for their normalization of anticommunism, then they construed the formal equivalence of their heterogeneous "anticommunist" positions as their political norm. But in enacting the state's will to exclude communism, U.S. citizens also shifted their primary mode of governmental belonging from the ideal nation to the State of Exception. No matter what the specific contents of their political views, U.S. citizens were obliged to enact the state's will to exclude communism as the precondition for their becoming viable political subjects.

Hage has described active governmental belonging as the result of white Australians' inhabiting and enacting the national will to manage the spatial field. American exceptionalism differed from Australian managerial nationalism in that it enabled Americans to practice U.S. citizenship as an exception to the national norms of nations like Australia, and to practice politics by removing their enemies from the political field.

U.S. "nationals" were also unlike white Australians in that they were not national citizens. They were the subject-citizens of the State of Exception. After it excluded its national enemy, the fantasy of exceptionalism positioned U.S. citizens within a vantage point whereby they enframed world events within the cold war state's way of picturing the world. Having positioned them there, the fantasy of American exceptionalism enabled U.S. citizens to imagine themselves as enactors of the state's will to govern the affairs of other nations.

U.S. citizens inhabited their political culture by enacting the state's exceptions, and they recast the state's governance of them as if it were an expression of their managerial control over the political field. They thereafter participated in and enacted the rule of the U.S. State of Exception by identifying with the state's violation of the rules of the nation-states under its protective governance. In shifting their positions from the national political sphere to the State of Exception, U.S. citizens transformed themselves from competitors for political dominance into the protectors of U.S. politics as an American way of life. The object cause for their struggle to transform themselves from an interested party in a political struggle with its own specific order into the disinterested protector and guardian of the political order was the threat communism was imagined to have posed to the viability of the American way of life.

It was in fact the state's declaration of the State of Exception that had violated U.S. citizens' normal political practices of liberal inclusiveness. But the cold war state's projection of the "enemy within" the individual citizen as the possible outcome of an individual citizen's political expressivity led U.S. citizens to reflect upon their political practices from the perspective of the National Security State, and to renounce and repudiate any signs of this imagined enemy within their individual psyches as well as within the political sphere.

Ironically, this structure enabled citizens to achieve this normalization through the enjoyment of the transgression that the state's violent exclusion of communists posed to their norms. Citizens enjoyed the state's violation of their political norms by shifting their relationship to the state's violence from that of an actual target to an imaginary agent of the state's surveillance technologies.

Rather than considering themselves targets of the security state's surveillance apparatus, U.S. citizens who construed themselves as actively belonging to the national governance routinely reperformed, in their relationships with immigrants, racialized minorities, and minoritized populations, the state's surveillance practices. When the National Security State required ordinary U.S. citizens to take up practices of surveillance that had formerly been restricted to the officials at the nation's borders, these policies erased any meaningful distinction between INS agents and U.S. citizens. By redirecting the state's surveillance apparatus against minoritized bodies and against their own minority allegiances, U.S. citizens became the eyes of the state. And when they looked at the world through the eyes of the security state, they believed that their participation in the state's governance of immigrants constituted a form of self-governance.

By staging fantasies that produced an imminent justification of the National Security State's power to construct exceptions to its own rules, American exceptionalism articulated the interconnection among law, war, and citizenship in ways that fostered U.S. citizens' primordial attachments to the State of Exception. It was from this vantage point that they authorized differential modalities of national belonging and played determining roles in deciding who did and who did not belong to the nation.[30]

If the cold war constructed the magical artifice through which the state pronounced itself the will of the nation and the protector of its order, American exceptionalism named the fantasy structure through which the events in that war were reimagined as demonstrations of U.S. citizens' successful supervision of the planet. U.S. citizens who felt empowered to occupy the State of Exception inhabited, participated in, and enacted the will of the National Security State at home and abroad. The fantasy of American exceptionalism took hold when it induced U.S. citizens to cultivate two incompatible and nonconvergent attitudes toward the United States. On the one hand, U.S. citizens envisioned the United States as an ideal nation whose model the state propagated across the globe. On the other hand, they understood themselves responsible to do the work necessary to achieve that ideal. Exceptionalism also split the difference between these two attitudes by enabling U.S. citizens to believe that they could achieve their national ideals by enacting the will of the state. Overall the fantasy of American exceptionalism enabled U.S. citizens to see themselves as exceptions to the rules that regulated the World of Nations and to identify their will with the will of the State of Exception that governed the (inter)national political order.[31]

American exceptionalism, as we might summarize these operations, named the process whereby citizens established an exemplary national order in a way that reciprocally valorized the State of Exception. By practicing exceptionalism, individual citizens did not merely practice the ruling norms, they enacted the exception to the norms that undergirded the national order. Exceptionalism also named the mode of governmental belonging through which U.S. citizens practiced nationalism as a form of state governance. The state's exceptions got disavowed by U.S. citizens through the psychosocial processes that were activated within the fantasy of exceptionalism. At the site of the state's declaration of exceptions to its constituting laws, the vast majority of U.S. citizens did not seek relief from these illegal suspensions of their constitutive bonds. They did not do so because the state fantasy of exceptionalism took hold of their psyches at the site of these exceptions. Rather than protesting against the state's abrogation of its rules, U.S. citizens fantasized themselves as the sovereign power that had suspended the law in the name of securing the nation.

American exceptionalism worked at different scales and in different registers to effect the same overdetermined outcome. American exceptionalism authorized U.S. citizens to imagine the nation as a fulfilled

ideal, and its exceptions provided them with the structures of disavowal through which they conceptualized it as a constantly renewed
aspiration. In representing the United States as an ideal nation, American exceptionalism elevated its exemplarity into the proof of the state's
power of imperial rule. When it worked in tandem with the state's
imagined war with Russian communism, exceptionalism authorized the
state's power to decide upon the rule that regulated the norm. When it
supplied U.S. citizens with the psychosocial structures through which to
disavow the state's exceptions, American exceptionalism turned the nation in which the exception had itself become the norm into the State
of Exception. All of these registers performed their work in the oscillation
between an understanding of the state as an exception to the nation
and the State of Exception as the fulfilled nation. American exceptionalism operated as the principle of organization of the State of Exception to whose will it gave expression and as the horizon of intelligibility
of the fulfilled national political order it valorized.

The cold war state produced a normal domestic situation out of the
permanent State of Exception needed to protect and defend the domestic population against Russian aggression. The U.S. state's construction
of exceptions appeared to liberate the individual citizen from imprisonment within the Soviet Union. But when the Soviet Empire came apart
and the United States lost its enemy Other, the entire overdetermined
structure of the state fantasy was dismantled. When the cold war stopped
justifying the state's production of exceptions, Carl Schmitt's diagnosis
of the instability of the liberal political sphere proved all too accurate.
Unable to project the antagonisms that plagued the exponents of incompatible political positions within the U.S. political sphere onto an
external enemy, the state was confronted with the irreconcilable differences internal to the liberal political realm. Since the state could no
longer disavow the contradictions and ruptures that were internal to the
liberal state as exceptions to its rules, they returned as juridically action-
able wrongs that demanded redress in the very real time of the liberal
political sphere.

Law played a key role in the formation of the U.S. imperial state in
that it supplied the state with the power to impose its rule in the name
of the law's adherence to exceptionalist norms. Throughout the cold
war, social movements emerged whose members drew attention to the

disparities between the nation's exceptionalist ideals and the state's discriminatory practices against domestic minorities and its acts of imperial aggression in the arena of international politics. But after redescribing these policies as exceptions to its norms and ideals, the state redescribed members of these social movements as anti-American and forged "guilt by association" linkages between their demands for changes in the political apportionment of rights with the state enemy's threat to the "American way of life." It was in part because the members of the antiwar movement of 1968 did not participate in the same state fantasy as did the Nixonian Republicans or the Hubert Humphrey Democrats that their nonstatist associations were pathologized as manifestations of what would later be referred to as the "Vietnam Syndrome."

But when the state's psychosocial structures of disavowal lost their purchase at the termination of the cold war, the members of these social movements acquired the power to confront the State of Exception that had declared these exceptions with the limits to the exercise of its power. The disjunction between the law's claim to universal power and the disclosure of its limits in the face of these alternative sites of power also opened up spaces for the reconfiguration of the social order.

It was not the pluralism of political positions that precipitated the irreconcilable rifts within U.S. political culture. It was the absence of a war with an external enemy onto which the antagonisms that emerged in between these positions could get projected that caused these deep fissures to appear within the U.S. political sphere. When the state's exceptions could not be disavowed by the state or the psychosocial process of disavowal through which U.S. citizens participated in the logic of the state, the political antagonisms that the exceptions had foreclosed from recognition reemerged as irreconcilable constituencies.

The Prolonged Transition

The primary work that American exceptionalism performed during the cold war was discernible in the problems and questions with which U.S. citizens were confronted after its entire fantasy structure was dismantled. A range of disparate and incompatible fantasies appeared at the site of this foundational rift in U.S. culture that opened up at the site of the long transition from the cold war to the Global War on Terror.

The fantasies that emerged at this site turned around variations on the themes of law, war, and the exception.

In this book, I shall take up the state's declarations of war, individual works of expressive culture, political spectacle, cinema, and journalism, and attempt to explain how the state fantasies underpinning these artifacts shaped and directed U.S. citizens' impossible desire for a relation to a fully realized U.S. national culture that would be as answerable to their needs within a globalized world economy as the fantasy of American exceptionalism had been during the cold war. The chapters that follow are all concerned with events—the Persian Gulf War, the Oklahoma City bombing, the return of Alexis de Tocqueville, the Southernification of the American Revolution, 9/11, Cindy Sheehan's occupation of Crawford, Texas, and Barack Obama's political campaign—that have solicited and in the case of Obama's "movement" become alternative state fantasies. I have not merely selected these events because they took place at the site in between the cold war that governed U.S. society and culture for a half century and the Global War on Terror that has recently been founded to replace it. I have organized this discussion around these events because they disclose the stakes of the legislation that these state fantasies would naturalize.

The order of the chapters reflects the chronology of the transition from the inauguration of the New World Order of President George H. W. Bush in chapter 1 to the efforts by President Bill Clinton and Newt Gingrich to organize antagonistic political constituencies out of their followers' different reactions to the events that took place in Waco, Texas on April 19, 2003, and in Oklahoma City on the same date two years later. Having examined the ways in which their utterly incompatible reactions to the dismantling of the cold war state had rendered Clinton's and Gingrich's constituencies virtually unrecognizable to one another in the second chapter, in chapter 3, I undertake a consideration as to why both of these lawmakers along with many other symbolic engineers turned to Tocqueville's Democracy in America to supply a representation of Americanness that would allow the members of these two groups to become recognizable to one another. When members of Clinton's New Covenant America became unrecognizable to the Americans who had signed on to Gingrich's Contract, they recontracted their Americanness by becoming recognizable to Tocqueville.

Throughout the opening three chapters, I also examine how each of these figures—Bush, Clinton, and Gingrich—had fostered a war with "Islamic extremists" in Iran and Iraq in an effort to create an official state enemy and an oppositional mentality out of which to organize a state of fantasy with the encompassing provenance and the mass appeal of the cold war. In chapter 4 I take up Roland Emmerich's 2000 film *The Patriot* and try to formulate the psychosocial rationale for the more pervasive state fantasy of the "southernification of America" in which the film participated. More specifically, I offer an explanation as to why *The Patriot* relocated the origins of the contemporary war against terrorists in the paramilitary wing of a South Carolina regiment during the War of Independence against England. In chapter 5, I analyze the mythological foundations of the State of Exception that President George W. Bush did succeed in installing after he declared a Global War on Terror after September 11, 2001. I wait until the final chapter to explain how a contemporary avatar of the extrastate social movements that had agitated to overthrow the State of Exception throughout the cold war harnessed a series of events—the revelation of the prisoner abuse at Abu Ghraib, Cindy Sheehan's peaceful occupation of Crawford, Texas, the globally circulated photographs of the survivors of Hurricane Katrina—to Barack Obama's movement in 2008 and successfully accomplished the undermining of Bush's newly forged State of Exception by changing the state fantasy.

State fantasies do not altogether conceal the inconsistencies that they mask. State fantasies disclose and open up irreconcilable rifts that provide the state's subjects with a space wherein they can change their relationship to what is worst about the U.S. imperial state formation and start to let go. The stakes of the state fantasies under consideration in this book became most clearly evident in the limit figures—the televised beating of Rodney King, the misrepresentation of the agency responsible for the Oklahoma City bombing, Cindy Sheehan's playing Antigone to President Bush's Creon during her occupation of Crawford, Texas, the reports of prisoners tortured at Guantánamo—to these state fantasies. It was because these figurations had been abjected from within the state's fantasies that they performed the "knowledges" that these state fantasies had foreclosed. As figures that could not be included within these fantasies without bringing them to their limits, these extraneous figures did not merely reveal the profound social antagonisms that these fantasies structurally disavowed, they also opened up sites in which an alternative state of justice might emerge.

American exceptionalism is a transgenerational state of fantasy, and like a family secret it bears the traces of a transgenerational trauma. Resembling an ongoing nightmare into which we occasionally awakened, this transgenerational trauma bore the psychic reality of the obscene underside to the victory culture that was structured in the fantasy of American exceptionalism. The content of this transgenerational trauma haunted the historical record with events that could neither be claimed nor completely foreclosed in the state of fantasy. The traumatizing images that insist within American exceptionalism's transgenerational fantasy reach back to events that accompanied the nation's founding—Indian massacres, the death worlds of the slave plantations, the lynchings and ethnic cleansing of migrant populations—and project themselves into the present as images that confront historical narratives with what violates their conditions of representation.

These traumatic images remember everything inside the psyche of the state fantasy that it wills its subjects not to know. In spontaneously recovering these memories from the unrecorded texts of American history, these traumatizing images perform the representational function of the figures of thought Walter Benjamin called dialectical images. A dialectical image functions like the opening shot in a montage in that it solicits an entire series of related images each one of which breaks from its fixed historical context to bear partial documentary witness to the whole image montage of a historical event that suddenly flashes up into visibility and demands redress.

When the film from the handheld video camera that documented the LAPD's beating of Rodney King was broadcast across television screens in 1991, this image could not be integrated within the state fantasy of the New World Order that the Gulf War was designed to inaugurate. Rather than settling into the image repertoire of the newly forged state fantasy, this documentary instead spontaneously recovered the memories—of slaves beaten by their masters, of migrant laborers forced into transfer centers, of Indians slaughtered by the thousands, of Vietnamese families dragged from their huts and shot and burned, of Iraqis forcibly separated from their homeland—that haunted the present with this record of injustice from the historical past at the very moment when the New World Order was systematically expunging that record from official historical narratives.

The Rodney King film opened up an empty space in between the dismantling of one state fantasy and the emergence of another. A revolutionary moment suddenly became possible within this space as images from an unacknowledged past suddenly burst into the present as if rising from the wrongs suffered at the hands of dominant fantasy. The dialectical images inhabiting this revolutionary space continue to haunt the state fantasies that have emerged in the long transition from the Persian Gulf War to the election of Barack Obama. Their acknowledgment constitutes one of the motivations for my writing this book.

1

Staging the New World Order: Hiroshima, the Vietnam Veterans Memorial, and the Persian Gulf War

During the cold war, television supplied U.S. viewers with a frame that "contained" national and international events within the cold war's picture of the world. This television frame empowered these viewers to visualize the world through the eyes of the National Security State's values by transmitting the representational effects of its viewpoint into their homes as the evening news.[1]

In his effort to fill the space of transition from the cold war to the New World Order, President George Herbert Walker Bush staged a war in the Persian Gulf that was designed to supply U.S. citizens with tele-visual representations of a military victory that the conclusion to the cold war lacked. As images of the war were broadcast across the tele-vision, these media representations eliminated the distance separating the viewer's perspective from the state's military action.

The state's aestheticization of this display of force enabled the sov-ereign people to participate in the war as an extension of the technol-ogy through which it was visualized. The televisual record of the war did not represent the action. It produced a fantasmatic structure that embed-ded U.S. citizens in the project of war. As the television screen repli-cated an incoming missile's aerial view, the conflation of the television screen and the smart bomb's lens secured the fantasy that this was not a representation but an enactment of the sovereign power to remake the world in the image of U.S. democracy. And once the war's enactments were articulated to the nation's patriotic fiction, that fiction represented the state's show of force as an expression of the sovereign will of the U.S. people to propagate the U.S. model of democracy worldwide.

Perhaps because the Persian Gulf War was the most highly mediated in the nation's history, it has elicited at least as much commentary about the media coverage as the historical events. Uncertainty over the appropriate focus of media attention was in part the result of ambiguities in the Bush administration's stipulation of the government's motives for Operation Desert Storm. From its inception the Persian Gulf War constituted a military enterprise designed to forestall Saddam Hussein's aggression against Kuwait, and at the same time was an attempt, in the aftermath of the cold war, to solicit spontaneous assent to the alternative means of enframing historical events Bush named the New World Order. But the event crucial to the success of the new consensus was symbolic rather than actual. It entailed overcoming what was called the Vietnam Syndrome.

Understood from within the context of U.S. foreign policy, the Vietnam Syndrome referred to the antiwar consensus that had resulted from media coverage overwhelmingly critical of the war in Vietnam and had subsequently deprived U.S. intervention in the affairs of third world countries of its moral justification. To recover from the syndrome, Presidents Ronald Reagan and George H. W. Bush recast Vietnam as "the war the media would not allow the U.S. to win," and the course of their direct military interventions in Grenada, Libya, Nicaragua, and Iraq designated control over the media's coverage of events as crucial to military victory.

Unlike campaigns in Grenada and Nicaragua, the Bush administration could not depend on the sociopolitical presuppositions embedded in the cold war as the frame of referents through which the Persian Gulf War could be viewed. With the disappearance of this context that had enabled the nation's citizens to make mythological sense of historical events, a gap had opened up between historical facts and their agreed-upon meaning, between what happened and how to make sense of what had happened. This generalized alienation, in the aftermath of the cold war, between the facts of war and their significance turned the media coverage, as the instrument for ascertaining the relationship between those facts and their meaning, into the "real story" of the Persian Gulf War.[2]

Dick Hebdige has analyzed cogently the war's capacity to supplant critical observation with the spectacle of consensus:

> but now more than ever vicarious contact with the front line via blanket news coverage fails to guarantee comprehensibility, still less access to the truth. The battlefield today is electronic. Wars are waged, as ever, over real territories and real spheres of influence. But conflicts between "major players" are now conducted in a "virtual space" where rival hypothetical scenarios, "realized" as computer simulations, fight it out over the data supplied by satellites. Meanwhile, hygienically edited highlights of the action get replayed nightly on the news through ghostly green videos shot through the night-sight viewfinders of airborne artillery. In this space anything can happen but little can be verified.[3]

The Bush adminstration, in its effort to overcome the Vietnam Syndrome, had not only limited the U.S. media's access to coverage of the war, but struggled to convert the events actually taking place during the war into the virtual reality of purely symbolic forms—instruments for the construction of a new consensus—rather than historical facts. In short-circuiting the relay between events and their factual observation, Operation Desert Storm elided their historical witness. In place of events actually happening in Iraq, Operation Desert Storm turned the signifiers from "bodies of discourse" that the end of the cold war had rendered superfluous—soldiers missing in action (MIAs), prisoners of war (POWs), mutual deterrence, missile crises, the Vietnam Syndrome, nuclear holocaust—into its objects of reference. In refiguring these signs within the hyperreality of computer simulations, rather than the raw reality of the battlefield, the Bush administration appealed to the cultural code developed during the cold war as the basis for the New World Order. Rather than transmuting events in the Gulf War into the mythos of the cold war, the U.S. news media's coverage of Operation Desert Storm transmuted the cold war into a virtual reality and returned national spectatorial publics to the viewing positions they occupied in the aftermath of World War II.

Positioned within the "smart bomb's" pinpoint view of their trajectory right up to the point of impact, U.S. televisual publics were deprived of the critical distance necessary to adopt a standpoint on the war. Having been deprived of access to any facts other than this media simulation, these spectators were instead embedded in the unfolding of this spectacle, as part of its production.

Before they could disembed themselves from their position within this generalized spectacle, U.S. citizens had to develop a critique of the war coverage itself. Although several commentators mounted criticism of the media during their coverage of the war, the most significant opposition to the war took place as the spontaneous response to an event that took place more or less contemporaneously with the war's conclusion. I refer to the eyewitness video recording of police brutality in what has been called the Rodney King affair. The crude status of the technological apparatus added to the truth of this historical witness and established its crucial contrast to the professional media's coverage of the war.

The Rodney King incident exposed the LAPD's excessive use of force as the instrumentalization of a repressive and racist state apparatus; its recording opened up a correlative critical standpoint on the police action in Iraq. One consequence of this critical standpoint was a change in the public's relation to the newly configured state fantasy, which opened up the possibility of creating an alternative to it. This contestatory state fantasy emerged in part through the exposure of the ruse through which the New World Order had taken control of the visual field.

Christopher Norris has provided the documentable facts about the war that interfered with the efficacy of the official state fantasy:

1) that Saddam Hussein was brought to power and maintained over
a long period by US intelligence and "long-arm" strategic agencies;
2) that his regime was backed up *until the very last moment* by constant
supplies of weapons and resources (not to mention diplomatic support)
provided by the US and other Western powers; 3) that this invasion of
Kuwait was prompted—or at least given what appeared to be the green
light—by indications that the US would not intervene since it also
wished to push up the oil-prices by exerting pressure on Kuwait; 4) that
the Gulf War was fought *first and foremost* as a war of retribution against
an erstwhile ally who had proved too difficult to handle; 5) that its
conduct involved not only enormous military and civilian casualties
but also—contrary to professed "Allied" war-aims—a full-scale campaign of aerial bombardment launched against electricity generating
stations, water-supply systems, sewage disposal plants, and other

components of the urban infrastructure whose collapse could be predicted to cause yet further death and suffering through the breakdown of emergency services and the spread of infectious diseases; 6) that the attacks on retreating Iraqi forces (along with civilian hangers-on and hostages) continued to the point where any justifying talk became merely a cover for mechanized mass-murder; and 7)—still within the realm of documentary evidence—that the war might well have been averted had the "Allies" held out against US pressure and listened to those well-informed sources who argued that sanctions were already (in early January) taking their toll in Iraqi war-fighting capabilities.[4]

The strategic positioning of Operation Desert Storm, at the intersection of the end of the cold war and the fiftieth anniversary of Pearl Harbor as well as the quincentennial celebration of the Discovery of America, and the claims for its symbolic efficacy as the inaugural moment of a New World Order, constituted a symbolic burden the Gulf War finally could not support. Intended to represent U.S. supremacy in the aftermath of the cold war, the Gulf War, in the two-year interval following its inception on January 16, 1991, has instead itself become the occasion for intense critical scrutiny.[5] The reversal in its semiotic fortunes was in part the result of conflicting symbolic investments. The identification President Bush ritually adduced between Saddam Hussein's "rape of Kuwait" and Adolph Hitler's invasion of Czechoslovakia disclosed the administration's stakes in this representation: an imaginative reinvestment of the symbolic moral and political inheritance of the Second World War onto a Middle Eastern topography previously the source of hostage and oil crises, religious wars, territorial disputes, and Irangate. Official Pentagon representations of the Gulf War drew upon such otherwise unrelated collective anxieties as the flag-burning controversy, steady economic downturn, Japan's and Germany's emergent economic superiority, the Vietnam Syndrome, the loss after forty-five years of the Soviet Union as the national enemy, and rumors of Saddam Hussein's nuclear capability as the raw materials for the official state fantasy. The staging of the Persian Gulf War was designed to project a spectacular image capable of discharging these anxieties as well as the pervasive dread of a nuclear holocaust underwriting the entire cold war era.

"We are determined to knock out Saddam Hussein's nuclear bomb potential," Bush announced to the nation in his televised address of January 16, 1992. Acting upon the president's suggestion that the cold war could properly end only with a reprise of the Hiroshima scenario with which it properly began, the conservative columnist Cal Thomas wrote the following policy recommendation in his "Time to Think Nuclear" piece for the February 7, 1991, op-ed pages of the *Boston Globe:* "The United States should use tactical nuclear weapons against Iraqi forces occupying Kuwait in order to bring the Gulf War to a speedy conclusion and save the lives of American and allied fighters."[6]

In a *Monthly Review* interview with Mojtaba Sadria, Doug Lummis spelled out the Pentagon's fantasy with remarkable precision: "The war had to be staged in such a way as to seem unambiguously just, with all the law and justice on the U.S. side, and it had to be winnable, which as they learned from the war in Vietnam, means that it had to be short.... The propaganda was Second-World-War language: Saddam Hussein was called Hitler; the troops fighting him were called the Allies, the demand was for unconditional surrender like the Potsdam declaration.... Their hope was clearly that by reenacting the Second World War, the society could become as strong and healthy and dominant in the world again as it was just before the cold war began."[7] But the aftermath of the Gulf War exposed this as an impossible symbolic task. As a strictly "imaginary war," the cold war depended on a projected "end of the world" nuclear scenario for its control of the public imagination. This scenario transmuted U.S. citizens into survivors of a nuclear catastrophe. But the spectacle enacted in the Persian Gulf solicited the belief that the cold war could have ended without a nuclear holocaust, and what was still more astonishing without visible signs of bodily mutilation.

If recast as a transitional object designed to wean the nation of its cold war mentality, however, the Persian Gulf War produced a compelling scenario. When such by-products of the forty-five years of weapons buildup as smart bombs and Patriot missiles hit their targets, a civilian population (in Israel) was in fact defended against possible nuclear attack, and, as a consequence, the U.S. spectatorial publics were encouraged to give up nuclear anxiety and to start appreciating such strategic defense initiatives. As Operation Desert Shield had quite vividly demonstrated, the U.S. military industrial complex had in fact successfully developed a prophylactic device capable of rendering a civilian population immune to terrorism no matter whether nuclear, fundamentalist, economic, or (by way of the Nicaragua Iran-Contra connection) narcotics-induced. Just as the U.S. ground forces had been shielded in the Iraqi desert, this psycho-logic had it, so would the U.S. public be by the Strategic Defense Initiative (SDI).[8] Throughout the war, the U.S. public was interpellated from within the target sites of smart bombs, and actual combat situations were restaged as if sites for the SDI's more sophisticated military hardware. In his January 28, 1992, State of the Union address, President Bush linked U.S. victory in the Gulf War with the SDI. "We must not go back to the days of the hollow army," Bush warned. "I remind you this evening that I have asked for your support in funding a program to protect our country from limited nuclear missile attack. We must have this protection because too many people in too many countries have access to nuclear arms. And I urge you again to pass the Strategic Defense Initiative, SDI."[9]

President Bush hoped to capitalize further on this identification of national security with military success in the Persian Gulf when he observed "that the veterans of the Gulf War were safer in the Middle East than in the streets of their own cities."[10] In correlating urban violence with Saddam Hussein's putative nuclear terrorism, President Bush reactivated an understanding of civil defense that presupposed the sacrifice of urban population to the "first strike" capabilities of the enemy. Dean MacCannell has described this "internal" foreign policy as an aspect of the "nuclear unconscious" with chilling clarity:

> Nuclear technology, even without another Hiroshima, has already had
> a profound impact on social structure and consciousness, perverting
> them both in discernible ways. Beneath the surface of fear of the sup-
> posedly unthinkable prospect of millions of deaths in the United States
> of America, one can find growing evidence of the desire to experience
> the bomb. The United States' official policy of . . . sacrificing our
> cities . . . suggests that the configuration of every detail of domestic life
> in the United States is the product of a transformation of our internal
> affairs into a quasi-military nuclear foreign policy.[11]

But this ideological identification of U.S. internal security with the SDI began to come apart on March 3, 1991, when a U.S. citizen videotaped the brutal police beating of Rodney King. In its vivid representation of an individual citizen savagely beaten by LAPD officers, this home video supplied the images (of excessive force, bodily mutilation, a civilian target) missing from official coverage of the Gulf War. The Rodney King affair opened up a public countermemory of the Gulf War that George Mariscal has succinctly described:

Clearly none of these inhumane events were isolated (or, as Chief
Gates would have it, aberrant) occurrences, but, rather the unmistakable
symptoms of a society deeply dependent upon racism and brute force
for its reproduction. The violence perpetrated against Rodney King
cannot be disassociated from the massive destruction wrought by the
United States Government against the Iraqi people.[12]

In the aftermath of the Rodney King affair, Saddam Hussein's "rape of
Kuwait" was replaced by reports of the rape of women in the U.S. military; reports of the Bush administration's technological assistance both
during and after the war severely compromised the official representation of Saddam Hussein's "secret" development of a nuclear device; the
stories of the deaths of U.S. troops as a result of friendly fire recalled
similar episodes in Vietnam; the endless homecomings of flag-waving
troops in "yellow-ribbon parades" ended and were replaced, following
the verdict in the King affair, with demonstrations in Los Angeles and
purple ribbons declaring "No Justice, No Peace." The composite of
these reversals in the symbolic fortunes of the official state fantasy irretrievably damaged the Bush administration's efforts to accrue the
moral capital of World War II. Operation Desert Shield became Iraqgate. The images of Los Angeles burning recalled not only Baghdad but
Dresden and Nagasaki and the moral dilemma left over from the decision to drop an atomic bomb on Hiroshima.

As the proper names enumerated in its title indicate, in the remainder of this chapter I will not be concerned solely with either the Gulf
War or its aftermath but with the vast stretch of the cold war state fantasy through which the United States had previously represented its
role in world history and with the state's aspirations to use its victory in
the Gulf War to bring the cold war to a satisfactory conclusion. The
cold war officially began with the atomic diplomacy that followed in
the wake of Hiroshima; it was officially superseded in 1991 with George
H. W. Bush's declaration that the Persian Gulf War inaugurated what
he called the New World Order. The massive scale of eventuation infer-
able from this trajectory calls attention to the difficulties these names—
Hiroshima, the Vietnam Veterans Memorial, the Persian Gulf War—
posed individually and collectively to the cold war's capacity to reproduce
and account for historical memory.

When redescribed as illustrations of this problem, the second and third
terms in the title rehearse difficulties in commemoration and projection

respectively. The Vietnam Veterans Memorial was designed to restore to official national memory events that took place in a war that in fact undermined the assumptions informing the cold war state fantasy, and the Gulf War "took place" so as to endow the otherwise fantasmatic "end of the cold war" with all the trappings of a historically factual event. These observations indicate that each of these terms also harbors ongoing contestations over their significance. Individually and collectively they designate monumental national memories expressive of an ahistorical supranational essence and a metasocial national subject as well as traumatic historical matters inassimilable to this state of fantasy.

Despite my inclusion of its events within a single metanarrative, the cold war cannot accurately be described as either monolithic or unchanging through history. I wish to acknowledge at the outset of this effort to offer an account of its mode of eventuation as a metanarrative that I run the risk of denying the historicity of the cold war. It may appear foolhardy to postmodern skeptics of grand narratives to ascribe narrativity to a conjunction of historical actions and their outcomes that were actually diffuse and quite disorganized. It might even be persuasively argued that the power of the cold war as a compelling mentality was predicated on the fact that its events lacked coordination and that its outcomes were never entirely totalizing. But since the primary intention of this project entails spelling out the role that state fantasy played in organizing the political efficacy of the cold war mentality, I intend to sketch out the contours of grand national narrative that that fantasy presupposed as the imagined underpinning for the events taking place in U.S. history between the years 1945 and 1991.[13]

When articulated in relation to this grand narrative, these names render visible an otherwise occluded antagonism between the nation-state and the National Security State. From 1945 until President Bush's January 28, 1992, State of the Union address, the cold war supervised the nation's postwar recovery by securing the citizenry's willingness in peacetime to submit to wartime discipline. The beneficiary of this collective surrender of will was "the National Security State," whose form of governmentality derived from generalized nuclear panic and from its right to produce exceptions to the nation's rules and laws.

The instrument responsible for the cultivation of this panic included the state fantasy that had removed Hiroshima from its position as a historical event that had in fact taken place on August 6, 1945, at the conclusion of the Pacific campaign and that had resulted in the deaths of over 100,000 Japanese soldiers and civilians, and recast it as the possible fate of U.S. citizens if Soviet imperialism remained unchecked.

As the representation of the complete destruction of a civilian population, "Hiroshima" occupied a position in the primal scene of the fantasy of American exceptionalism that I described in the Introduction. As such, its mode of eventuation partakes of the dual temporality that I earlier described as the defining trait of the national Thing. Like the national Thing, "Hiroshima" comes into being as an "object" whose "absolute annihilation has already taken place yet not yet happened." Because the historically factual event called "Hiroshima" involved the near total annihilation of a civilian population by the United States, it was inassimilable to the assumptions underwriting the fantasy of American exceptionalism. In that fantasy, the United States always successfully liberated other nations from the nuclear threats posed by Soviet imperialism. Since "ultimate" responsibility for Hiroshima was projected onto the potential nuclear aggression of the imperial Soviet, "Hiroshima" became a purely symbolic referent for a merely possible event, which was reassigned the duty to predict what "will have happened" had not the United States already mobilized the powers of nuclear deterrence against the Soviets.

Unlike other historical anachronisms, this fantasmatic representation of a nuclear holocaust in the future anterior entailed the destruction of any recollective agency capable of recording its historical actuality. In the following passage Jacques Derrida explains the dizzying temporal status of such a nuclear holocaust whose future existence depends upon its anticipatory recollection from a present time, which is itself in danger of never being recorded as a memorable past:

> Unlike other wars which have all been preceded by wars of more or less the same type in human memory . . . nuclear war has no precedent. It has never occurred itself; it is a non-event. The explosion of American bombs in 1945 ended a "classical" conventional war; it did not set off a nuclear holocaust. The terrifying reality of the nuclear conflict can only be the signified referent, never the real referent (present or past) of a discourse or text. At least today, apparently. And that sets us thinking about today our day, the presence of our present in and through that fabulous textuality. . . . For the moment, today, one may say that a non-localizable nuclear war has not occurred; it has existed only through what is said of it only where it is talked about. Some might call it a

fable, then a pure invention, in the sense in which a myth, an image, a fiction, a utopia, a rhetorical figure, a fantasy, a phantasm is an invention.[14]

Hiroshima signified the no-place the United States might have become had it not proleptically opposed, as the precondition for the postwar settlement, the Soviet Union's nuclear capacity. Hiroshima also pre-signified the geopolitical fate of those nation-states that had not identified the foundational cold war fantasy ("U.S. liberation from Soviet imperial aggression") as their geopolitical destiny. The name of this always already displaced event that every other cold war event at once deferred yet anticipated, Hiroshima held the place of what I described as the national Thing in the primal scene of the cold war fantasy. Because Hiroshima will have taken place only if the terrible reality of an all-out nuclear war did indeed take place as such in some possible cold war future, its historical "referentiality" at the conclusion of World War II would, according to the fantasmatic logic of the nuclear imaginary, also undergo derealization if the cold war lost its future.

As we have already seen, just such a symbolic return from the future informed the specular logic of the Gulf War. Capitalizing on the un-canny temporality informing the cold war and effected by a framing narrative that at first disavowed any possible referent for Hiroshima within the U.S. national narrative and subsequently identified Soviet totalitarianism as the potential historical agency for this nonevent, Operation Desert Storm enacted a simulacral return to the testing site of the first atomic explosion at Alamagordo, New Mexico, at 5:29:50 a.m. on July 16, 1945. Following this ex post facto deactivation of the nuclear device Saddam Hussein was prevented from testing, the U.S. public was to have been relieved of a forty-six-year-old nightmare:

> And so now [President Bush reassured the nation, in his January 28, 1992, State of the Union address] for the first time in 35 [sic] years, our strategic bombers stand down. No longer are they on round the clock alert. Tomorrow our children will go to school and study history and how plants grow. And they won't have, as my children did, air raid drills in which they crawl under their desks and cover their heads in case of nuclear war. My grand-children don't have to do that and won't have the bad dreams children had once, in decades past. There are still threats. But the long, drawn-out dread is over.[15]

Following the supersession of the cold war by the New World Order, the nuclear anxiety originating from Hiroshima was to be understood as if retrospectively crucial to the dismantling of the cold war mentality it had engendered. As the actual historical enactment of the "spectacular annihilation," the cold war at once affirmed yet denied, Hiroshima had acquired the U.S. public's spontaneous consent for the containment ideology of the cold war epoch and a vivid justification for the policy of nuclear deterrence. As a historic national spectacle, Hiroshima had turned the entire U.S. social symbolic system into the afterimage of a collectively anticipated primal scene, a self-divided (rather than self-present) instant, that always had not yet taken place (hence always anticipated) but had nevertheless always already happened (in the lived experience of anticipated disaster).

The difference between the cold war's fantasmatic ordering of events and social relations more usually attributed to the pervasive structure Guy Debord has called the society of the spectacle entails a further transformation of the spectator.[16] As an anticipated total disaster, Hiroshima transmuted cold war spectators into symbolic survivors of their everyday lives, able to encounter everyday events as the afterimages of ever-possible nuclear disaster. The spectacle of an anticipated nuclear disaster activated the logic of the primal scene, which converted events in everyday life onto screen memories of that unrepresentable scenario. In the aftermath of disasters on the scale of Hiroshima, its actual survivors could not exchange their experiences for already existing images in the national repertoire. Such exchanges have rendered the absolute singularity of nuclear disaster continuous with these other cultural representations. In place of such a generalized exchange, the cold war derived its authority from the displacement of scenes of nuclear disaster, incommensurate with the official scenarios out of which the national narrative constructs its representations, with a generalized global conflict. As a geopolitical spectacle that represented the security state's ability permanently to deter the nuclear holocaust, for which it served as a screen memory, the East-West conflict reactivated the spectator in the national survivor, but also thereby authorized a division between what was representable and what was of necessity unrepresentable in the national narrative. In its office as the official signifier of the unrepresentable dimension of the national narrative, Hiroshima occupied the sociopolitical unconscious of the National Security State. The symbolic reward that U.S. citizens granted the National Security State for the continuous noneventuation of the nuclear holocaust "authorized" it to carry out illegal covert activities. Upon performing the secret tactics necessary to impede nuclear war, the National Security State turned the U.S. publics' specular relations with nuclear holocaust into what Michael Paul Rogin has called their "vicarious participation" in the cold war state fantasy:

> Most obviously, the specular relation to political life has implications for democratic governance. Spectators gain vicarious participation in a narrative that, in the name of national security, justifies their exclusion from information and decision making. Covert operations as spectacle purify domestic as well as foreign audiences, for they transform the political relation between rulers and citizens from accountability to entertainment. . . . Vicarious participation in the spectacle of the covert secures in fantasy and preserves in fact the separation of those who plan from those who kill and are killed.[17]

When the cold war state fantasy reappropriated Hiroshima within this social logic, it transmuted nuclear panic into the opportunity to stage a technological spectacle corroborative of the nation's invulnerability. An invisible but pervasive supplemental scene accompanied U.S. citizens in their daily experiences. This "end of the world" cold war scenario enabled U.S. citizens to reexperience everyday doubts, confusions, conflicts, and contradictions as the cold war's power to convert indeterminacy into an overdetermined opposition.

Paul Virilio has spelled out some of the political consequences of this identification of personal with national security: "There is no more need for an armed body to attack civilians so long the latter have been properly trained to turn on their radios or plug in their television sets. No need for solid, laboriously moving bodies when their spectral images can be projected anywhere in an instant. From now on military assault is vaporous in time and the population's organic participation is no more than the irrational support of a techno-logistical supra-nationality, the final stage of delocalization, and thus of servitude."[18]

In its forty-six years, the cold war can be described as having assumed two distinct aspects. It was at once a spectacular fantasy capable of organizing national life and a geopolitical paradigm capable of determining international policy. Although these two functions were certainly not equivalent, they were linked. As a state fantasy responsive to the public's need for vicarious participation in the decision-making powers of the National Security State, the cold war exhibited its powers of spectacular persuasion precisely in those historical moments when the cold war as a paradigm failed to account for political complexities. When the cold war paradigm became productive of doubts, the cold war spectacle repositioned that doubt itself as a threat to the national security, and thereby effectively depoliticized the relations between U.S. citizens and the security state's mode of governance. It displaced situations that citizens could change into an arena of decision making wherein the unthinkable scenario of nuclear holocaust was a possible outcome. When it staged this encompassing state fantasy, the cold war did not represent the significance of political events but reduced them to the status of the ever-possible nuclear afterimages (the fate of every event in the cold war epoch) hence in need of covert operations for their survival.

Whereas the cold war as paradigm confined totalizing oppositions to the work of the Other superpower, the cold war fantasy spectrally identified its own totalization as that Other at work. The fantasy thereby reduced freedom either to the activity of positioning oneself within this structured opposition or to the "freedom from" the need to decide. It thereafter relocated the free citizen within a spectacle in which all discussion had been decisively premediated if not quite settled and the only unfinished business that of becoming the "national character" through whom the paradigm could speak.[19]

I began this discussion of Hiroshima by describing its double register as at once the object cause of the cold war's powers of displacement as well as the countermemory belonging to an order of events other than the official historical record regulated by the National Security State. But thus far I have devoted all of my attention to the cold war's capacity to deny the difference between its powers of historical framing and this different order of historical eventuation. As long as it functioned as the objective cause of the cold war's power to appropriate and redescribe the agency responsible for nuclear holocaust, Hiroshima legitimized the suspension of the system of checks and balances underwriting the U.S. Constitution, and authorized, in the name of national security, a shadow government comprised of unelected officials engaged in covert activities and undeclared wars. When successfully waged, these wars redeployed the containment power inherent to the cold war as the frame

necessary for the unfolding of a formulaic drama (of a heroic democratic
people overcoming a despotic, totalitarian power) whose entertainment
value derived from a collective desire to find nuclear panic reduced to
the manageable dimensions of conventional warfare.

The usual beneficiary of such cold war spectacles was the National
Security State, but during the Vietnam War, the cold war's failure to
correlate acts of war with this formulaic scenario resulted in collective
national trauma. Combat veterans who returned from the battlefields
in Vietnam to oppose the state policies that sent them there delegiti-
mized the National Security State's authority by finding it in violation
of rules of international law, and rendered suspect the cold war as the
putative agency of ideological identification. Intense critical scrutiny of
U.S. foreign policy during the Vietnam War explicitly associated military atrocities against civilian populations with Hiroshima. In a prescient
article, Marita Sturken described the Vietnam Veterans Memorial as an
unsuccessful attempt to overcome the national trauma resulting from
actions incompatible with the prevailing image of U.S. foreign policy.

> The incommunicability of Vietnam War experience has been modified
> by the communicability of its memorial. Yet we cannot understand
> the role played by this memorial, by its *difference* as a memorial, unless
> we understand what made the war it memorializes different. In the
> Vietnam War the standard definition of warfare had no meaning. This
> was a war in which the enemy was not always known, and in which the
> master narratives of "free" world versus communism and First-World
> technology and Third World "peasantry" were no longer credible. The
> rupture in history made by the Vietnam War is ... [of] the ability of this
> country to impose its will on others.[20]

The monument commemorated what was commonly referred to as the
Vietnam Syndrome, the loss of the nation's resolve to intervene overseas. When understood as an effort to disremember the Vietnam War,
Operation Desert Storm could be redescribed as a deferred reenactment
and subsequent working through of the traumatic events in this "unfinished war" and an attempt to relegitimize the foreign policies subject
to intermittent reevaluation in the aftermath of Vietnam (and Hiroshima). If "the memorial acts as a screen for projections of a multitude
of memories," Marita Sturken concluded this line of reasoning,[21] the
Gulf War provided the figures capable of being projected onto that
screen. When the United States failed to win the Vietnam War, the state

fantasy lost the power to screen the memory of nuclear holocaust, and as a direct psychological consequence of this failure, startling numbers of Vietnam veterans identified themselves with the survivors of Hiroshima. By way of a growing number of testimonials, autobiographies, and improvised narrative accounts, these combat veterans did not sacralize the nation's military violence by effacing its signs, but bore witness to images of war (charred bodies, dismembered limbs, eyeless skulls) that were utterly heterogeneous to the national narrative.

The technology of warfare displayed in the Gulf was designed to eradicate the negative afterimages remaining from the Vietnam War. Unlike their predecessors in Vietnam, the combat soldiers in Desert Storm seemed surplus appurtenances whose bodily integrity was assured rather than betrayed by a war machine productive of a new chain of national memories, replacing the bodies in pain recollective of Vietnam with bodies shielded from danger. As the public watched the war on television, the transgenerational trauma inherited from Vietnam seemed to have been conjured up to be "worked through" in the hyperreality of the Iraqi desert so that it might be completely obliterated from the national psyche.

It was the state's decision to occlude actual scenes of human carnage during the Gulf War that constituted its chief difference from the War in Vietnam. After they were harnessed to the war machine, the new computer technologies' contribution to the war effort was aesthetic in that it regulated the representations of the enemy's obliteration within the scenes through which these media transmitted the war. These state-of-the-art technologies facilitated an official state fantasy that at once celebrated the state's awesome powers of annihilation yet regulated the representations of its horrific effects.

But when the videotape of the Rodney King beating restored the image of a civilian's body in pain, that image reactivated the memory of other traumatizing images that resisted the state fantasy's powers of forgetting. This delayed reaction exposed the contradictory effects of the Gulf War: as a supplemental recollection of the Vietnam War, the Gulf War "completed" the screen memory initiated in the Vietnam Veterans Memorial, but it also stirred up traumatic images (including the recollection of mass death at Hiroshima) that screen memory unsuccessfully repressed. In the Gulf War the Bush administration tried to project Vietnam veterans like Norman Schwarzkopf and Colin Powell onto that screen of forgetting. Whereas the Veterans Memorial had screened out negative images of Vietnam veterans, the Iraqi desert projected over 500,000 official substitute images of U.S. men and women whom the U.S. military had shielded from enemy attack.

In linking the Gulf War to Hiroshima by way of the Desert Shield the Pentagon had hoped thereby to represent the nation as immune to nuclear attack. The pictures transmitted from the desert suggested that the U.S. public should understand itself as having been liberated from the forty-six years in which it was the hostage of nuclear panic. The state's correlation of the Gulf War with Hiroshima by way of the Vietnam Veterans Memorial also activated a way of remembering these forty-six years other than the selective amnesia authorized by the New World Order.

W. J. T. Mitchell indirectly alluded to this contrary linkage when he shrewdly observed that the power of the memorial derives from its violation of the cold war's conventional means of repressing (and expressing) violence:

> The Vietnam Veterans Memorial is antiheroic, antimonumental, a
> V-shaped gash or scar, a trace of violence suffered not of violence
> wielded in the service of a glorious cause (as in the conventional war
> memorial). It achieves the universality of the public monument not by
> rising above its surroundings to transcend the political, but by going
> beneath the political to the shared sense of a wound that will never
> heal, or (more optimistically) a scar that will never fade. Its legibility is
> not that of narrative: no heroic episode such as the planting of the flag
> on Iwo Jima is memorialized, only the mind-numbing and undifferen-
> tiated chronology of violence and death catalogued by the fifty-eight
> thousand names inscribed on the black marble walls. The only other
> legibility is that of the giant flat V carved in the earth itself, a multi-
> valent monogram or initial that seems uncannily overdetermined. Does
> the V stand for Vietnam? For a Pyrrhic "Victory"? For the Veterans
> themselves? For the Violences themselves?[22]

Throughout this account, Mitchell draws attention to the difference between the figures the monument memorializes and their inassimil-ability to the national narrative. Like Hiroshima, the Vietnam War oc-cupies a position in national history wherein historical facts are the outcome of conflicting representations of their significance. It is an undisputed fact that the Vietnam War refers to the historical events that took place during the U.S. occupation of South Vietnam between 1945 and 1973. But as a contested cultural representation, the Vietnam War refers to the massive transformation in the nation's self-understanding that took place during those same years. In *American Myth and the Legacy of Vietnam*, John Hellmann explained this transmutation as the nation's loss of its mythological rationale. The national mythology to which Hellmann refers originated with James Fenimore Cooper's "Leatherstocking Tales." It retold the sacred story of America's origination in the savage wilderness and its violent regeneration through its many campaigns against an Evil Empire. But their experiences in Vietnam brought this mythology to an abrupt conclusion when, instead of taking possession of their memories of the Vietnam experiences by projecting this "inner romance" upon them, U.S. combat soldiers entered into a psychic landscape "that overwhelmed the American idea of frontier [as liberated territory]."[23] When televised on the evening news, incidents in the Vietnam War refused to become referents in the composite fantasmatic event that cross-identified Columbus's discovery of the New World with the American colonists' successful revolution against the British Empire.

Unlike previous geographical sites on which the American Revolution was successfully restaged, Vietnam resisted this frame. After the government failed to provide a coherent moral justification for U.S. presence in Vietnam, combat soldiers lacked a moral rationale for their actions. In the absence of such a rationale they lost the power ethically to discriminate between war crimes and incidents of war. The belief structures informing the Vietnam combat veterans' understanding of the national mythology of war was incommensurate with their wartime experiences. Because their experiences did not corroborate the assumptions undergirding national myths, these returning veterans undermined the assumptions informing the national mythology as well as the security interests they served.

Their collective difficulties resulted in a profound change in the dominant cultural image of the American soldier, from that of a heroic adventurer to that of a vulnerable survivor unable to recover from wartime trauma. This transformation in the agents and settings of war was accompanied by related changes in the cold war fantasy that had failed to integrate them within the national mythology. Their inability to correlate the atrocities produced by the U.S. war machine with representations within the official mythology led the vast majority of U.S.

citizens to construe Vietnam as an unjust war. That construal resulted, in turn, in a reconceptualization of Hiroshima, as a prefiguration of the Vietnam Syndrome.

In an essay he published in the aftermath of the Russell International War Crimes Tribunal, Noam Chomsky designated "genocide" as the historic linkage:

> Hoopes [a former undersecretary of the Air Force who resigned after the Tet Offensive] does not tell us how he knows that the Asian poor do not love life or fear pain, or that happiness is probably beyond their emotional comprehension. But he goes on to explain how "ideologues in Asia" make use of these characteristics of the Asian hordes. Their strategy is to convert Asia's capacity for endurance in suffering into an instrument for exploiting "a basic vulnerability in the Christian West." They do this by inviting the West "to carry its strategic logic to the final conclusion, which is genocide...." At that point we hesitate, for remembering Hitler and Hiroshima and Nagasaki, we realize anew that genocide is a terrible burden to bear.[24]

Here and elsewhere in his analysis of the war, Chomsky refused official history's explanations of events. Identifying the characteristics assigned indiscriminately to all "Asian masses" as a symptom of "official racism," Chomsky proposed racism as the general equivalent that correlated U.S. efforts to construct the Japanese people as the nation's "official enemy" during World War II with the policy of genocide in Vietnam and with the mass destruction of civilian populations in Hiroshima and Nagasaki. Chomsky invoked this finding to delegitimate the course of U.S. foreign policy since World War II and to suggest that, as the responsible agency, the architects of the National Security State should be tried for violations of international law.

When combat soldiers involved in action in Vietnam struggled after the war to disavow this identity, their efforts only implicated them further in a compulsive cycle of violence. In his commentary on the war, Jean-Paul Sartre provided the following account of their reaction-formation:

> They [the American soldiers] came to save Vietnam from "communist aggressors." But they soon had to realize that the Vietnamese did not want them. Their attractive role as liberators changed to that of occupation troops. For the soldiers it was the first glimmering consciousness. "We are unwanted, we have no business here...." They vaguely understand that in a people's war, civilians are the only visible

enemies. Their frustration turns to hatred of the Vietnamese; racism takes it from there. The soldiers discover with a savage joy that they are there to kill Vietnamese they had been pretending to save. All of them are potential communists, as proved by the fact that they hate Americans. Now we can recognize in those dark and misled souls the truth of the Vietnam War: it meets all of Hitler's specifications.... Whatever lies or euphemisms the government may think up, the spirit of genocide is in the minds of the soldiers. This is their way of living out the genocidal situation into which their government had thrown them.[25]

According to Sartre's account, these combat soldiers constructed a false self system that they divided off from their experience of the genocidal structure of the war. But this false self (the figure in these soldiers only "pretending" to save the Vietnamese people from communist aggressors) was the only subject the U.S. government officially recognized.

In his monumental study of Vietnam veterans, Robert Jay Lifton discovered profound similarities between their collective experiences of social abjection—ontological insecurity, desymbolization, general distrust of the counterfeit nurturance of the environment, psychic numbing, flashbacks to the experience of death immersion, psychic disconnections between affect and experience, shock syndrome—and those of *hibakusha*, the survivors of Hiroshima, who had undergone the collective experience of Death-in-Life. Neither the experiences of *hibakusha* nor the veterans Lifton examined could be represented in the image repertoires of their respective national narratives.

As psychic materials in excess of any narrative's power to derive significance, these profoundly disturbing experiences remained unforgettable and unrepresentable somatic symptoms and returned *hibakusha* and Lifton's Vietnam veterans alike to the respective scenes of their traumas. Unable to surrender their past experiences to a narrative enchainment able to redescribe terror as valor, pain as courage, mutilation as integrity, and thereby transmute physical distress into the abstractions cultures reward, the survivors of Hiroshima as well as the Vietnam War, Lifton explained, instead felt absolutely disassociated from their culture's social symbolic orders. Without belief in the official narratives with which the government justified its Vietnam policy, the Vietnam veteran became, in the national mythology, the representative of a spectacle of atrocity—napalming, holocaust, assassination, torture—the cold war state fantasy could not assimilate.

The Vietnam veterans, in remaining inassimilable to the state fantasy, precipitated an order of discourse incommensurable with a culture's habitual self-explanation. The nation's inability to associate its wartime atrocities in Vietnam with the imperatives of the National Security State constitutes one of the indirect causes of the national adjudication of the difference between that shadow government and the U.S. Constitution called the Watergate trial. As it apprised the nation of the difference between its two constitutions (the U.S. Constitution proper and the emergency measures of the National Security State) that trial also suspended the cold war's power to enframe historical events.

The Watergate trial depended for its efficacy upon the U.S. public's previous construal of Vietnam as an unjust war, and that reconceptualization resulted in turn in a revisionist understanding of Hiroshima as the first symptom of what was to be called the Vietnam Syndrome. Robert Lifton proposed the My Lai massacre as a dialectical image that was able to interlink Hiroshima with the Watergate scandal as well as the Vietnam War with the following observations:

> At My Lai the atrocity involved the killing of five hundred non-combatants, Watergate involved subverting the electoral process—an atrocity of its own—in a way that makes more likely the kind of military atrocity that occurred at My Lai.... Like Hiroshima and Auschwitz, My Lai is a revolutionary event: its total inversion of moral standards raises fundamental questions about the institutions and national practices of the nation responsible for it.... One finds in Watergate and My Lai a simplistic polarization of American virtue and communist depravity.... There was a self-perpetuating quality to the whole Watergate style [which also applies to My Lai and Hiroshima]. One had to keep on doing more things to prevent a recognition of what one had done from reaching oneself or others.[26]

Because such veterans as these experienced themselves, on their return home, as the objects of public repudiation (for their failure to fulfill the imperatives of the state fantasy and liberate Vietnam from totalitarian aggressors), some Vietnam veterans reinvented themselves as Vietnamese survivors, or Japanese *hibakusha*.[27] Other veterans represented the cause of the Vietnam people against the imperatives of the U.S. government, and they struggled for the rights of Asian minorities. Having discovered the figure of the Vietnamese survivor within their own psychic experience of the war, many veterans became antiwar dissidents, in open conflict with a government (and a public) that had betrayed them by failing to understand their predicament. In assigning the moral responsibility both for the war's atrocities and for their inability to recover from the memory of them to the National Security State, these Vietnam veterans became representatives of the political alternative to the cold war mentality known as the Vietnam Syndrome.

That syndrome exerted a profound inhibitory influence on U.S. foreign policy until Ronald Reagan took office in 1980 with an understanding of his mandate as involving the recovery from the Vietnam Syndrome. Reagan's understanding of the cultural significance of the Vietnam veteran was significantly different from Lifton's. During his presidency, Reagan recast the combat soldiers who had returned from what he described as their heroic action in Vietnam as the prisoners of an antiwar sensibility, which had deprived the U.S. public of its patriotic pride. His efforts to undermine that sensibility led to his participation in the creation of the "mythology of the MIAs."[28]

After the Truman administration oversaw the establishment of the cold war state, the tolerance of conflicting opinions within the domestic political field was sustained by intolerance toward the political disposition of the state's enemy. The fantasy of a National Security State involved in a permanent war with a geopolitical enemy produced an overlapping consensus from within the nation by representing real political differences into the rationale for an imagined war with an alien state onto whom all the fundamental political antagonisms of the social arena were projected. The threat of an all-out nuclear war introduced an apocalyptic dimension to the people's conception of the state's power that could not be compromised. The National Security State thereby prepared the citizens under its charge to enjoy the spectacle of such a war. This state fantasy maintained its reflective hold on social relations by situating U.S. citizens within a spectatorial community that enabled them to participate in the state's power to represent the world within its terms. The fantasy did so by staging the connection between law, war, and national identity within a spectacle that fostered the belief that U.S. citizens were themselves the producers of the laws and regulations to which the state had subjected them. When news coverage of the Vietnam War disrupted the cold war's picture, however, the Vietnam Syndrome undermined the state's capacity to represent world events within scenarios through which its citizens could imagine themselves in the position to control their outcome.

From the day he took office, Ronald Reagan understood his presidency as a mandate to restore the National Security State fantasy that the Vietnam Syndrome had disrupted. With initiatives that ranged from support for Nicaraguan "Freedom Fighters" to the funding of the SDI and the demand that "Mr. Gorbachev tear down this (Berlin) Wall," Ronald Reagan systematically reaffirmed the image of America that had been installed after World War II—as the "Shining City on the Hill" whose citizens had been commissioned by God to restore the rule of law across the planet. The homology that he adduced between the state's exceptional role in the world and the exemplary family values displayed by U.S. citizens across the economic spectrum fostered the formation of a political constituency that he called the "silent majority" whose members internalized the military values of the National Security State. Reagan included blue collar workers, Christian evangelicals, antiabortion activists, cold warriors, and market fundamentalists within the silent majority.

After World War II, America became a State of Exception. But in the wake of the War in Vietnam, America's State of Exception was trailed by a constitutional movement that repudiated the extralegal status of the State of Exception. Ronald Reagan repudiated this emergent force as something destabilizing that would not go away. Reagan's reimagining of the Vietnam War was essential to his rehabilitation of the State of Exception. Reagan dubbed the state fantasy that he produced to bring about a change in the images through which the public recollected the Vietnam War "Operation Homecoming." No images were more powerful to Reagan's fantasy than those of the American POWs and the American MIAs.

The popular feature films *Deerhunter* and *Rambo* contributed to Reagan's effort to change the public's reaction to the war by securing a correlation between the image of an American GI taken prisoner by the Viet Cong and images of a U.S. nation imprisoned by greedy bureaucrats, corrupt politicians, and shadowy secret agents in business who demeaned and betrayed its true heroes. According to H. Bruce Franklin, the core stratagem of Reagan's mythology "was to take images of the war that had become deeply embedded in America's consciousness and transform them into their opposite." The primary target of this reversal was the annulment of the political power of the Vietnam veterans who opposed the war. For the myth "rejects and repudiates not only the history of the Vietnam War, but also what it portrays as the quintessential every-day life in post-Vietnam America. The idealism, virility, warlike powers and heroism of men who dedicate their lives to rescuing their abandoned comrades, sons, and fathers are presented as the alternative to a weak, decadent America subjugated by materialism, hedonism and feminism."[29]

The myth of the MIAs served a double function. As a specific mytho-logical figure, the MIA replaced the negative image of the Vietnam veteran with this account of heroic sacrifice. But the significance of the term MIA did not merely refer to the soldiers who were lost in action. The signifier referred as well to the discourse of American exceptional-ism as the sole discursive space in which the MIAs could be safely re-turned to their home and country.

Reagan's motives for commissioning the erection of the Vietnam Veterans Memorial drew upon his conjoined desire to accomplish the psychological rehabilitation of these combat veterans and to enable the nation to recover from the syndrome these soldiers represented. Reagan never wavered in his intention to return the United States to the psychological euphoria of the pre-Vietnam cold war:

> Restoring America's strength has been one of our Administration's highest goals. When we took office, we found that we had ships that couldn't leave port [and] planes that couldn't fly.... In the last five and a half years we've begun to turn that desperate situation around. We've restored the morale, the training, and the equipment of our armed forces. And let me just say that around the world and here at home, I've met many of our young men and women in uniform over the last several years. It does something to you when you're standing up there on the demilitarized zone in Korea and a young fellow standing there in uniform says, "Sir, we're on the frontier of freedom."[30]

The Wall, as the Vietnam Veterans Memorial was commonly called, was to have represented Reagan's new frontier of freedom. What W. J. T. Mitchell described as a scar, memorializing the fact that the Vietnam experience had been separated from any other official form of recollec-tion, Reagan understood contrastively as a badge of courage, a national war wound representative of many acts of valor deserving of national commemoration. Erected during the second year of Reagan's presi-dency, the monument was intended to achieve two outcomes: (1) the erasure of the negative chain of recollections associated with the Vietnam Syndrome and (2) the replacement of the Vietnam veteran with the representation of the POW as the symbol of an imprisoned American citizenry, struggling to return to the political certitudes of World War II.

Reagan turned the Vietnam Veterans Memorial into the gigantic screen onto which he encouraged U.S. citizens to project their collective wish to recover national pride. But the agency responsible for the success of this screening of the past was not Ronald Reagan the president, but Ronald Reagan the actor, who provided his spectatorial publics with representative heroic actions—freedom fighting in Nicaragua, the bombing of Libya, the invasion of Grenada—and encouraged U.S. citizens to realign themselves with the doctrine of American exceptionalism and the moral imperative to fight a Just War. One result of this realignment was the disavowal of any similarity between U.S. combat veterans and Japanese *hibakusha*.

Being recalled to the imperatives of the cold war entailed the nation's collective forgetting of Vietnam and Watergate as analogies of Hiroshima. As long as the cold war scenario successfully recoded these historical events into its frame of reference, this collective amnesia remained in force. But in the last two years of the Reagan presidency, glasnost and perestroika threatened to bring the cold war itself to an end, thereby depriving Reagan of his habitual way of explaining away such illegalities as the arms for hostages deal that surfaced in the Iran-Contra hearings. If we understand the Gulf War as a spectacle in which the Pentagon aspired to represent the end of the cold war as a U.S. victory, we can also understand it as the Bush administration's effort to justify the National Security Council's role in Irangate. The Gulf War was after all a way of diverting the national attention away from covert operations and redirecting it to a purely symbolic war.

In trading arms to Iran in exchange for money to conduct unauthorized wars in Latin America, the National Security State had turned an ideological enemy into an ally in an illegal war. Because of this and related political contradictions it brought into the open, Irangate recalled Watergate and encouraged an understanding of the Reagan presidency as comparable with Nixon's. Without the cold war to justify its covert operations, the National Security State had become the subject of more critical scrutiny than any other period since Vietnam. To recover the integrity of the National Security State, the Bush presidency staged a scenario that depended upon "arms for hostages" as its grounding rationale. As combat soldiers returned home from the Gulf, they became representative as well of the hostages released from Lebanon and indirectly of the national citizenry released from the cold war. As U.S. military technology systematically disarmed Saddam Hussein's nuclear capability, the U.S. public was invited to return to the Alamagordo of 1945 by way of the Saudi desert in 1991 and witness the removal of the cold war from the U.S. national narrative, and its miniaturization as the discourse exchanged by the principals in the Middle East. Instead of remaining mnemonically bound to the traumatic historical images—the Dresden and Tokyo firebombings, the Cuban Missile Crisis, My Lai, Three-Mile Island, Chernobyl, the Iran hostage crisis—etched in the cold war archive, the Gulf War "worked through" cold war hysteria by repeating all of these events in the infinitely fast-forward of an "end of History" scenario, understood this time as an overtaking of the cold war past by way of a U.S. future, which rediscovered the cold war in an underdeveloped temporality (the Middle East) understood as historically incommensurate with the New World Order. By refinding the cold war in Kuwait's relationship with Iraq (rather than the United States' with the Soviet Union), the televisual public was encouraged to undergo what might be described as para-amnesia: it was to remember to forget its own cold war history by learning to remember Middle Eastern history in the terminology of a miniaturized cold war.

With the compulsive repetition of the troops' triumphant homecoming (from World War II, Korea, Vietnam, Grenada, and Panama as well as the cold war), the United States was to have entered the New World Order with the same ideological assurance accrued after World War II, and the cold war was to have been recycled as the history of the Middle East in the epoch of Pax Americana. Able to see everything about the enemy without being seen, SDI was to have turned each viewer into an agent of a Transnational Security State, with surveillance responsibility for the globe. Invulnerable because invisible, this transnational consciousness was to have enabled viewers to transform Iraq into a peripheral U.S. border and the Middle East (as well as every other "developing" nation) into the United States' political unconscious.

But, as I have already suggested, the concrete fantasy that underwrote the Gulf War entailed the projection of moral responsibility for Hiroshima onto Saddam Hussein and the symbolic disavowal (in SDI's systematic dismantling of Hussein's nuclear capability) of Hiroshima's ever having actually taken place. Through this symbolic undoing of the United States' role in the forty-five-year cold war, Operation Desert Storm repositioned the nation in the aftermath of World War II, the "war to end wars," and assigned it the responsibility for preventing nuclear wars in the future. But since the United States was in historical fact the only nation ever to have preemptively used a thermonuclear device in wartime (and would have, and for the same ostensible reason—to save U.S. lives—used one again in the struggle with Hussein), this denial of responsibility exposed the United States' undeterred preeminence as a version of the imperial power its national narrative was sworn to oppose. Which is to say that in the absence of the enemy superpower onto whom the United States was used to assigning responsibility for its crimes, the United States had become its own undeterred Other in the New World Order.

As a state fantasy, the Persian Gulf War depended upon the selective forgetting of the criticism directed against the Vietnam War as well as a new national mythology, the quest for MIAs held captive (in Vietnam, Korea, the Soviet Union) since World War II. As "hostages" released at the conclusion of the cold war, MIAs fostered an understanding of the nation itself as a hostage released after a forty-six-year captivity. The hostages released after the Gulf War fostered this identification. But as we have seen, the Rodney King incident activated alternative memories.

Mike Davis has underscored the historical dimensions of this alternative memory with the following observations about the Rodney King affair:

> The balance of grievances in the community is complex. Rodney King is the symbol that links unleashed police racism in Los Angeles to the crisis of black life everywhere, from Las Vegas to Toronto. Indeed, it is becoming clear that the King case may be almost as much of a watershed in American history as Dred Scott, a test of the very meaning of the citizenship for which African Americans have struggled for 400 years—as a veteran of the 1965 riot said while watching SWAT teams arrest some of the hundreds of rival gang members trying to meet peacefully at Watts's Jordan Downs Housing Project: "That ole fool Bush think we as dumb as Saddam. Land Marines in Compton and get hisself re-elected. But this ain't Iraq. This is Vietnam, Jack."[31]

The resident of an environment closer in its demographics to Baghdad than say La Jolla, Rodney King complicated the picture of a New World

Order that identified urban populations with failed Middle Eastern states and other "seedbeds of terrorism." When citizens set Los Angeles aflame in May of 1992 as a protest against the police actions, the Rodney King incident reanimated questions about the legality of actions justified in the name of the National Security State dating as far back as Hiroshima. The images of a city burning in protest against police brutality seemed in retrospect a response to the official representation of Baghdad, as the appropriate staging ground for U.S. prominence in the New World Order. Like Hiroshima, Los Angeles represented one of those cities designated by nuclear strategists as expendable. Images of police brutally clubbing Rodney King recalled a series of related images left over from police actions in Vietnam, Korea, Panama, Grenada, and the Persian Gulf. By including within the fantasy space of the New World Order this obscene supplement to the official representations of a war that was uncontaminated by signs of violence, the video-taped representations of the Rodney King beating revealed what the state fantasy had covered over. Before the state's fantasy could solicit the citizen's desire to identify with its capacity to enjoy the humiliation and defeat of the national enemy, the fantasy must seduce the citizen into believing that it is the national enemy rather than the state who is responsible for the transgression of the state's laws. But in offering visual proof of the LAPD brutally violating a U.S. citizen's legal rights, the Rodney King incident brought about a change in U.S. citizens' identificatory relationship to the state's fantasy work.

These images included the representations of the state's use of excessive violence that the state must perforce exclude before its law can appear coherent and merely regulative. The addition of extraneous images to the image repertoire of the New World Order effected the disintegration of the entire fantasy. If Baghdad was bombed to demonstrate U.S. technological superiority at the outset of a New World Order, the burning of buildings in South Central Los Angeles raised important questions that recalled the related moral dilemmas attending the decision in the name of international security (and an earlier New World Order) to drop the atomic bomb on Hiroshima at the end of World War II. Whereas the Bush administration had aspired to divert attention away from just such questions as these, the aftermath of the cold war returned the nation to them as an unfinished collective task.

2

America of the Two Covenants: The Waco Siege and the Oklahoma City Bombing

The cold war did not end with a nuclear apocalypse but with the nation's insertion into a New World Order. President George Herbert Walker Bush had introduced the phrase New World Order to bring a new consensus into existence. But as we have seen, the restricted war in the Persian Gulf with which he inaugurated the New World Order proved ineffective for the symbolic order that had depended upon the permanence of an imaginary war to sustain the allegiance of its members.

Moreover what Bush called the New World Order did not reflect existing public opinion. The New World Order linked the norms and values forged within American civic order into the basis for a global civil society, which was to be comparably organized. The New World Order installed a model of international relations that proposed that states construct foreign policies out of the globalization of assumptions forged within U.S. civil society.

During the cold war, the fantasy of American exceptionalism had legitimated America's dominance within the dichotomized world order by supplying the rationale for America's superiority to Russian communism. However, after the conditions that lent this version of American exceptionalism its plausibility had passed away, two interrelated dimensions of the disavowed underside of American exceptionalism—American imperialism and America's global interdependencies—emerged simultaneously into view. With the disappearance of relations that were grounded in the cold war's polarization, the demands of a newly globalized world order required an understanding of America's embeddedness within transnational and transcultural forces rather than the reaffirmations of its splendid isolation from them.

The cold war state had produced an image of America in which gender, class, race, and ethnic differences were massively downgraded as threatening to national unity. U.S. citizens who had organized their national identities out of exceptionalist norms had deployed the coordinated myths of the Frontier and the Melting Pot in which the state's assimilationist paradigm overrode questions of diaspora, cosmopolitanism, and multiculturalism. But racial, ethnic, and gender minorities who refused to be aggregated within these geographies of exclusion have recovered the forgotten histories of U.S. imperialism to bring the exceptionalist norms forged during the cold war into crisis.

Following President Bush's inauguration of the New World Order, the racial and ethnic minorities whose ancestors had been the forgotten victims of American imperialism retrieved these histories of imperial subjection so as to demand redress within America's newly multiculturalized civil society. After they were linked with the anti-imperialism that had become the multicultural norm, these global processes did not merely incite the democratization of Americanist minority cultures and subcultures; globalization also fostered an understanding of the relationship between these intranational and subnational social movements to migrant and diasporic communities across the globe.

The interminable liminality of the New World Order did not triumphantly sum up the grand narrative of the nation's manifest destiny that had endowed the events that took place over the preceding half century with their historical purpose. Nor did it gratify the desire for order and fullness that narrative animated. The nation's entry into this new geopolitical arrangement did not conclude the cold war; it displaced the grounding assumptions that had constituted its coherence. Following this displacement the events that had taken place during the cold war just stopped happening, and the story that had endowed historical events with their intelligibility simply broke off. Among several other consequences, this termination posed problems of closure for the national metanarrative that had legitimated historical events over the preceding fifty years.

The New World Order's disruption of the cold war state's ruling fantasy provides a kind of case study on the role fantasy has played within the state's juridical apparatus. Law binds citizens to its rules by way of state fantasies that produce an imminent justification for its rules. Such fantasies should not be construed as a disposable representation of the state's procedures of governance. The fantasy through which a population takes up a different juridico-political order constitutes an essential dimension of the order's symbolic efficacy. What's at stake in these fantasies is not simply the legislator's construction of an imaginary relationship to the real conditions of state governance. Legislators depend upon such fantasies for their legislations to take hold. In taking hold, the state fantasy regulates the processes whereby U.S. citizens acquiesce to the legal identities through which the state manages the population.

After the cold war came to an end, however, the state lost the fantasmatic power to project insuperable political contradictions outside its domestic environs. As a consequence of the state's loss of the powers of disavowal, contradictory economic and social questions returned as intractable political realities. The global economy may have transformed the world into a single, interconnected space, but the disparate socioeconomic processes that traversed nations and locales with different histories resisted any effort to subsume them within the U.S. perspective on the world. When U.S. exceptionalism as a geopolitical logic came unhinged from globalization as an economic logic, the two logics became incommensurable rather than mutually corroborative.

After the narratives that had invested them with significance stopped performing this function, every one of the events that had taken place over the preceding forty-five years threatened to become a series of meaningless contingencies rather than a fulfilled order of temporality. Defining "narrativity" as the imaginary form that readers impose on historical facts to enrich them with the qualities of coherence and finality, Hayden White has argued that the authority that its addressees cede to narrativity in the representation of real events originates from their deep-seated desire to have real events display the values of coherence, integrity, and closure that are otherwise reserved for images of life that are and can only be imaginary. It is only insofar as "historical stories can be completed," in the sense that they "can be given narrative closure, can be shown to have had a plot all along" that their authority can be acknowledged.[1] It is the process of making events that might otherwise seem contingent or arbitrary seem to possess coherence and closure that enables narrativity to make the real seem desirable.

The provision of an appropriate formal closure to the cold war would have performed the essential political function of providing the national metanarrative with a model of order capable of bringing its end into concordance with its beginning. This model would have supplied U.S. citizens with the sense of an ending out of which they could separate themselves from the fantasy to which they had formerly been attached. Only the gratification of this demand for closure could legitimate the sequence of events that had taken place over the preceding half century and reinstate them as elements in the state fantasy through which the official historical narrative had taken possession of them. With this violation of the cold war's narrative contract, U.S. citizens were deprived of the pervasive psychological and social structures out of which they had constituted their national identities. In the absence of an ending concordant with the state's official account of its beginning, two opposed state fantasies emerged that set U.S. citizens who advocated the emergence of a multicultural nation against citizens who remained loyal to the imperatives of the National Security State.

Clinton's New Covenant with America

When he became president in 1992, Bill Clinton set the stage for the formation of a new state fantasy when he introduced a series of legislative measures that changed the terms of the cold war settlement from liberal individualism to liberal multiculturalism. U.S. citizens took up the legislation through a fantasy in which they imagined dissevering themselves from the nation's shameful monocultural past. Recognition of the nation's past wrongs became for the Clinton administration the moral precondition for the redistribution of social and symbolic as well as economic goods within the multicultural polity.

In his July 16, 1992, acceptance speech for the Democratic presidential nomination, Clinton articulated his vision in terms of what he called a "New Covenant with America" that would offer a place to all disenfranchised individuals:

For too long politicians told the most of us that are doing all right that what's really wrong with America is . . . Them. Them, the minorities, Them, the liberals, Them, the homeless, Them, the people with disabilities. Them, the gays. We got to where we really "themed" ourselves to death. Them and Them and Them. But this is America. There is no them. There is only us.[2]

Clinton inaugurated his New Covenant as a part of a war of position during the organic crisis within a historical conjuncture when the neoliberalization of the global economic order was supplanting the cold war's organization of the globe into three worlds. When the age of globalization supplanted the age of the three worlds, culture became a site for the maintenance and reproduction as well as the contestation and revaluation of social processes. At this conjuncture, the authoritarian populism of religious fundamentalists and the free market fundamentalist within the commercial sphere posed grave threats to democratic institutions—unions, social movements, welfare apparatuses—across the planet.

Reaganism and market neoliberalism were the forces that hegemonized the crisis of the post–World War II welfare state and reshaped the whole political landscape. Reagan's attack on the welfare state led to less social security, less guaranteed social care, less affirmative action. In correlating the deregulation of markets abroad with the criminalization of the poor and the alienated at home, Reagan's enterprise culture severely undermined the aspirations for progressive social and political change. The multiculture emerged at a time when the proliferation of neoliberal imaginaries redrew the political landscape of the global economic order by threatening the democratic institutions of liberal democracies worldwide. However, the liberal multiculture did not significantly undermine the relationship between the U.S. citizens who understood themselves to enjoy a supervisory relationship to the identity groups within the multiculture over whom they continued to exercise governance. Rather than significantly disturbing the relationship between what Ghassan Hage called the "governmental belonging" of white Americans and the "passive belonging" of nonwhites, President Clinton conceptualized the liberal multiculture as an initiative brought about by progressive white American nationals, like himself.

Clinton's New Covenant overlapped with the publication of Francis Fukuyama's *The End of History*, which described neoliberalism as the telos of every country on the planet, and with cultural events like Tony Kushner's *Angels in America*, Ken Burns's week-long docudrama *The Civil War*, and the Smithsonian Institution's "The West in America: Reinterpreting Images of the Frontier, 1820–1920" that represented the nation as undergoing a collective disassociation from its shameful past. The public's acknowledgements of these shameful deeds constituted the emotional precondition for the citizens' binding themselves to the New Covenant. The recognition of what was shameful about the historical past would enable its victims and their oppressors to take up a different position in the future. The shame would involve acceptance of the fact that America was an imperial society predominantly populated by white settlers who pirated land, exploited and enslaved subaltern laborers, bullied and sometimes murdered whoever got in their way. But if binding oneself to the New Covenant required loosening one's bonds to the cold war security state by repudiating its ruling "Us versus Them" mentality as a shameful inheritance of a discredited past, most of the members of Ronald Reagan's silent majority refused to accept the terms of the New Covenant.

Indeed Clinton's New Covenant did not merely presuppose that some of the dramatis personae within the national scene of reparation could not undertake the transition from the national to the transnational order of things. His New Covenant required the representation of internal threats to his new social bond as the precondition for its construction. Those who were either unable or unwilling to undertake the transition to purge themselves of their residual cold war attachments took up positions within this immobilizing site of nonpassage by way of fantasies that were very different from the ones that organized the people of the New Covenant.

Clinton articulated his new political formation in terms of the covenantal logics of the religious fundamentalists to which he was ostensibly opposed.[3] He went on to describe the social prejudices and chauvinist nationalism of the Religious Right as posing a threat to the emergence of a liberal multiculture. But Clinton's ostensible embrace of a Third Way that transcended what he called the "politics of difference" enabled him to conceal the structural violence at work in his programmatic elimination of welfare state institutions in the name of market imperatives. He effected the transition from welfare state to market rationalities by positioning Far Right populism as his political antagonist.

The fact that the United States was a multicultural nation had very little to do with the initiatives of its governmental nationals. In the wake of the cold war, the globalization of the economic order made it necessary for the state to abandon its assimilationist policies and to "celebrate" the heterogeneous ethnic groups within the United States as signs of its socio-economic advantage in a global economy. The state no longer viewed the nation's pluralized ethnic minorities as threats to national unity. Clinton's New Covenant redefined "Them" as opportunities for the state to open up market relations with each ethnic group's country or region of origin.

Multiculturalism had been an entrenched part of U.S. social reality from the nation's origin. The newly globalized economy now made it necessary for the government to recognize it in order to derive profit from multiculturalism. The acculturation of members of heterogeneous world cultures into American society was less affected by governmental procedures than the everyday decisions of the members of these communities. They defined the conditions of belonging to U.S. society according to criteria that were autonomous of the supervisory will of U.S. citizens who identified with Clinton's notions of multicultural governance.

The Right supplied Clinton's multiculture with the negative common denominator of its entire political spectrum. But Clinton's repudiation of the right wing's intolerance did not install a new ethos of tolerance of the given order, and his exclusion of the Us/Them mentality that had supervised the state's exclusionary powers throughout the cold war did not result in a discernible democratization of the polis. Clinton tactically deployed the fantasy of right-wing terrorism to discipline his real adversary, which was the radical left. The radical left was opposed to Clinton's neoliberalization of the financial markets and his downsizing of the social welfare as well as his "Don't Ask Don't Tell" policies within the military.[4]

But Clinton's New Covenant with America did bring about a drastic shift in the position that Ronald Reagan's silent majority occupied within the political order. Whereas the silent majority supplied Reagan's spectacular renewal of the fantasy of American exceptionalism with his political foundation, Clinton castigated its members as a socially backward and politically dangerous constituency "on the wrong side of history." Rather than identifying with these degrading positions, the silent majority took up fantasies of a different order.[5]

Americans from the Wrong Side of History

For them, the cold war had not merely failed to conclude with a cataclysmic Day of Reckoning in which the wicked were damned and the good rewarded. Its terminal events included a public stocktaking of the preceding fifty years of state governance that resulted in an enumeration of the national shames—plantation slavery, the bombing of Hiroshima and Nagasaki, the Jim Crow legislation, colonial violence—that, in the aftermath of the cold war, required reparation. The negative evaluation directed against these events led members of this growing political constituency to conclude that if the cold war had indeed terminated with a victory, the victors were the cold war state's enemies rather than its loyal patriots.

As a transitional scenario that did not gratify the demand for the closure of one political formation and that lacked the ceremonial rituals for representing as meaningful the transition to an alternative geopolitical structure, the United States' entry into a New World Order violated the premises of two of the nation's organizing narratives: apocalyptic nationalism and the cowboy western. Both narrative formations effectively linked the nation's citizens to the imperatives of the National Security State. The security state secularized the apocalypse, and it positioned the western cowboy, who was sometimes forced to take the law into his own hands, as the imaginary figure with whom U.S. citizens were encouraged to identify as they acquiesced to the state's demands.

The cold war state subjectivized its citizens' national identities out of the imperatives of the security apparatus. The United States did not exist outside the National Security State, and security did not exist outside the state. The epistemic mastery that it promised the national citizenry was indistinguishable from the security state's technology of power, which obligated citizens to imagine political change within the state's terms. Politicians and citizens alike regularly deployed concepts and themes from the biblical apocalypse and the cowboy western to secure U.S. citizens' spontaneous consent for state policies. In both its apocalyptic and western formulations, the cold war state invoked security as its foundational principle and sought to specify how security might be attained.

Both of these narrative formations adhered to the codes regulating Americans' behavior during the cold war. Since they also presupposed norms that sutured their constituencies to the patterns of domination, subjectification, and governmentality of the National Security State, however, the hegemonic value of both of these cold war narratives requires a brief reflection on the usage to which they were put by the cold war state.

The cold war state adapted the apocalyptic imagination to represent its sovereignty and to legitimate its monopoly over legitimate acts of force. Likening the United States to the Israel of the Old Testament, state officials drew on figures borrowed from biblical apocalypse to justify policy decisions. Indeed, according to Lee Quinby, "it was the convergence of apocalyptic beliefs concerning the end of time with utopian fantasies representing the United States as the perfection of universal history that culminated in the phrase 'American Apocalypse.'"[6]

As a result of the work of cold war Americanist scholars, the fantasy of American exceptionalism that had taken hold in the twentieth century was retroactively applied to a series of disparate historical epochs, beginning with the Puritans. In the estimation of the founders of American studies, the Puritans were better suited than other colonial settlers to meet the needs of this invented tradition. The American studies scholars who selected the Puritans' Exodus as the origin story for the tradition of American exceptionalism endowed the apocalyptic fiction that America had inaugurated a new order for the ages ("Annuit coeptis novus ordo seculorum") with the Puritans' representation of their pilgrimage to America as a divinely ordained "errand into the wilderness." The Puritans' mission thereafter became the theological matrix of the reason of the cold war state.[7]

These commentators chiefly drew upon the sermon "A Model of Christian Charity" (1630) that John Winthrop delivered to his congregation on the Puritan flagship *Arbella* as it was approaching the shores of America as their foundational text. Winthrop's sermon described biblical Jerusalem as the prefiguration of the "Shining City on the Hill" that his congregation would erect in America. In forging this typological linkage, Winthrop sought to overcome the difference between America and biblical scripture so that he could resituate the Puritans' historical realities as scriptural revelation. The special compact that Winthrop thereby drew up between the Puritans and Divine Writ commissioned the Puritans to create in America a church that would reform Europe.

Winthrop's Puritans saw themselves as exceptions to the European betrayal of Christian principles, and they believed that they were conducting an exercise in exceptionalism. Winthrop believed that the Puritans' exceptional spiritual standing granted them biblical warrant to use whatever means they deemed necessary to accomplish their mission. Indeed it was his sense of historical danger that inspired Winthrop to set his City on the Hill outside any constituted order, as the model and standard for a new order of things. The relationship between the American apocalypse and Puritan law that Winthrop established became the theocratic precedent for the cold war state's declaration of necessity as an autonomous source of law.

The Puritan magistrates cited passages from the book of Genesis and John's apocalypse to legitimate their theocracy as well as the regions of exceptions they produced to extend their dominion. Throughout its history, the U.S. imperial state appealed to what could be described as the cultural reserve of apocalyptic anxieties to justify its sovereign powers to declare war, pass judgment, and execute criminals. It was the convergence of the Puritans' apocalyptic beliefs concerning the end of time with the founders' utopian representations of American Revolution as "a transformation *of* history *in* history that would consummate and so give meaning *to* history" that endowed the nation's founding the status of a sacrosanct event.[8]

The Great Awakening of the 1770s allowed the nation's founders to channel the Puritans' evangelical enthusiasm into the American Revolution. The Puritans believed that Americans were exceptional because they were charged by God with the special spiritual and political destiny to create in the New World a church that would reform Europe. The American founding fathers created a different cultural identity by combining their newly forged political beliefs in liberty, egalitarianism, individualism, and laissez-faire with the Puritans' vision of America as a model of a religious rebirth. George Washington believed that the success of the American Revolution confirmed his belief that the almighty had erected in America a "rising empire," which was the "last stage of perfection to which human nature is capable of attaining."[9]

Projected onto the national landscape, the myth of the apocalypse inscribed a disjunct temporality on what happened there. Events that took place in historical time simultaneously intimated the traces of the end of time. One outcome of this disjunct temporality was the belief, destined to become canonical, in the United States' unprecedented relationship to history. Their belief in the apocalyptic aspect of the nation's historical progress provided U.S. citizens with a religious justification for the violence the state exerted to accomplish it.

The apocalyptic imagination described the collision of end-time with events in U.S. history as the quintessential sign of American exceptionalism, which represented America itself as an eschatological event. The assignment of ultimate responsibility for such eschatological events to divine judgment revealed the state's juridical apparatus as the chief beneficiary of its citizens' beliefs. By way of this law-preserving measure, the state established a boundary between what counted as legally binding within the national community and what lay outside it. Like God's apocalyptic judgments, the state's power to make and uphold the law could not be subject to the norms it enforced without submitting itself to those norms.

Americans who invoked the authority of an American apocalypse have, depending upon the course of action they wished to recommend, emphasized one or another of the elements that this phrase conflates: End of Time, Day of Judgment, Great Beast of the Apocalypse, Armageddon, Millennium. Each of these terms predicts the correlation of a historical event with the sacred catastrophe that it would also provoke. Declaring it metaphysically superior to America's opponents', the apocalypse endowed the violence Americans expended to found as well as rejuvenate the nation-state. The apocalyptic imagination enabled its American practitioners to disavow catastrophic outcomes of its exercise—like the Pequot massacre, or slavery, or Hiroshima, or the forcible dispossession of entire populations from their homelands—as Divine Writ inscribing exceptions to law to make manifest America's special destiny.

Throughout the cold war, the security state also invoked the cowboy western to displace actually existing social and political contradictions onto a strictly imaginary site where they underwent symbolic resolution. Set in an open national landscape that fostered the construction and realization of self-reliant individuals, the cowboy western staged spectacles that compensated U.S. citizens for their sacrifice of violence to the state. These spectacles were expressive of the cultural code through which normative behavior was representatively shaped as the actions of a rugged individual set against the backdrop of the Frontier. In its ratification of preconstituted themes—American Adam, Virgin Land, Errand into the Wilderness—from the national metanarrative, the western also legitimated the founding myth of American exceptionalism.

According to Alan Nadel, the adult western condensed within its narrative at least three disparate sets of cultural representations: it represented the real west in a historical sense and the American spirit in a mythical sense and the western bloc in a geopolitical sense.[10] John F. Kennedy's "New Frontier" speech provides ample proof of this claim. Under the banner of the "new frontier," Kennedy explicitly correlated the west of America's mythic history and the west of the cold war alliances and its history and destiny.[11]

The National Security State fostered a symbolic pact whereby the citizenry confirmed its primary linkage to the state through a willingness to surrender their civil rights and political values in the name of national security needs. This imagined act of collective sacrifice effectively realized the image of a totalized national community. It also effected a symbolic economy whereby the security state compensated the citizenry's willingness to substitute their democratic rights and democratic values in exchange for the illusion of collective security. The willingness to sacrifice "democratic" values for security interests had established U.S. citizens' primordial attachment to the cold war state. However, in the wake of the cold war a range of substitute formations—religious fundamentalists, paramilitary organizations that called themselves militia and "Christian patriots," and talk radio—emerged to take up the fantasmatic place of the lost security state.

The Emergence of Two Americas

The dismantling of the cold war state resulted in two very different configurations for U.S. citizens' symbolic identification. Talk radio callers and multicultural citizens designated social positions that it was representationally impossible for the same person to occupy. The Gaze organizing what was desirable in the visual field of multicultural America remained unrecognizable when viewed from the vantage point of monocultural America. Each vantage point was structured at the site of the "blinding" of the alternative to it. Rather than entering the multiculture, talk radio opened up a site of nontraversibility in between the two political dispositions. The talk radio community remained tethered to security state presuppositions long after Clinton authorized the state's transnational alliances and multicultural values.

Religious fundamentalist and militia organizations who put in calls across talk radio gave expression to the belief that the Clinton administration's dismantling of the National Security State had threatened their entire way of life. They construed Clinton's historical stock-taking as an act of state aggression directed against the fantasy structure through which they organized their enjoyment of being American. It was the government not the enemy that had dismantled the myths about their country these Americans held as sacred truths. Rather than enhancing their privileged positions, Clinton's New Covenant had directed a blow against their privileged sense of governance.

The shift in their site of symbolic identification from that of the cold war state to the new transnational world order did not merely involve the state's reconfigurations of the silent majority's way(s) of life. It also disrupted the affective attachments they had forged in taking up their positions within the National Security State. The change in the perspective from which they imagined themselves taking up their new social identities—from the U.S. security state to the transnational world order—resulted in a generalized state of panic among the callers to talk radio.

The attitude that the callers to talk radio adopted toward the transnational state might be better understood if it is interpreted in the light of Renata Salecl's observation that the aim of the aggressor in a war is to destroy the fantasy structure of the enemy's national identification.[12] Since the discontinuation of the cold war destroyed the frame through which they organized their national identity, the callers to talk radio construed the agency responsible for it as a state enemy. The state of panic that emerged with their felt loss of what Ghassan Hage described as "governmental belonging" might be understood as having emerged in the gap between the felt force of state power and their inability to make fantasmatic (i.e., American exceptionalist) sense of it. Talk radio callers gave expression to their panic through fantasizing their relation to the state in highly degrading scenes of violent subjection.

The Literalization of the Cowboy Western

Following the loss of the fantasy that had managed social antagonisms during the cold war, actual events that seemed to have borrowed characters and setting from apocalyptic fictions as well as the cowboy western emerged in real time as lurid scenarios in which the state and the talk radio community negotiated the terms of their juridical and political relationship. During a Wild West–style shootout with federal agents, in Ruby Ridge, Idaho, in 1992, Randy Weaver killed one of the FBI agents who had been tracking him for murder-conspiracy charges. Weaver was the suspected member of a neo-Nazi, white supremacist, militia group. The state agents who tracked him also shot and killed Weaver's wife and teen-aged son in the stand-off. The federal government later settled a wrongful death case with the family for $3.1 million.

Then on April 19, 1993, federal agents raided David Koresh's Branch Davidian compound in Waco, Texas. The Branch Davidians' leader, David Koresh, believed that a violent apocalypse was at hand and included an arsenal of automatic weapons and explosives in his compound in preparation. It was Koresh's belief in an American apocalypse that aroused the state's attention. When state agents from BATF (Bureau of Alcohol, Tobacco and Firearms) converged on the Waco, Texas, compound of the millenarian zealot, they declared his apocalyptic beliefs and practices as the actions of an enemy within the state. Seventy-six members of the Branch Davidians died from either bullets or fire in the conflagration at Waco. President Clinton described the Branch Davidians who died in the conflagration as responsible for having murdered themselves. Critics of the state's actions, who were not restricted to the callers to talk radio, condemned the state for the mass murder of its own citizens.[13]

The state's actions against Koresh seemed to callers across talk radio a weird reenactment of the shoot-out federal agents had initiated at the home of Randy Weaver at Ruby Ridge, Idaho, a year earlier. After these events from the cowboy western and biblical apocalypse through which the National Security State apparatus had formerly justified its power took place in real time and within actually existing frontier spaces like Ruby Ridge and Waco, the Clinton administration repudiated right-wing militia and religious fundamentalists for their complicity in these crimes against the state.

Talk radio's reaction to the government's siege in Waco resulted in congressional hearings on the event. The *Contract with America*, which was released by Newt Gingrich shortly after congressional hearings were held on the legality of the government's actions in Waco, led to the Republican takeover of the 104th Congress and to the consolidation of a political constituency that became increasingly influential. Gingrich's Contract included ten bills that promised to implement major reform of the federal government. Several of the bills bore titles—the Taking Back Our Streets Act, the Violent Criminal Incarceration Act, the Personal Responsibility Act, the American Dream Restoration Act, the National Security Restoration Act, the Family Reinforcement Act— that turned complaints voiced across talk radio into the bases for legislative action.

The particulars of the National Security Restoration Act drew upon the Christian militia's fears that the United States was about to be subjected to governance by the member states of the United Nations. To defend against this fantasized event, the bill included provisions that explicitly prevented U.S. troops from serving under United Nations command and that would cut U.S. payments for U.N. peacekeeping operations. In its specifics as well as its overall design, Gingrich's Contract with America convoked a constituency whose members held views about the United States' national purpose that were antithetical to the New Covenant.

An Event without a Witness

The conflagration at David Koresh's compound in Waco, Texas, and the shoot-out at Ruby Ridge competed with the Persian Gulf War over whether the state or these apocalyptic westerns would supply the ending that was missing from the site of the cold war's termination. But when the image of the bombed out Alfred P. Murrah Federal Building in Oklahoma City first flashed across the television screen on April 19, 1995, it revealed the vast scale of the crisis in self-representation that had ensued with the loss of the cold war fantasy. The event happened at the border between the dismantled cold war frame and the absence of an alternative narrative framework capable of making sense of the event. While the Oklahoma City bombing was shockingly visible, no ready-made viewpoint was capable of comprehending it. The difficulty in positioning it within any official narrative capable of making sense of the fact that it had taken place at all became the event's defining trait. The excess referentiality of this image-event rendered it irreducible to any of the interpretive frameworks that were supposed to make sense of it. As it passed through the available frames of interpretation, the Oklahoma City bombing failed to become explicable within any one of them.

The narrative that Clinton's Justice Department officials initially proposed to explain the event—involving Muslim extremists in a war of terrorism directed against the American people—enjoyed the hegemonic potential of the cold war state fantasy it was designed to replace. Its credibility derived from its power to unite a society against a credible national enemy. But a very different account of the events leading up to the bombing was beginning to take shape among callers to talk radio, who proposed the state's actions in Waco as the probable cause and Christian militia the likely agents.

The date of the explosion, April 19, 1995, coincided with the event that had taken place in Waco, Texas, two years earlier and ratified the callers' linkage between these events. But whereas seventy-six members of the Branch Davidians had died from either bullets or fire in the conflagration at Waco, the truck bomb that exploded in the Alfred P. Murrah Federal Building killed 168, injured 503, and damaged 320 buildings. The asymmetry in the results of these acts of violence brought into visibility a phantom war machine known as the "militia," comprised mostly of former members of U.S. Special Forces from the Vietnam War, who had formed cells across the country to replace the national security apparatuses that had been dismantled with the break-up of the Soviet Union. Members of the militia represented themselves as patrilinear descendants of the patriots from the epoch of the nation's founding who felt summoned back into active duty as a result of the state's imagined violation of the supervisory clause in the founders' social contract—the promotion of collective security in exchange for the citizens' submission to governmental rule.

It was the accounts of the callers to talk radio of the bombing in Oklahoma that brought the existence of the so-called militia movement to national attention. Rumors circulated there had it that Timothy McVeigh was a likely member of the Michigan Militia Corps, which claimed more than twelve thousand members. The federal government's subsequent investigation led to the discovery that up to one hundred thousand Americans in more than thirty states belonged to militia groups. Most of the militia members viewed federal gun control legislation as an attack on their constitutionally protected right to bear arms, and many of them hated the BATF, which was responsible for the enforcement of these gun laws. In their attack on the Waco millenarians, state agents had converted Koresh's and the militia's shared belief in this basic tenet from the cold war state's religion (of apocalyptic nationalism) into a crime against the post–cold war state. According to the members of these militia groups, the Oklahoma City bombing, in having answered violence with violence, had refused to recognize the legitimacy of the state's monopoly over the legitimate use of violence. This act of violence had founded a substitute for the National Security State.

But when this unofficial story of domestic paramilitary organizations engaged in internecine battle with the United States government replaced the initial explanation of the bombing as the work of Arab terrorists, a different communications network also emerged. Michael Harrison of the National Association of Radio Talk Show Hosts (NARTSH) explained the political significance of the alternative narratives circulating across talk radio to John Tierney of the *New York Times* (April 30, 1995): "The mainstream press is out of touch," Harrison explained. "That's why it didn't see the Waco connection right away."[14] Harrison, who is also editor of the talk radio publication *Talkers*, made this observation to mark the contrast between talk radio callers, many of whom had cited the Branch Davidian disaster as the probable cause of the bombing, and the talking heads on the network news channels, who represented Arab terrorists as likely suspects for the deaths in Oklahoma City. Talk radio's repudiation of federal intervention in Waco was expressive of the understanding that responsibility for the American people's collective security had now been displaced from existing state structures and transferred to the paramilitary organizations populated in part by former members of the national security community.[15]

Talk Radio's Community of Intimate Audibility

From the moment CNN's global satellite network connected the visual facts of the Oklahoma City bombing with its local stations throughout the world, this highly volatile event linked these stations to the violence of images that would not be situated within existing systems of intelligibility. By connecting the actual violence of the event with the symbolic violence directed against the frames that would make sense out of it, the Oklahoma City bombing produced a short-circuit between its mode of eventuation and these official interpretive frames. In taking place through the loss of the frame through which it might become a meaningful historical event, the bombing—as if it were itself the missing scene of its "catastrophic conclusion"—enacted the traumatic loss of the cold war frame.

The resistance of this event to recognizable visual images led news commentators to turn to the callers across talk radio stations to make sense of it. This emergent medium, which was the work product of two technologically outmoded communications systems—the telephone and the radio—originated in the 1980s as a medium that promised to give a voice to Ronald Reagan's silent majority. The change in the mode of transmission from the television to the radio symptomatized the loss of the cold war fantasy as the dominant way of positioning events. Throughout the cold war, television buttressed the state's fantasy by supplying television news networks with a visual field that enabled their viewers to visually enframe world events within the cold war's way of picturing them.

As news of this event interrupted television programming across the globe, the Oklahoma City bombing rendered this disconnection from the cold war frame hypervisible—yet utterly extraneous to available frames of reference. When transmitted through the rumors and panicked invective of talk radio, the event emerged into audibility as the remains of a fantasy that had come violently delinked from one frame of reference, the national symbolic order undergirded by the cold war global rivalry, yet could not yet be wholly anchored to another. Vacillating, in its mode of eventuation, between a sheer contingency that could not be claimed by a frame of reference and the destruction of modes of enframement as such, the Oklahoma City bombing disarticulated its glaring violence from the power to make sense of this event then imploded these separated factors into the white noise transmitted across talk radio.

When connected to the generalized rage of talk radio's callers, the event set into play scenarios that could not be accounted for in the pre-existing categories or articulated to the preconstituted relays of official news networks. The bombing also threatened to absorb talk radio into its process of eventuation, not as a standpoint on the Oklahoma City bombing or as an explanation of its causes, or the transmission of information concerning it, but as the site for the generalized implosion already triggered by that event.

The New World Order had discontinued the state fantasy out of which the members of the talk radio constituency had constructed their identities. The desymbolization that emerged in its wake evacuated the social positions that had once sustained the ideal self-images of the talk radio community, leaving them bitter and resentful. The operators of this network shared the belief that with the end of the cold war, they had lost the fantasy out of which they had previously made sense of their world. The fanatical nationalism of the listeners and producers of this alternative communications network was in part the outcome of their hysterical demand for the restoration of that state of fantasy.

Talk radio emerged as a medium through which the callers could communicate their efforts to continue the cold war state's fantasy by other means. Individually and collectively, their calls aspired to recover the callers' imaginary identifications. But in the wake of the cold war, callers to talk radio had to resort to another medium to sustain their residual mode of understanding world events. After their preferred mode of self-representation lost the condition of visual viability, the talk radio community resorted to the realm of audition to take their revenge.

The abrogation of the cold war state's sovereign power to make events take place according to its dictates led members of the talk radio community to fashion what Judith Butler has called "sovereign performatives"—speech acts that simulated the power of the state's speech to inflict real harm.[16] The sovereign names a figure of power whose intention is wholly invested in its real and efficacious practices. When it is correlated with a state's speech acts, this efficacious, transitive, unilateral, generative, sovereign power guarantees the state's accomplishment of them. Endowed with the power to do what it says, the state possesses a power of absolute and efficacious agency and performative transitivity that can deprive U.S. citizens of their rights and liberties, and, in the case of death sentences, their lives. The hate speech and racist invective transmitted across talk radio constituted acts of speech that impersonated the sovereign power of the state's speech acts. If construed from the perspective of the spectatorial fantasy the callers had lost, these sovereign performatives would appear to constitute forms of compensation within the field of audibility for the callers' and listeners' imagined loss of supervisory control over the visual field.

The fanatically embattled nationalism of the listeners and producers of talk radio was in part the outcome of their hysterical demand for the return of cold war certitudes. Talk radio transmitted what had to be elided from the official news media; namely, a preexisting and generalizable anxiety over the loss of the cold war frame. In its exploitation of these anxieties, talk radio adopted an antagonistic relation to the official mode of news production. Talk radio did not distribute already existing bits of information into digestible sound bites; it transmitted fierce and sometimes frightening nonnegotiable demands—racist invective, howls of outrage, death threats, curses, and the conspiracy fantasies through which these vocalizations circulated—that its subscribers did not address to anyone in a position to respond. These enunciations forcibly reduced the entire intersubjective symbolic order to the dimensions of "you" and subsequently removed that interlocutor from the circuit of communicative exchange.

The purveyors of these negative speech acts produced this alternative communications network whose callers and listeners were at once the producers and consumers of its information. In its early years, talk radio recruited major players from the cold war state fantasy, like the hero of the Senate Hearings on the Iran-Contra, Oliver North, and G. Gordon Liddy, to "receive" the call-ins. G. Gordon Liddy was the most notorious of the early talk radio hosts. This convicted felon from the Watergate era openly represented himself as the leader of an armed movement and instructed the listeners across the 250 stations that subscribed to his program in how to shoot federal agents in the head.

As a composite speech act, talk radio was addressed *to* and enunciated *as* its listeners' rage over the loss of their capacity to enframe the world within the cold war's picture. Talk radio's callers constructed a community of intimate audition out of their shared collective demand for the return of the power to appropriate the world to this superseded framework. Talk radio's listeners understood themselves as still inalienably linked to the picturing power of the cold war imaginary that had, with the globalization of the U.S. economy, been voided of any ground whereon its "reality" might be negotiated. Deprived of the national metanarrative whereby the cold war had secured the stability of their identities and lacking a generally accepted alternative, the subscribers to this "independent" radio network constructed intensely nationalistic fantasies to enunciate this demand. The cultural authority of talk radio was predicated on its power to represent its callers and listeners as the producers of their own news reception apparatuses. Because it took place by way of the loss of any preexisting frame of reference or preconstituted categories, the Oklahoma City bombing literalized as real the violence transmitted across talk radio.

Insofar as it brought talk radio into the dominant discourse of the post–cold war symbolic order, the bombing also symbolized the political significance of talk radio. In the affective and symbolic economy of these callers, the Oklahoma City bombing at once provided an image of the catastrophic conclusion that the cold war lacked. It also represented what would not be integrated within the New World Order. For the callers to talk radio, the Oklahoma City bombing participated in the ongoing violence of this desymbolization and gave vivid expression to their demand for the return of the power to enframe the world in the cold war picture of it. Upon expressing its callers' generalized anxiety over the loss of the cold war fantasy, the Oklahoma City bombing also incited a plague of fantasies.

Negative Interpellations

Underdetermined as to its significance, the bombing solicited accounts on the unofficial talk radio networks that were underwritten individually and collectively by the return of an abandoned state fantasy. In "Ideology and Fantasy," Rastko Mocnik has proposed an Althusserian explanation for the impossible demand for the return of such a fantasy:

> The mechanism of ideological interpellation (the mechanism whereby individuals are sutured to the State as subjects of/to its processes) may be described in the following way: in order to pronounce a meaningful utterance, the speaker identifies her/himself with a structural position (the subject supposed to believe) from which a meaningful, i.e., interpellative, utterance might be pronounced.[17]

The "subject supposed to believe," Mocnik reasoned, was the outcome of a preconscious activity—the overdetermination of two separable mental processes, condensation and displacement. Freud described the conflation of these processes as the precondition for the production of

fantasy. In fantasy, Freud claimed, the desire that an utterance be meaningful coincided with an otherwise unrelated need—the compulsion to
believe that the utterance was true.[18]

With the dismantling of the cold war, the "subject supposed to believe" in its fantasy was unable to shift credence to the very different
fantasies that had emerged in the New World Order. Although the "subject who was supposed to believe" in the cold war's ideologemes had
come unstitched from the symbolic order through which its demand for
sense had been gratified, the callers to talk radio remained committed
to cold war state fantasies.

The differences between talk radio's callers and the audience for the
global news turned on the latter group's ability to disconnect from
the "subject supposed to believe" in the National Security State. As the
locus for what has not been interpellated as a subject within the New
World Order, however, the "subject that was supposed to believe," who
had lost the official state fantasy to which it could tether its credibility,
reinvested its credence in the lurid rumors and fantasies with which the
callers to talk radio had supplanted that fantasy.

One of the most pervasive of the fantasies, which was circulated over
talk radio after President Clinton took office, warned of an imminent
takeover by agents of the United Nations whose secret plans included
the reintroduction of slavery and the opening up of concentration
camps for targeted U.S. dissidents. The description of President Clinton
as "the sworn vassal of a coven of Communist lesbian members of the
Tri-Lateral commission" held a key position in this fantasy.[19] Rather
than becoming interpellated to the discourse of the New World Order,
talk radio's callers resituated the "subject who is supposed to believe" in
collective fantasies like these, which demanded shelter from the imagined paramilitary operation putatively organized by the United Nations,
whose mission entailed their captivity as a slave labor force.[20]

The narrative logic underwriting this fantasy supplied the talk radio
community imaginative compensation for the transnationalization of the
state security apparatus. This fantasy capitalized on the generalized domestic insecurity that had emerged in the wake of the cold war and
cathected it onto the rumor that President Clinton intended to dismantle the U.S. military apparatus in the name of the antiwar movement that
originated with the 1960s counterculture and whose members (now in
the White House) were presently involved in a world-wide conspiracy

designed first to enslave and later to exploit "mainstream" U.S. citizens as an unpaid labor force.

This fantasy overwhelms the question of the truth. What matters to the talk radio community is the way desire is organized in response to the anxieties opened up by the callers' collectively shared fantasy structure. Whether or not any of these scenarios is factually true is of little importance because the fantasy underwrites the desire *for* the "subject who is supposed to believe" them. Since the fantasy itself is structured at the site of an impossible demand, it is always factually untrue, even as it reveals the truth of the impossible demand. It can never actually be experienced as raw fact because of the traumatic character of the demand to which it gives expression.

Reduced to the political demand underwriting it, this fantasy can be restated as a collective demand to be separated from President Clinton's multicultural state. Without the promise of collective security in symbolic exchange, talk radio listeners feared that their survival had been jeopardized in the liberal multiculture. The phrase "coven of Communist lesbian members of the Tri-Lateral commission" in the aforementioned fantasy condensed several signifiers—(militant) gays in the U.S. military, single-parent families, feminists subversive of white patriarchal dominance, communists masquerading as multiculturalists, the transnational enemies of the National Security State—to the enframing anxiety over the Clinton administration's threat to their survival.

The cold war had displaced social catastrophe onto the nation's Other and condensed all other social antagonisms at the resolution imagined at this displaced site. With the breakdown of the mechanism that structurally repressed these unclaimed images from the past—the institution of slave labor camps for Africans in the nineteenth century; concentration camps for Japanese-Americans in the twentieth; fire bombings of civilian populations in Dresden, Tokyo, and My Lai; nuclear holocausts in Hiroshima, Nagasaki, and the Bikini Islands—these images returned as traumatic national memories. In the distance separating the historical fact that these events had indeed happened from the loss of the powers of their foreclosure, the unspent force of foreclosure had become the communicative medium for callers to talk radio.

In *Modernity and the Holocaust*, Zygmunt Bauman supplied a historical rationale for these fantasies.[21] Bauman has described the nation-state's

systematic denial of death as one of the unclaimed legacies of the Enlightenment. Because death threatened the conceptual order founded
in a belief in reason, the state projected the anxiety associated with
death onto persons relegated to what Edith Wyschogrod has called
"death worlds," that is, social regimes whose inhabitants were compelled
to undergo experiences that were structured in the imagined conditions
of death.[22] The Enlightenment posited the state's symbolic immortality
as the difference between the enduring value of its institutions and the
evanescence of events undergone in the death worlds. According to
Bauman this structure was secured through the symbolic order's designation of certain figures—slaves, prisoners of war, the sick and homeless—
as socially dead, and thereby externalized death from the social categories
whose reproduction ratified the symbolic immortality of the socio-
symbolic order.

Representing itself as symbolically voided of the order of mortality,
the post-Enlightenment cold war state produced what might be called
an empty category within the social order. It was at this non-place that
the mortality of the social order was at once acknowledged (as the "life
world" of the socially dead) and disavowed. When the state refused a
viable social position to these "exceptions" to the liberal state's policy
of inclusiveness, it produced a mortality structure for these socially dead
figures whose radical externality to the workings of the symbolic order
enabled that order to believe that it had already surpassed the death
that it had simultaneously instituted.

Having lost the cold war fantasy anchoring their life worlds, the
callers to talk radio might be imagined as having experienced themselves
interpellated to this mortality structure. Without a national Other
onto whom responsibility for this order of trauma could be projected,
the return of these traumatic images (I am thinking in particular of the
hysterical reactions of World War II veterans to the revisionist historians'
accounts of Hiroshima and the Enola Gay) have become themselves
representative of the interpellative powers of the death worlds.

The nonspace of the death world houses those figures whose constitutive externality to its workings produces the assimilative structures of
the symbolic order. This superfluous category reveals the priority of the
trace of exteriority over any already constituted order and a relation to
the figure of the exception within—or what might be called "internal
externality"—that precedes the interpellated self (the "individual"

Althusser conceptualized as prior to the subject but who assumed sub-jectivization as the effect of the hailing).[23]

Because they experience themselves in the place of internal exter-nality where this call is most audible, the callers to talk radio at once disclosed this site at which alterity calls from within an already existing symbolic order and also initiated a struggle to drown out this different order of responsibility. In their hate-filled hailings, they are reenacting the trauma of alterity's reception as the abject loss of the power to re-figure alterity as an opposition. In reducing this call to a crisis of inter-pellation that their alternative field of audibility would shout down, these callers have thereby turned the "interpellation" of exteriority into the occasion to protest the loss of their power to reduce it to the order of the self-same opposition. By way of their enraged voicing, the call that had emerged in between the death of the cold war's sociosymbolic order and the eradication of the subject positions for those who had been subjectivized within its terms has been rearticulated as the de-mand for the return of those lost interpellations.

Relegislating the State's Fantasy

As we have seen, the Oklahoma City bombing served these callers as a transitional object. It empowered them to transfer their residual cold war state fantasies onto this event whereon the loss of the cold war power to control its conditions of intelligibility had become visible. This event detached post–cold war political rationalities from the state apparatuses that guaranteed their legitimacy and opened up intense nego-tiation between their desire for recognizable meanings and the Clinton administration's efforts to discredit them. Oscillating between antagonis-tic modes of juridical enframement that associated the bombing with the "illegal violence" of the militia movement on the one hand and the "legalized violence" of the multicultural state on the other, the event operated within an adjudicative calculus that threatened to transform this incompatibility into opposed legal rationalities.[24] The struggle to make sense of the event assumed the form of an opposition between interpellative powers: the listeners to talk radio, who believed that the federal government had organized the event to discredit their phantom substitute for the National Security State, and the officials in the Clinton administration who recharacterized the event as an example of the senseless violence talk radio's "lunatic" beliefs had summoned forth.[25] Clinton represented talk radio as the agency responsible for articulating the meaning of the event, and he condemned talk radio callers for their refusal to join the state in its repudiation of the event. Clinton thereafter correlated talk radio's collective indignation with the violence that David Koresh and Timothy McVeigh had directed against the state, and he turned all of these examples of illegal violence into the occasion for the state's recovery of its monopoly over the legitimate use of retributive justice.

Talk radio callers directed their hate speech against the government in the name of this secret security state that had emerged in the wake of the cold war. But after receiving the FBI's official explanation of the event, Bill Clinton refused to acknowledge the legitimacy of the linkage talk radio callers had adduced between the state's actions in Waco and the disaster in Oklahoma City. In recharacterizing such efforts at constructing a rationale for this action as the retroactive justification for "absolute evil," President Clinton first delinked the Waco conflagration from the Oklahoma City bombing, then he connected his legislation with the rejection of talk radio's vituperative nationalism.[26]

President Clinton established the post–cold war state's monopoly over the legitimate use of symbolic violence in the very act of separating these two events. When the Oklahoma City bombing was forcibly separated from the government's siege of the Branch Davidians' compound in Waco, President Clinton voided it of its quality of retributive justice and redefined it as a senseless act of violence. Through this diminution of the scale of the Oklahoma event, Clinton removed the bombing from talk radio's contested representation of it. By way of this same act of symbolic violence, however, Clinton also retroactively sanctioned the state's actions at Waco. Disconnecting the Oklahoma bombing from the Waco burning entailed a reaffirmation of the state's authority to enframe that incident within a juridical logic of constitutionally sanctioned state violence.

Having correlated talk radio's rage over the state's violence in Waco with the aggression motivating McVeigh's bombing of the Murrah Federal Building in Oklahoma City, Clinton fashioned a defense of the state's actions in Waco out of the state's refusal to recognize the legitimacy of any connection between the two events. He then addressed this complex speech act to the talk radio network, whose operators had invoked the specter of vigilante justice to explain its relationship to Waco. Having dissevered the Oklahoma City bombing from the narrative authority of this countersymbolic order, Clinton accused the participants in talk radio's alternative security state apparatus as bearing indirect responsibility for the event.

Within days of the bombing in 1995, President Clinton made a speech criticizing the "many angry voices" of talk radio "as purveyors of hate and division" who "leave the impression, by their very words, that violence is acceptable."[27] He also concluded that such voices encouraged actions like the Oklahoma bombing. After thus resituating the bombing in a series comprised of the most extremist voices on the talk radio circuit, Clinton founded the legality of his governmental rule upon the representation of talk radio's shadow security state as involved in a crime against the state. In sentencing Timothy McVeigh to death, Clinton transmuted the militia's illegal violence into the founding violence of the multicultural state.

The significance of Clinton's description of McVeigh's crime as deserving capital punishment should be considered within the context of the state's refusal to ask for the death penalty in the case of Aldrich Ames, a CIA agent whose sale of state secrets to Soviet counterparts had resulted in the deaths of several fellow agents. Had the Ames case taken place during the cold war, the state's demand for his public execution would have corroborated the power of the National Security State. After the breakup of the "Evil Empire," the National Security State had lost its rationale. President Clinton founded the post–cold war state's security upon this displacement of the National Security State's rationale.

The operators of talk radio stations quickly disavowed any relationship between their callers and the bombing, but they affirmed the collective fantasy through which the callers represented the bombing as an act of retributive justice for the government's use of excessive force in Waco, Texas, two years earlier. Following this ratification of their previous description of the event, however, the talk radio constituency gave renewed expression to their indignation over the aggression the state directed against U.S. citizens. Clinton's official version of the bombing was represented as a campaign against talk radio.

Clinton had in fact founded the state of the New Covenant at the contradictory site where he represented the religious nationalism of the Christian fundamentalists and the violent nationalism of the militia movement as illegitimate expressions of U.S. nationalism. President Clinton described Christian fundamentalists and nongovernmental militia groups as threats to the national order. He urged them to unbind themselves from their residual attachments to the illegitimate violence they advocated and to bind themselves to the images and representations within the New Covenant community. In building his New Covenant out of the legitimate violence the state directed against Timothy McVeigh, Clinton was also founding the covenant community out of the exclusion of these constituencies. In foreclosing them from his new America, Clinton had also literalized the fantasy—of having been consigned to a death world—that had been widely circulated among the members of these sects. Clinton thereafter referred to the outrage to which they subsequently gave expression across talk radio as the authorization for the legitimacy of his new compact. Clinton had forged his New Covenant at the site at which they felt consigned to a hell, and Clinton enjoined the members of his fellowship to enjoy their pain.

Newt Gingrich constructed his Contract with America out of his constituency's demand to punish President Clinton for crimes against the people. As we have seen, Gingrich's Contract with America was not merely constructed as the Republican Party's answer to Clinton's New Covenant. Gingrich composed its bill of particulars out of the demands for recognition of the Christian fundamentalists and the militia Clinton had excluded from his national compact. When Gingrich published his Contract, the rift that had emerged in the wake of the cold war was consolidated into an internal war that had opened up in between two irreconcilable national factions. Both forms of legislation—Gingrich's Contract with America and Clinton's New Covenant—depended upon the construction of state fantasies to hegemonize these social compacts.

Since the value of Clinton's New Covenant was premised on the rejection of monocultural nationalism, Clinton was in search of an event that would enable him to found this community at a site where it supplanted this discredited compact. Gingrich constructed his Contract with America out of the enraged responses of Christian fundamentalists and the militia to the Clinton administration's actions at Waco.

The terms of Clinton's New Covenant and of Gingrich's Contract were organized around antagonistic reactions to two cataclysmic events— the BATF siege of the Branch Davidian complex at Waco and the bombing of the Alfred P. Murrah Federal Building in Oklahoma City. While these two national communities were organized out of the different fantasies that cohered around these events, each state fantasy was constructed at the site of the enjoyment of the destruction of the other's state of fantasy. The position from which each of these fantasies got interiorized required imagining the ongoing negation of the Other's way of life.

The sites where these fantasies took hold were also places of intense contestation over the significance of these events. Clinton "felt the pain" of the members of the old covenant whom he characterized as having been so scarred by the historical traumas they inherited from the past that they could not move on. In their response, talk radio turned to hate speech and all too literal acts of violence to "feel the pain" of Clinton's covenantal community as an alternative way of organizing their desire for a national compact.

The difference between these compacts with America symptomatized the deeper rift that had emerged in the aftermath of the cold war. Unable to project their internal antagonisms outward, the members of the U.S. political sphere interiorized the rift that the fantasy of American exceptionalism had disavowed. The culture war that emerged out of the implosion of the cold war divided the nation into peoples of Two Covenants within red and blue states organized out of a fundamental conflict over the terms of inclusion within these contradictory fantasies. The members of the New Covenant who embraced transnational and multicultural values condemned the messages broadcast across talk radio as the rantings of white supremacists and racists. But the members of the talk radio constituency perceived themselves as normal, law-abiding, church-going citizens who were practicing the American way of life.

Clinton's New Covenant and Gingrich's Contract with America might be described as having deepened the site of the transition from the cold war to the New World Order into a nontraversable abyss. They are significant to the concerns of this book because each of these pieces of legislation is structured at the site of what might be called the organizing antagonisms of the liberal political order. This site cohered around the limit to the liberal order's desire for inclusiveness and it took the form of the radical disruption of every possibility of clearly distinguishing between membership and inclusion, between what was outside and what was inside, between exception and law.

America of the Two Covenants

The state's official legal response to the Oklahoma City bombing had consolidated these sites of symbolic identification into opposed political compacts that set the citizens of the talk radio constituency in a relation of opposition to the citizens within the multiculture who organized their identities from the perspective of a global economic order. The callers who expressed their indignation at Clinton's ruling were giving expression to their residual identification with the cold war's state of fantasy. When he composed what he called the Contract with America, Newt Gingrich repudiated Clinton for his abrogation of the cold war's social contract. And after the Waco Hearings, he encouraged his constituency across talk radio to understand their rationale for the Oklahoma City bombing as the foundational tenet for this revolutionary social contract.

In this chapter, I have tried to keep track of what was nonsymbolizable within a cold war fantasy by conceptualizing it in terms of the cataclysmic events that have literalized that traumatizing element in the cold war's wake. And I have arrived at a conclusion in which Bill Clinton and Newt Gingrich have conscripted that nonsymbolizable violence as the foundational event of two utterly incompatible social compacts. Neither Clinton nor Gingrich traversed the site of transition in between the cold war and a newly configured state. Each instead occupied the site of the intense political antagonisms in between the state and the political community to forge compacts that were expressive of these antagonisms rather than any social or political formation through which U.S. citizens could organize their relationship to what remained unrepresentable within these antagonisms. But the incommensurability between Clinton's New Covenant and Gingrich's reactionary contract brings us to a threshold moment of irreversible transition where a rite of passage that would not merely literalize this violence was all the more urgently needed. In the next chapter I will analyze the revival of interest in Alexis de Tocqueville as an effort to produce this rite of passage.

3

A National Rite of Passage:
The Return of Alexis de Tocqueville

Tocqueville, the Mullah of Surplus Containment

President Clinton was well aware of the problems that the Two Covenants had posed for the national political culture. And throughout his administration he forged a politics of recognition that might enable Christian evangelicals and liberal multiculturalists to acknowledge each other as heirs of a shared political tradition. Along with many other politicians and journalists he found Alexis de Tocqueville's analysis in *Democracy in America* of what rendered America exceptional especially suitable to this purpose. Clinton also believed that Tocqueville's condemnation of revolutionary terrorism would prove valuable in explaining and justifying the legislation he introduced in Congress condemning terrorism in its nativist as well as its Islamic extremist manifestations.

But in its February 2, 1998, issue, the *New Republic* published a column entitled "Tocqueville and the Mullah" in which the editors expressed their concern over the different usage to which *Democracy in America* had been put by the president of Iran. The editors gave expression to this concern after watching an interview that CNN had recently broadcast with President Mohammed Khatami. They described the interview as posing a significant "threat" to the U.S. policy of "dual containment."¹ The dual containment policy referenced in the column operated on two separate but intertwined levels. These levels inter-connected the national geography governed by state policymakers with the civil society inhabited by U.S. citizens.

As an official foreign policy, dual containment implemented the state's substitution of Iran and Iraq for Russia and China as the repre-sentatives, in the wake of the cold war, of the fundamental threats to the national security. In substituting Islamic terrorism for world com-munism as constituting a pervasive menace to the American way of life, the post–cold war policy conjoined the totalization of danger in the external realm with a reorganization of domestic civil society.

"Tocqueville" and the "Mullah" were condensed signifiers for the operations that produced both the threat and the territorial and civic spaces whereby the policy contained the threat. The enactors of con-tainment as an official foreign policy invoked Tocqueville's description of the exceptional standing of the United States in the history of nations to authorize the securing of its territorial borders against the threats posed by the Mullah's Islamic terrorists. Citizens found in Tocqueville's *Democracy in America* a representative account of U.S. civil society. Tocqueville described civil society as a social arena in which citizens could exercise their rights of voluntary association and free and open discussion as a consequence of the state's protection of its contours against the menace posed by the Mullah's civic violence and linguistic terrorism.²

But the threat that the editors characterized Khatami as having posed was neither that of the Muslim terrorist who justified the state's foreign policy nor that of the Islamic fundamentalist whose "incivility and irrationality" consolidated the contours of U.S. civil society. The greatest threat that Khatami posed to the editors grew out of his having declined to appear threatening. Khatami's carefully articulated refusal to identify either himself or Islam as a menace to U.S. democracy thereafter endangered both levels of the policy of containment that, as we have seen, depended upon these negative representations of the Mullah for their effective operation.

Khatami gave expression to his refusal to ratify this negative repre-sentation in three separate but interconnected articulations: he refuted the claim that the Islamic Republic constituted a threat to the United States' territorial borders; he proposed similarities between the religious

cultures of the United States and Iran; and he declared the dual containment policy a violation of internationally agreed upon codes of
civility and a threat to democratic cultures worldwide.[3]

The editors found in the fact that the CNN interview with Khatami
had taken place at all evidence of Iran's unwarranted reintegration
within civil society. But they were particularly vexed over Khatami's
citations from Tocqueville's *Democracy in America* to justify Iran's change
of status. Khatami had adapted his understanding of Alexis de Tocqueville's *Democracy in America* (a book he was "sure most Americans have
read") to the task of formulating this complex repudiation of the dual
containment policy. Proposing that U.S. citizens' devotion to liberty
was itself cultivated in the rites and traditions of what Tocqueville had
described as a national civil religion, Khatami drew the conclusion that
the U.S. civil religion was not altogether different from Iran's religious
nationalism that also "calls all humanity irrespective of religion and belief, to rationality and logic."

Khatami's deployment of Tocqueville's text to dismantle the containment policy should be understood as the inversion of the usage to
which policymakers had previously put it to work. From the time of its
initial publication in 1835, *Democracy in America* supplied the concepts, generalizations, and categories out of which U.S. citizens were
encouraged to experience and make sense of U.S. democracy. Its system
of representations anchored the presuppositions out of which citizens
and politicians formulated their opinions. *Democracy in America* was reproduced, perpetuated, and transmitted through such discursive practices.

Because Tocqueville's *Democracy in America* was reputed to have
codified the governing norms and assumptions that undergirded U.S.
democracy, political commentary on it elevated the text into a transhistorical representation of U.S. democracy's unchanging transcendental
essence. It was as a consequence of the text's standing that the governmental officials responsible for the dual containment policy invoked the
norms and rules informing Tocqueville's categorical understanding of
U.S. democracy as politically authorized criteria for deciding that the
United States and the Islamic Republic were absolutely opposed political formations.[4]

"Tocqueville" thereafter became the signifier of what was quintessen-
tially American, and the "Mullah" was made to represent a foreign will
that was constitutive of U.S. democracy's negative essence. Because

Islamic fundamentalism represented everything *Democracy in America* was not, it followed that Khatami's Iran was not only not democratic, it was not amenable to democratization and could never become so. Insofar as Islam represented the political formation out of whose exclusion U.S. civil society had established its integrity, the political effectiveness of U.S. civil society might be described as having depended in part upon Islam's ongoing negative valuation of its workings. Indeed, the "universal" value of the model of noncoercive communication underpinning U.S. civil society was produced out of its differential relation to its putatively negative valuation in Islamic countries.[5]

Consequently, when President Khatami quoted from passages in *Democracy in America* as evidence of the similarities between Islamic nationalism and U.S. civic associations, he transgressed the borderline between the two political orders that "Tocqueville" had formerly delineated and removed both cultures from the relationship of mutual exclusion in which they had been contained. When he constructed equivalences between the political aspirations of Iranian and U.S. citizens, however, Khatami had accomplished more than the disruption of the policy's capacity to sustain the mutual antagonism between Americans and Iranians.

Khatami's invocation of *Democracy in America* to express his refusal to subject himself to its powers of containment had transformed the policy itself into a matter for political deliberation. Upon materializing a common ground out of these homologies, Khatami deployed *Democracy in America* to open a place for Islamic fundamentalists *within* the U.S. democracy from which "Tocqueville" had prohibited them access. And in his CNN interview, President Khatami suggested that his heterodox reading of *Democracy in America* might become the basis for a free and open conversation between the two cultures.

But when the editors subsequently quoted passages from the interview, they did not agree or disagree with the particulars of Khatami's observations. Rather than engaging President Khatami in a discussion of either the merits of his reading of Tocqueville or the similarities between the two political cultures, the editors resorted to acts of verbal aggression that were apparently designed simply to annul Khatami's rights as an interlocutor within U.S. civil society.

The editors' symbolic violence involved the imposition of terms— "ayatollah," "mullah," "jihad"—the connotations of which cohered around the signifier of Islam's unchanging equivalence with international terrorism whose meaning Khatami had adamantly refused. Furthermore, when the editors did quote from the interview, they attributed to Khatami's statements significations that reversed their declared meanings and that were designed to prove his ignorance of democratic norms. After quoting Khatami's remark that "supporting peoples who fight for the liberation of their land is not, in my opinion, terrorism," for example, the editors interpreted this statement as evidence that Khatami had simply "resorted to the old semantics of revolutionary mischief." After thus substituting for Khatami's statement a signification that was precisely the reverse of the meaning that Khatami had declared, the editors proposed their substitution as proof of his failure to conceal his continued allegiance to Islamic terrorism.

The violence that the editors acted out in the process of removing him from the environs of the U.S. public sphere might be explained as a defensive reaction to President Khatami's having proposed equivalences between the two orders. His production of this symbolic common ground had trespassed the imaginary border that delineated each culture's totalized negation of the other.

However, in aggressively projecting onto Khatami the identity of "menacing terrorist" that he had so adamantly repudiated, the editors had also violated the norms of civility and noncoercive communication organizing the civic contract. Exactly why Khatami's interview should have provoked in the *New Republic*'s editors the threatening behavior and civil violence that the containment policy had formerly restricted to Islam requires some further consideration of the social work that the policy performed and the role of "Tocqueville and the Mullah" in its construction.

Claude Lefort has located one source of the editors' anxieties in what Tocqueville had called democracy's "limitless social power," a power that might be understood to underwrite the containment policy itself. Lefort draws the following description of the immense dimensions of this power from the following passage from Tocqueville's *L'Ancien Regime et la Revolution*: "It is the role of the State not merely to govern the Nation, but to shape it in a certain fashion; it is the task of the State to shape the minds of its citizens in accordance with the model that has been proposed in advance; its duty is to imbue their minds with certain ideas, and to inspire in their hearts such feelings as it judges necessary. In reality, no restrictions are placed upon its rights, and there are no limits as to what it can do; it does not simply reform men, it transforms them; and if need be, it will simply create other men."[6] What Tocqueville discovers in this passage is that it is democracy's "limitless power" itself that constitutes the greatest threat to the democratic order. In the wake of the French Revolution, Tocqueville designated the centralized state and the people as the two agents that democracy had historically empowered to exercise this terrifying power. In its recodification of the limitless powers that Tocqueville feared, the dual containment policy transformed the text through which Tocqueville had managed his fear into one of the instruments through which it produced an internal as well as an external limit to the exercise of this power.

The policy produced each of these limits out of a threefold operation. The policy alienated democracy's limitless power from its putative origins within the democratic people and the sovereign state, it divided this power into protective and aggressive manifestations, and then it externalized power's threatening aspects onto two substitute formations—the antidemocratic forces of foreign as well as domestic terrorists. After it projected what Tocqueville had found threatening about the state's limitless power onto the menace that Islamic fundamentalism posed to U.S. democracy, the policy repositioned the source of the state's limitless power as a violence external to the nation. The policy's projection of the state's excess force onto the violence the Mullah directed against its citizenry produced a symbolic limit to the state's power. This imaginary boundary line in between state violence and its externalization inscribed a limit that legitimated the state's use of force. This limit also enabled U.S. citizens to manage their fear that the state might direct its limitless power against them.

In addition to this external limit, the containment policy inscribed a limit to the democratic people's power that was internal to each individual citizen. The policy produced this internal limit out of the division of the citizen's potential expression of democracy's power into regulatory and menacing aspects. Citizens exercised the regulatory aspect of their power, according to exponents of the containment policy, when they redefined popular movements for democratic change as constituting threats to democratic governance akin to Muslim terrorists'. The policy thereby managed the citizenry's limitless power to effect democratic change when it recast collective democratic movements as themselves posing a threat to the democratic state.

"Tocqueville" and the "Mullah" thus named the condensed signifiers whereby the dual containment policy managed the citizenry's fear of the limitless powers posed by the state and radical democratic movements. When President Khatami refused to identify with the position of the Mullah through which the policy had inscribed the external and internal limits to democracy's limitless powers, he quite literally brought the containment policy to its limits. Without containment's powers to externalize this threat, the editors came face to face with a quite literally unlimited democratic force. Unable to subsume Khatami within any of the already constituted positions *within* the containment policy, the editors performed the acts of civic violence that apparently violated the distinction between "Tocqueville's" civility and the "Mullah's" terrorism upon which the dual containment policy had been founded.

Although the editors' aggressive actions seemed to violate the policy's founding prohibition of civic violence, these acts of incivility had in fact reestablished the distinction between Tocqueville and the Mullah upon which the policy had been founded. In reinaugurating the containment policy at the site of Khatami's annulment of its already constituted positions, the editors exercised what might be called the surplus power of containment.

By containment's surplus power, I mean to indicate the excessive power required for the inauguration of the dual containment policy. As the tour de force that produced the founding distinction between Tocqueville's civility and the Mullah's terrorism, this inaugural event could not be sorted either within civil society or within the realm of Islamic terrorism out of whose ongoing negation the civic order achieved its coherence. The act that was responsible for the inscription of the policy, that is to say, could neither be subject to the rules and norms through which Tocqueville regulated the democratic order nor could it be represented within the system of representations through which the Mullah threatened that order.

Because this act was responsible for the production of the relation of mutual exclusion organizing the integrity and coherence of both realms, it necessarily surpassed the powers of containment of each. When the policy subsequently subsumed all acts of civic violence under the aegis of the Mullah, however, it also tacitly proposed that the founding act of discrimination whereby the policy had irretrievably excluded Islamic violence from civil society had also designated itself as the single act of (civic) violence that constituted an exception to the Mullah's rule. As we have seen, President Khatami had compelled the editors to invoke this exception to the rule prohibiting them from performing acts of civic violence when he deployed Tocqueville to refuse the containment policy's suturing within the position of the Mullah.

The editors enunciated the exception that overruled Khatami's refusal when they pronounced the phrase "Tocqueville was not all you needed to know." The Tocqueville whom the editors had invoked as the authorization for this pronouncement was the very same Tocqueville whom Khatami had cited as the authority for his refusal to acknowledge the oppositional relationship that the containment policy had erected between the two cultures.

The exception that Tocqueville appended to his own prohibition against civic violence targeted President Khatami as the "you" to whom this exception was addressed. The exception required "you" to know that "Tocqueville" was not all that "you" needed to know. What President Khatami also needed to know was that the position of the Mullah that the containment policy had mandated "you" to assume had been defined as lacking any politically legitimate knowledge of Tocqueville. After the editors invoked Tocqueville to deauthorize the Mullah's knowledge of *Democracy in America*, they also reinstated the exclusion of the Mullah from the U.S. civic order.

"Tocqueville" thereby performed a double duty within the dual containment policy. Tocqueville materialized at once the internal limit to the limitless power of democracy and an exception to its rules and norms. But as the exception to his own rule prohibiting civic violence, Tocqueville was empowered to become the Mullah of the surplus powers required to recontain President Khatami within the position of Mullah. The *New Republic*'s editors should be understood as having acted upon the authority of "Tocqueville's" surplus powers of containment in their reinscription of the containment policy.

The fact that he provoked these extreme measures suggests that Khatami had also brought the editors face to face with the containment policy's inability fully to regulate the different kind of democratic politics that Khatami had employed Tocqueville to practice. In what follows, I shall try to explain the difference Khatami's use of Tocqueville might entail for the prevailing understanding of democratic politics. In searching for that explanation, I shall briefly address a number of inter-related topics: the affective dimension of dual containment as a foundational fantasy of democratic governance; a critical genealogy of Tocqueville's role in the staging of this fantasy; an analysis of Tocqueville's trip to America in terms of this governing fantasy; a redescription of *Democracy in America* as Tocqueville's fantasy of French governance; and an account of the political rationale for C-Span's 1998 retracing of Tocqueville's 1831 itinerary.

Tocqueville and the National Thing

Thus far I have analyzed the centrality of the Tocqueville project to the production of dual containment as a foreign policy and as a structure of domestic governance. But in doing so, I have failed to distinguish between containment as a historically specific governmental policy and containment as a horizon of intelligibility that supported a collective fantasy of democratic governance. The editors' anxiety over the loss of the power to project the political conflicts arising *within* democratic society onto the external threat posed by "Islamic terrorists" betrays a more profound anxiety. The anxiety arises from the editors' feared loss of the entitlement to manage U.S. democracy. This management involved the identification of conflicts over the political significance of democratic values as posing a threat to civil society akin to foreign terrorism so as to ostracize the political from the social. As an expression of this anxiety, "Tocqueville and the Mullah" is symptomatic of a more pervasive state fantasy about democratic governance.

While the fantasy required the dual containment policy for support, however, it placed Tocqueville and the Mullah in the service of psychic as well as political processes. When taken up as a collective fantasy of democratic governance, dual containment did not merely position Islam as a culture totalized out of its impermeability to U.S. civil norms. It also hollowed out a space within the social order wherein citizens could imagine themselves the agents of the national will that expressed itself through that policy. When the fantasy depicted Iranians as terroristic religious nationalists who were contemptuous of the democratic norms underwriting U.S. civil societies, it effected an individual's identification with those norms as the agent responsible for the fanatics' exclusion.

Whereas the officials responsible for the regulation of the nation's territorial borders were government office holders officially invested with the powers actually to practice containment as a state policy, however, the citizens who construed themselves as having been empowered by the fantasy to participate in the governance of the social order had not been governmentally mandated to carry out this duty. The governance these citizens exercised more closely resembled the unofficial opinion-making powers of the *New Republic*'s editors. Like the editors, the citizens' imaginary participation in the nation's management did not result in material changes in the realm of Realpolitik but entailed merely the feeling that they were entitled in the course of everyday life to make managerial statements about the nation's foreign policy.

Ghassan Hage has described citizens who share with the *New Republic*'s editors the belief that they possess the right to contribute personally to the nation's internal and external policies as enjoying a condition that he calls "governmental belonging." He distinguishes this mode of belonging from "passive belonging" in that those who imagine that they belong governmentally to the democracy perceive themselves as agents and enactors of the national will whose purposes they believe themselves to inhabit. Their regulation of the democratic culture entails the fantasy that they inhabit American democracy at the level of its grounding norms and assumptions and that they enact those norms in their practice of governmental rule.[7]

Hage draws upon Jacques Lacan's psychoanalytic explanation of fantasy to provide an understanding of the means whereby citizens transform themselves into the agents of the will responsible for the national governance. Following Lacan, Hage differentiates the fantasy that facilitates this collective transformation from daydreams in that this fantasy of governance does not result in hallucinatory worlds that are external to the subject but it does produce the subject out of the fantasy. The fantasy is unlike a daydream in that it reflexively constructs the subject who thereby embodies the fantasy. Citizens who believe themselves empowered to act upon the democratic norms and assumptions sedimented within the dual containment policy also believe themselves to be the authors and agents of the norms that they enact in their everyday management of U.S. democracy. These enactments materialize the fantasy spaces that they inhabit and of which they recognize themselves to be a crucial part.

This state fantasy thereby supplied citizens with the material and the psychic means through which they imagine themselves exercising managerial control over the spaces that the dual containment policy reproduced. Citizens did not "have" the fantasy of dual containment, they inhabited the spaces produced by the state fantasy of dual containment as itself an enactment of their national will.

Before the fantasy could endow the citizens' lives with this raison d'etre, however, the national will that supported and was supported by the fantasy had to be invested with a sense of meaning and purpose that could be communicated so as to be enacted by the subjects of the fantasy. Tocqueville and the Mullah named the psychic figures through whom the policy of dual containment was transposed into the fantasy that U.S. democracy was endowed with intrinsic values that made every citizen's life worth living.

Tocqueville and the Mullah accomplished this transformation of dual containment into a collective state fantasy through Tocqueville's conversion of the process that the Mullah threatened into what might be called the "national Thing." In referring to the psychic product of the transaction between Tocqueville and the Mullah as the "national Thing," I mean "Thing" in the Lacanian sense as what continues to bind the subject to the object of desire after the subject has finished with the desiring of it.

In its office as a fantasy of democratic governance, the state policy of dual containment would position the national Thing as what necessarily exceeds the "Mullah's" efforts to appropriate it. As the indissoluble remainder that persists after Islam attempts to consume this object of national desire, the national Thing names the specifically American form of democracy that supports the national uniqueness. I have drawn the notion of the national Thing from Slavoj Žižek who has described this Thing with admirable clarity:

> The element that holds together a given community cannot be reduced to the point of symbolic identification. The bond linking its members always implies a shared relationship toward a Thing, toward enjoyment incarnated. This relationship toward the Thing, structured by means of fantasies, is what is at stake when we speak of the menace to our "way of life" presented by the Other. . . . National identification is by definition sustained by a relationship toward the nation qua Thing.

This Nation-Thing is determined by a series of contradictory properties. It appears to us as "our Thing" (perhaps we could say *cosa nostra*), as something accessible only to us, as something "they," the others, cannot grasp, but which is nonetheless constantly menaced by "them."[8]

In this passage, Žižek describes the national Thing as the outcome of contradictory processes. It names that aspect of the U.S. citizenry's collectively shared experience of democracy that is impossible for another nation to appropriate; yet Žižek also proposes that the individual members of U.S. national culture can "enjoy" their national Thing only by means of the collective fantasy of an Islamic menace to their democratic way of life. The fact that Žižek understands the second of these processes to constitute the precondition for the first discloses the centrality of the U.S. containment policy to the reproduction of the national Thing.

U.S. citizens might be capable of enumerating the processes—liberty, egalitarianism, laissez-faire, individualism—constitutive of U.S. democracy. But, as we might plausibly infer from Žižek's theoretical fiction, it is only their shared fantasy of threats to those processes that secures the U.S. citizenry's connection to the national Thing. In finding their Thing threatened, citizen-subjects also undergo a change in the condition of belonging to a national order. Following the threatened intervention of this other order, national citizens experience their relation to the democratic objects of national desire as enjoyable restorations of the full significance of the national Thing rather than alienating signs of its loss.

When it is mediated by the fantasy of the possible loss of the national Thing, the entire symbolic order undergoes a doubling. The threat posed by Islamic fundamentalism recasts the citizen-subjects' relation to the democratic order. The threat to the survival of the national Thing then triggers a generalized process of transference whereby the citizenry cathect their fear over the loss of the Thing into the need to *rescue* and protect the national uniqueness.

However, the quality of "uniqueness" that the Mullah threatened was not merely the outcome of democracy's negation of Islamic terrorism. It more significantly described the value that Tocqueville had discerned in American democracy in 1831. Whereas the "Mullah" endowed the national Thing with the values that pertain to a threatened national object, the value that "Tocqueville" invested in the national Thing derived from the usage to which he wanted to put American democracy. When Tocqueville traveled to the United States in 1831, he came in search of a form of democratic governance that would facilitate the restoration of order to French democracy. The forces of political change that the democratic revolution had effected in France had resulted in the removal of the liberties and privileges that had formerly signified the social standing of the French aristocracy of which Tocqueville's family had been prominent members. Having experienced the power of democratic change as the traumatic loss of the Tocqueville lineage's mandated social position, Tocqueville studied American democracy in order to discover the laws at work within a democracy that he found exceptional in lacking a revolutionary dimension.

Tocqueville wrote *Democracy in America* as at once a scholarly analysis of the democratic institutions responsible for this unique form of governance and as a model for French democracy. It was the latter dimension of his project that would prove indispensable to the production of the fantasy of dual containment as well as the national Thing upon which it was grounded. In finding American democracy valuable in its possessing the property of meaningful order that other democracies lacked, Tocqueville endowed the U.S. national Thing with the property of uniqueness that became the envy of other political cultures. Although he was not a U.S. citizen, Tocqueville nevertheless became the model of democratic governance underwriting the dual containment fantasy.

The Thing of American democracy became the object cause of Tocqueville's desire—it named what Tocqueville desired and what caused him to exist as a desiring subject. In Tocqueville's case this Thing constituted his effort to overcome what French democracy was constitutively lacking. Democracy became a Thing when Tocqueville desired something more than the features that comprise democracy in America. As this something more, Tocqueville's Thing named what gave plenitude and meaning and vitality to the national life. As the object cause of desire, the national Thing also staged the fantasy space that caused Tocqueville to want to obtain it.

In *Democracy in America*, Tocqueville had transposed the national Thing into the object of his political desire as well as the cause of subjectivity through which he desired to obtain it. When he wrote about U.S. democracy he wrote from the position of the aristocrat that democratic processes had completed absented from the French social order. His act of writing constituted an effort to identify with the will of the democratic powers that had accomplished the complete disinheritance of the position he had formerly enjoyed so that he might inherit from democracy the political will responsible for his social disinheritance.

Writing became for Tocqueville a means of identifying his will with democracy's grounding rules and assumptions so that he might, upon his return to France, exercise the will of democracy itself rather than subject himself to the unruly forms it might assume in French democratic culture. In place of the aristocratic will that French democratic processes had utterly destroyed, Tocqueville imagined himself to coincide with the aims and purposes of U.S. democracy, to inhabit its norms and rules, and to be the agent of its will.

The fantasy through which citizens participated in the achievement of the containment policy's imperatives derived from their having imagined themselves as inhabiting the agency of the national will to which Tocqueville's *Democracy in America* had given them access. Like Tocqueville they imagined themselves inhabiting U.S. democracy at the level of its grounding norms and assumptions and that they enacted those norms in their practice of managing democracy's conflicts.

When they exercised these powers of governance, U.S. citizens took up the privileged position that the French aristocrat imagined himself to occupy when he perceived himself as the enactor and agent of the national will. Instead of analyzing the text's significance, they turned to Tocqueville to assume the managerial role through which the French aristocrat had given expression to the tacit norms and rules regulative of democratic culture.

In "Tocqueville and the Mullah," the editors derived from Tocqueville the symbolic entitlement to exercise managerial control of the national contours and to make statements about its governance. When they exercised these ruling powers, the editors assumed the privileged position that the French aristocrat imagined himself to occupy when he perceived himself as the enactor and agent of the national will.

The Return of Alexis de Tocqueville

In observing the role that Tocqueville has played in this fantasy, I do not mean to diminish his scholarly status. The part Tocqueville plays in

the fantasy depends upon the canonical value that the scholarly community has continued to invest in his work. Political scientists, literary
theorists, philosophers, and citizens alike have invested Tocqueville's
work with a metahistorical knowingness about U.S. democratic culture.

As a consequence of this collective transference, *Democracy in America* has endowed U.S. democratic culture with a framework of intelligibility. Its categories, rules, and concepts have provided the metalanguage
in which issues get identified, recognized, parsed, construed, ordered, and
concatenated. Revered as the archive in which are preserved the United
States' core metasocial significations, Tocqueville's *Democracy in America*
was believed to possess the keys to the culture's purpose and it has been
invested with the authority to effect the culture's self-transformation.[9]

Tocqueville's work released in commentators like the *New Republic's*
editors a kind of wishful thinking about its pertinence to the present
historical conjuncture. That thinking fostered the construction of a
political mythology surrounding Tocqueville's project. Exempting it
from the procedures of verification associated with other scholarly works,
the mythology has elevated *Democracy in America* into a secular scripture. *Democracy in America* has supplied the concepts, generalizations,
and categories out of which individuals were encouraged to experience
and make sense of their historical conditions. Its system of representations anchored the presuppositions out of which individuals formulated
their opinions. It was reproduced, perpetuated, and transmitted through
such discursive practices.

Because its terms were devoid of any necessary reference to the historical institutions Tocqueville had observed, they also outstripped the
code-regulated relationship of signifier and signified. The mythology
surrounding the book has construed it as containing instructions for
bringing about what it described, and this mythology has also entrusted
the book with the task of facilitating a rite of passage from one order of
cultural intelligibility to another.

Tocqueville's own prior usage of *Democracy in America* as a force crucial to achieving France's transition from a feudal monarchy to a democracy has encouraged the belief that his book could bring about the
social conditions it also described. After returning to France, Tocqueville
had himself reconceptualized problems specific to French national politics in terms of the compendium of precedents and examples he had

recorded in *Democracy in America*. In so doing, he corroborated a belief
that organized national aspirations throughout the cold war; namely,
that a successful conclusion to it would enable nations throughout the
world to adopt the U.S. model of liberal democracy.[10]

The fact that the end of the cold war did not eventuate in a World
of Nations modeled after the U.S. example threatened to discredit the
national narrative that had endowed antecedent events with significance.
In place of corroborating them, the terminal events of the cold war—
Russia's embrace of a market economy, the emergence of a globalized
economy, the resurgence of ethno-nationalisms—severely challenged
the nation's core beliefs. With the demise of the Soviet Union, the
United States had lost the antagonist whose efforts to impede its world
historical mission had entrusted everyday events with a quasi-mythological
standing. The sudden loss of the need to negate the Other's incursions
against them threatened the nation's primary symbolic goods—the free
market, democratic institutions, freedom of speech—with devaluation.

Throughout the cold war, each of these symbolic goods had acquired
their value in part from the desire to secure them against the Other's
aggressive negation of that value. But since the ex-Other now desired
the same things, this "undesirable desire" entered into such close proximity with the symbolic space of the national identity that it produced
"regression into structures of the mirror stage (associated with memories
of the disorganized body) or even farther back into psychotic dispositions." Anxieties over the feared loss of national distinctness and dissolution within an irreducibly alien universalism lay at the heart of a
xenophobia "triggered by the collapse of the fantasy of the whole,
unified, undamaged body in the space that is conceived of metaphori-
cally and metonymically as the body's extension or double."[11]

The nationalist anxieties released in the wake of the cold war should
be construed as the basis for the quasi-mystical forces condensed in the
phrase the "return of Alexis de Tocqueville." In its most expansive
sense, Tocqueville's "return" might be conceptualized as a symbolic compensation for the absence of an adequate conclusion to the cold war. As
the personification of attitudes that had prevailed throughout the cold
war and as a resource for alternatives to them, Tocqueville returned to the
symbolic space whose capacity to support the national identity had been
severely jeopardized by the war's terminal events. Having previously

turned U.S. democracy into the model for the future of France, Tocqueville had in fact already performed the action that would have provided the cold war with a felicitous ending. But his work had been no less crucial to the founding of the cold war settlement.

But while his work provided a model for U.S. democracy that could be emulated worldwide, neither Tocqueville nor his work was subject to its conditions of historicization. Because his work constituted the means of effecting these disparate historical dispositions yet had not become identical with any of them, the retrieval of it constituted a transhistorical resource for the production of a passage from one historical condition to another.

Within yet seemingly beyond history, Tocqueville produced historical continuity. Surviving as a living remnant, this master signifier performed the dual function of a part-object still connected to the cold war mentality and as a transitional object that permitted of its separation. Having participated in founding the cold war epoch yet survived its termination, Tocqueville could be imagined as having returned to the foundational scene to inaugurate an alternative order. Resituated there, Tocqueville reduced the cold war past to the dimensions of the force it contributed to effect a historical transition.

After having prophesied the cold war, then, *Democracy in America* has reemerged at its conclusion to add this magical scene of national transformation that the cold war's terminal events significantly lacked. In accomplishing this transition work, Tocqueville has shifted his core identity from that of the interpreter of U.S. exceptionality to that of the legislator who would subsume new cultural instances under more general regulative laws. In selecting "civic associations" as the new regulative ideal, Tocqueville's legislation has transferred U.S. citizens' cultural allegiances from actions on the scale of global Armageddon to the dimensions of the local town meeting.[12]

The Tocqueville revival has also reduced historical change to the selection of different passages from *Democracy in America*. After the shift of emphasis from Tocqueville on American exceptionalism to Tocqueville on civic associations, the "resurgence of Islamic fundamentalism" has replaced the threat of world communism as the repository for cultural processes that are intrinsically opposed to such initiatives. Khatami's repudiation of the positioning of Iran as the signifier of negative civility disclosed his understanding of the role *Democracy in America* had played in the replacement of the nation with civil society as the space in which U.S. citizens consolidate their national belonging after the cold war.[13]

Among its pluralized contemporary manifestations this intertextual terrain includes the following: Bill Clinton in espousing the tenets of the liberal multiculture, Newt Gingrich writing in support of a politics of law and order, William Connolly on the territorial rights of indigenous tribes, Arthur Schlesinger in opposition to a disunited nation, Anne Norton on feminism, David Campbell against the security state, Michael Sandel on communitarianism, Seymour Lipset in support of neoliberalism, and Cornel West in defense of a politics of difference.[14] This enchainment of argumentative positions is not governed by causal relations, and their means of association cannot be accounted for by a single explanatory principle. In fact there is no order of concatenation that binds these elements into a repertoire of examples except their appurtenance to a proper name. "Tocqueville" serves as the master signifier for the association of these apparently irreconcilable arguments. But the role Tocqueville plays as their master signifier is to turn each of these otherwise antagonistic political positions into equivalent efforts to achieve validation in Tocqueville's eyes.

After *Democracy in America* subjects them to its specific forms of reorganization, the Tocqueville canon controls the way these arguments get interpreted and received. Articulating them to its framework of intelligibility, it nets the worth of their serial associations by describing the outcome as a representative civil society. "Tocqueville" thereafter reworks these arguments into terms that would appear to have achieved their reconciliation and designates civil society as the space in which such reconciliations have been transacted.[15]

The pertinence of Tocqueville's nineteenth-century model of a civil society to the political imaginaries of the twenty-first century discloses the transhistorical value of his work. At a time in U.S. political culture when the civil society was itself internalizing the irreconcilable political clashes that had formerly been projected outwards, Tocqueville performs the indispensable political work of rendering the talk radio constituency upon whose rebellion Newt Gingrich had forged his Contract with America and the members of Clinton's New Covenant community into equivalent representations of *Democracy in America*. But in order to

understand how Tocqueville's politics of recognition has become trans-
ferrable across history, we need briefly to examine the work to which
Tocqueville had put this model in nineteenth-century France.

After Democracy in France

A member of the French aristocracy that had been superseded with the
revolutionary overthrow of the feudal order in France, Tocqueville characterized the emergence of democratic forces as a potential danger to
the dominance of the French ruling elite. As a loyal French monarchist,
Tocqueville owed his seat in the July monarchy to the votes of country
landowners who counted him as a hereditary member of their territorial
aristocracy. Prominent among his intended addressees, that class read
Democracy in America as a defensive weapon useful in that historical
moment's war of cultural positioning.

After Tocqueville had become a magistrate, he was commissioned to
travel to America as an official of the French state. Alexis de Tocqueville
journeyed to America in order to ascertain the regulatory principles responsible for the construction of a people that "while all the nations of
Europe have been devastated by war or torn by civil strife . . . remained
at peace"[16]

Tocqueville accepted temporary leave from his office as an assistant
French magistrate with the understanding that the information he gathered during his trip to America concerning governmental rule in general and penitentiary reform in particular would become instrumental in
regularizing democratic institutions in France. In *Democracy and Punishment: Disciplinary Origins of the United States*, Thomas L. Dumm has
argued that the penitentiary system importantly contributed to Tocqueville's understanding of liberal democracy and deeply influenced the
organizational matrix of *Democracy in America*.[17]

Democracy and America and the U.S. penitentiary system constituted
comparable yet autonomous symbolic practices that aspired to the rehabilitation of the persons who undertook them. The penitentiary
system created the behavioral conditions responsible for shaping the
political subjects required to internalize liberal and democratic values
and fostered the creation of individuals who had learned how to rule
themselves. Tocqueville's notion of civic associations resembled the

penitentiary system in that the texture of attitudes embedded within both social formations would reproduce behavior so as to reform it.

Tocqueville addressed *Democracy in America* in the last instance to the governmental bureaucrats who granted him leave from his official duties. In fulfilling this mandate, Tocqueville accumulated a mass of details about democratic institutions in the United States that he painstakingly related to what he understood to be the central theme of *Democracy in America*; namely, the art of governmental rule. In his efforts to discover in the United States a form of democratic rule, Tocqueville devised a complex rhetorical strategy that enabled him to recover the persona of the French aristocrat as an analytic perspective required to formulate the differences between democracy in France and America.

In enunciating the social and cultural conditions surrounding America's distinctive form of democracy, Tocqueville habitually assumed an aristocratic attitude toward American democratic ideas and customs. Writing from this subjective standpoint authorized Tocqueville's signature detachment from the political phenomena that he described, and at key moments turned his exposition of the American political economy into a reflection on the generalized crisis that had emerged in France after it had undergone the loss of the institutions that had formerly legitimated the feudal order. By way of the masterful survey that Tocqueville had compiled of its customs and institutions, *Democracy in America* became the socially regulative ideal through which he displaced the violence of the French Revolution from aristocratic memory.

Writing thus became a kind of transferential process whereby he translated the social position lost after the French Revolution into the literary standpoint through which he practiced his historic movement throughout the United States. In codifying Americans' contradictory attitudes toward freedom and equality by way of formulaic phrases such as the "tyranny of the majority" and "salutary servitude," Tocqueville's political analyses disclosed an anxious desire to recover the aristocratic tradition in the displaced form of the historical perspective wherefrom he discerned what was significantly absent from American democracy.

As a representative of a superseded feudal tradition he construed American history as exceptional in lacking, Tocqueville also thereby added to Jacksonian America the class position that French democracy had replaced. This class supplementation was conveyed in the analytic distinctions Tocqueville adduced between political and civil society. The difference between civil society and political society was sustained, Tocqueville reflected, by the irresolvable conflict between "private interests" and "public liberty." Given this contrast and American individualists' "natural" predisposition to gratify their individual interests, political society depended upon a residual feature of feudal society, namely, respect for liberty in its aristocratic aspect, as a precondition necessary for its emergence.[18]

Paradoxical as it may seem, Tocqueville believed that the democratic individual's love of political liberty "presupposed the presence of a kind of virtue of which the proud independence of feudalism was an anticipation."[19] Claude Lefort has recently traced Tocqueville's unworked-through attachments to the aristocratic tradition by examining the paradoxical status of American "individualism." American individualism, under Tocqueville's description, oscillated from an "abstract" subjectivity whose resolutely private interests alienated it from any meaningful political form to a social subjectivity so "lost in the crowd" of prevailing opinions as to be void of any subjective point of view. In Tocqueville's representations of his dilemma, the American individual had on the one hand "been released from the old networks of personal dependency and granted the freedom to think and act in accordance with his own norms," but had on the other been "isolated and impoverished and at the same time trapped by the image of his fellows, now that agglutination with them provides a means of escaping the threat of the dissolution of his identity."[20]

Writing thus became the means whereby Tocqueville translated the social position his family had lost after the French Revolution into the literary standpoint through which he practiced his historical movement across the United States. In writing about American political culture as if he were a living embodiment of aristocratic liberty, Tocqueville reconstituted the aristocratic psyche that had been debilitated in the democratic process. Tocqueville struggled thereby to recover, albeit in the displaced form of his literary style, from the loss of status the aristocracy had undergone in France.

Democracy in America performed the work of displacing the trauma of class conflict onto a place lacking the feudal tradition's sophistication. When he adapted its sociological generalizations and its temporally expansive claims to the work of regulating the French social order he also displaced the violence of the French Revolution from aristocratic memory.[21] By "working through" residual class anxieties Tocqueville turned the feudal tradition that he had associated with the displacement he feared into a backdrop against which he could project what he perceived American democracy as lacking.

Claude Lefort has spelled out the dimensions of the trauma that he discerns at the very heart of Tocqueville's account of U.S. democracy. Upon encountering in the United States a democratic culture that was voided of the feudal order's transcendental guarantees, Lefort believes, Tocqueville reexperienced the trauma of the French Revolution as the gap between a fully achieved civil society and the terror of civic violence:

> When social power is divorced from the person of the prince, freed from the transcendental agency which made the prince the guarantor of order and of the permanence of the body politic, and denied the nourishment of the duration which made it almost natural, this power appears to be the power society exercises over itself. When society no longer recognizes the existence of anything external to it, social power knows no bounds. It is a product of society, but at the same time it has the vocation to produce society; the boundaries of personal existence mean nothing to it because it purports to be the agent of all.[22]

Insofar as it closes around the exclusion of the traumatic violence that it aspires to control, Tocqueville's civil society constitutes a permanently incomplete task. It can never be fully achieved but only reconstituted through the externalization of the forces threatening its order. But its reconstitution required a shift in Tocqueville's persona from an interpreter of democratic culture in America into its legislator in France.

The absences—of class conflict, of political turmoil—Tocqueville had perceived in the U.S. political society contained what Tocqueville had wished removed from French democracy. In his relentless depoliticization of U.S. political topography Tocqueville's *Democracy in America* produced a perceptual faculty that Freud has described as responsible for "negative hallucination," the capacity *not* to see what is actually there. In perceiving what he claimed were absent in U.S. democratic culture Tocqueville accomplished a "democratic" desire to except those same elements from French democracy.

After returning to France, he implemented his interpretation of U.S. democratic culture as if it comprised a legislative paradigm for the future of French democracy. Having already interpreted its accomplished formation in America, Tocqueville the legislator transferred onto *Democracy in America* the full amplitude of normative power required to manage the emergence of a democratic culture in France. *Democracy in America* provided Tocqueville with a normative metalanguage from which he generated by negation the social forces that he disallowed the condition of belonging to French democratic culture. Because *Democracy in America* had predesignated residual feudal forces as what were lacking democracy, Tocqueville thereafter deployed that designation as warrant for the exclusion of class antagonisms and related manifestations of civic violence from French democracy.

Democracy in America in France

In "Medusa's Head: Male Hysteria under Political Pressure," Neil Hertz borrowed the story of Perseus's encounter with Medusa to explain Alexis de Tocqueville's anxious reaction to the political events that ensued after the fall of the Second Empire. Hertz included an anecdote from Tocqueville's *Souvenirs* within a series of related examples of the Medusa fantasy drawn from Courbet, Hugo, and Burke. By way of the Medusa fantasy these authors experienced the threats that democratic changes posed to their position and property as castration anxiety in which fear of female sexuality conflated and gave metaphorical expression to the losses they feared.

Hertz selected the following entry from Tocqueville's *Souvenirs* recording an event that took place on June 24, 1848, as a representative instance of a Tocquevillean Medusa fantasy. On this second day of street fighting that had broken out after attempts to overthrow Louis-Philipe I failed, Tocqueville was walking toward the Chamber of Deputies:

> When I was getting near and was already in the midst of the troops, an old woman with a vegetable cart stubbornly barred my way. I ended by telling her rather sharply to make room. Instead of doing so, she left her cart and rushed at me with such sudden frenzy that I had trouble defending myself. I shuddered at the frightful and hideous expression on her face which reflected demagogic passions and the fury of civil war. I mention this minor fact because I saw it then and rightly, as a major symptom. At moments of violent crisis even actions that have nothing to do with politics take on a strange character of chaotic danger.

These actions are not lost on the attentive eye and they provide a very reliable index of the general state of mind. It is as though these great public emotions create a burning atmosphere in which private feelings seethe and boil.[23]

The experience Tocqueville recorded in this souvenir would appear to confirm Hertz's classification: it entailed Tocqueville's momentary loss of representational control and his attribution of the disempowerment to the peasant woman's unruly energies. Instead of following Tocqueville's order to get out of the way, the peasant stunned Tocqueville with the violence of a gaze that resembled Medusa's in that it threatened to reposition him within an antagonistic visual field. As a consequence of this encounter, Tocqueville temporarily experienced the loss of both his footing and the ground whereon he might have taken the succession of steps from the public square to the assembly hall.

But the event Tocqueville recorded here was also important for its vivid representation of the democratic scenario of revolutionary violence he most feared and in the usage to which he put the themes and categories of *Democracy in America* to manage this fear. The scene took place at a border in between antagonistic dispositions of the future of French democracy and under two different forms—as an event within Tocqueville's perceptual field and as the illustration of the themes that Tocqueville recorded in *Democracy in America*.

Tocqueville's second mode of apprehending this event turned it into a tableau vivant of passages from *Democracy in America*. However, when he "visualized" the event's significance by way of the metalanguage inscribed in *Democracy in America*, Tocqueville did not perceive what was taking place—he interpreted its significance. This substitution enables Tocqueville to transform the visual perception into the occasion for visually recalling the themes from *Democracy in America*. Tocqueville's reading of the event's significance silently reinscribed *Democracy in America* into the visual field. By way of this second take, he turned this contemporary event that took place in French democratic culture into a representation of the "demagogic passion" and the "fury of civil war" whose causes he had already thoroughly researched in his journey to the United States nearly two decades earlier. After he reconstituted this scene within his already recorded reflections about American democracy, those figures of memory transformed what Tocqueville had earlier found frightening about the peasant woman's countenance into the orderly manifestation of the hidden laws of democracy.

As the raw material for the transmutation of the scene, *Democracy in America* translated the event Tocqueville was presently undergoing into what *Democracy in America* will have made of it. The presuppositions and preconstituted representations of Tocqueville's master work supplied the means whereby he made sense of the unfolding events. Its themes transformed him from an individual who was subject to the vicissitudes of revolutionary democracy into the metasocial subject who could read events that illustrated the premises of *Democracy in America*. Following this transposition, these events ceased to terrify him and became instead the occasion to verify his understanding of the workings of democracy.

Re: *Traveling Tocqueville's America*

As we have seen, Tocqueville could only imagine the United States as a totalized representation of civic order against the backdrop of the absented social forces that threatened to overwhelm that order in France. When he travelled to America, Tocqueville transferred onto its landscape the semblance of his desire for a fully realized democratic order.

The Tocqueville revival might be construed as having performed a related transference at the present historical conjuncture. In returning to the Tocqueville who had validated the ideological assumptions of the sequence of events that had taken place during the cold war, interpreters of him at the site of the transition from the cold war to an alternative geopolitical order have effected a transposition of Tocqueville's function that is perhaps best understood in terms of the time loop paradox familiar to lovers of science fiction. Understood in the logic of the time loop, the "return" of contemporary interpreters to an aspect of the Tocquevillean archive that was significantly different from the doctrine of U.S. exceptionalism that had "caused" the sequence of cold war events could trigger the cancellation of the entire sequence.

On May 9, 1997, C-Span, the Cable Satellite Public Affairs Network, to turn now to what has replaced the cancelled series, launched a project they called *Traveling Tocqueville's America*. It involved retracing the nine-month journey throughout the United States that Alexis de Tocqueville had undertaken with his companion Gustave Beaumont in 1831.

After a year of planning, C-Span turned a forty-five-foot-long yellow bus into a high-tech network production vehicle from which they transmitted live C-Span's fifty-five-stop tour through seventeen states. In addition to the sixty-five hours of programming, C-Span operatives distributed annotated road maps, set up an interactive Web site, and organized local town hall meetings and classroom teach-ins of the series, as well as scholarly conferences, week-long symposia, and a national essay contest on the subject of Tocqueville's *Democracy in America*. The tour guide C-Span distributed along with the series included synopses of Tocqueville's and Beaumont's recorded impressions, sketches and folklore about the places and people Tocqueville visited, photographs and brief descriptions of famous local sights, and information about dining and accommodations.

Traveling Tocqueville's America installed Tocqueville's recorded memoirs of his initial trip through America as an intermediary between its television audience and America. It transformed the act of watching television into an interactive rereading of the themes and conceptual categories that Tocqueville described as having discerned within the U.S. landscape. But C-Span's rendering Tocqueville's text available to the television audience's pluralized readings also legitimized as the final and the true reading the one given by the socially authorized intellectuals who theatricalized their understanding of its significance.

By describing it in metaphors borrowed from the mystery of the Incarnation, Jacques Rancière has invested this transferential process with a quasi-mystical dimension. Tocqueville had travelled to America, Rancière claims, in order to found a civil religion that borrowed its secular authority from the mystery of the Incarnation. Proposing that his travel narratives merged "the great mystery of the Word become flesh" with the "little scenes of everyday life," Rancière argued the importance of the transformation of the reader into a traveler who retraced the itinerary of these "little narratives of everyday life" to the accomplishment of the central mystery of Tocqueville's civil religion.[24]

According to Rancière, *Traveling Tocqueville's America* would overstep the all but invisible boundary distinguishing between the inside of Tocqueville's journal and the landscape that has enfleshed its words. In the very slight movement whereby reading becomes traveling, what is written undergoes a change of emplacement from the inside of the book into the thereness or what Rancière calls the "ecceity" of the landscape.

Traveling thereby became the acquisition of a quasi-sacramental faculty: "the power of mapping together a discursive space and a territorial space, the capacity to make each concept correspond to a point in reality and each reality coincide with a point on the map."[25]

When the traveler reencountered Tocqueville's descriptions in the sudden thereness of them within the living flesh of the landscape, the residual reader within the traveler became the vessel for the achievement of the coincidence of Tocqueville's words and the ecceity of their incarnation in and as the scenes so encountered. When Tocqueville's journal was thereby lodged in the popular consciousness it intermediated between places, scenes, and historical events and the viewers' perceptions, transforming the latter into revisualizations of Tocqueville's democratic culture.

Tocqueville had not himself simply discovered the traces of his conceptual model already inscribed in American things. His model was not derived from nature, as Rancière suggests, so much as it was inscribed on it. He produced this model of democratic culture so that it could be thereafter written on the body politic of democratic societies as Tocqueville's means of regulating their experience of democracy.

In keeping with this description, reading Tocqueville's *Democracy in America* might be reconceptualized as the symbolic embodiment of a spatial practice. Tocqueville's text composed the America through which he journeyed into an itinerant yet regulated and progressive spatial practice. The categories, rules, and procedures into which he had transformed America could be operationalized as either reading or traveling. Both forms required the support of the flesh of the reader that the text changed into the bodies conforming to this regulated movement. The writing constituted a symbolic action, an encoded behavior, for which the bodies of the readers and travelers were postulated as interchangeable agents.

After Tocqueville had collected and classified the exterior world into his system of representations, this text thereafter regulated his perceptions of American things. When C-Span later aspired to adapt that model of democracy into a form of governance that would persuade its audience to conform to its rules, it accommodated Tocqueville's itinerant apparatus to the multiple and diverse resistances of the bodies to be conformed by fragmenting it into proverbs, sayings, retroactive dialogues, and other types of knowledge about the bodies that it would remap.

Like the basic unit of symbolic exchange underwriting Tocqueville's treatise, the C-Span Tocqueville tour animated a relationship with American democracy that was relentlessly circular and reciprocal. Tocqueville wanted to deliver to his readers a coherent image of America's national identity. Only metaleptically, however, and after a reading of America through the lens of Tocqueville's classic could Americans reacquire a coherent self-image. Call-ins could append additional classifications to Tocqueville's discourse on democracy and specify more precisely their relationship to Tocqueville. *Traveling Tocqueville's America* situated Tocqueville's work within an expansive and interlocking set of intertextual relations that influenced how it might be used and how it was read.

What Tocqueville was looking for in America, as Jacques Rancière has remarked apropos of this intertextual process, was "good democracy, reasonable democracy for he comes from the land of bad, unreasonable democracy."[26] The United States, in the post–cold war epoch, as we might plausibly extrapolate observation, had become a place that, in "having become opaque to itself," required Tocqueville's guidance to reclaim the transparency of its institutions.

C-Span's Tocqueville tour entailed the reaffirmation of an essential Americanness by declaring the tour empowered to retrieve it. C-Span restaged America's nineteenth-century past as a means of recovering from contemporary crises in the national identity. Each of the elements in the tour guide built upon the collective wish to remake U.S. political culture in the image of Tocqueville's foundational text. The site from which Tocqueville returned would, according to this description, reconstitute the television viewer within the field of intelligibility regulated by Tocqueville's previous visualization of U.S. culture.[27] But this field of intelligibility was inclusive enough in its representational compass to invite callers from talk radio to exchange their opinions about the state of the nation with television viewers who shared none of their assumptions. The Tocqueville tour thereby produced the material space within which even the most antagonistic members of the nation could "agree to disagree."

Understood as a response to the post–cold war dissociation of its conceptual mapping from the cultural terrain for which it had formerly provided an orientation, the tour might be described as a response to the desire to recover the cultural typology through which U.S. citizens had formerly taken conceptual possession of their surroundings. But the C-Span tour may also have reintroduced television viewers to the challenges to its civic order that Tocqueville had not managed fully to exclude from his field of vision.

In a splendid essay entitled "Narrating Space," the cultural geographer Patricia Yaeger has associated the desire to inhabit themed space, as evidenced in projects like *Traveling Tocqueville's America,* with the loss of any sense of place altogether. Yaeger described Americans' loss of credible (or what she calls persuasive) space as the outcome of the sense of placelessness that she believes was one of many consequences of the 1995 Oklahoma City bombing.

In testing this hypothesis, Yaeger asked a range of Oklahomans why they reacted to the tragedy that eventuated in the wake of this catastrophic event by expressing an obsessive concern over whether the space they inhabited was real. Upon interpreting their responses, Yaeger discovered that one by one they answered with some variation of the statement, "This does not happen here—in Oklahoma City. It happens in other countries. Maybe it happens in New York City."[28]

Yaeger cited this field sample to warrant her conclusion that places only became persuasive enough to incorporate people in them because, as did the C-Span retracing of Tocqueville's local communitites, they were constantly reinvented, made up, again and again out of the stories, rumors, themes that repeatedly produced a sense of locatability. The citizens who comprised Yaeger's sample claimed that they recovered a sense of inhabitable space through their sublimation of catastrophes like Oklahoma City, Waco, and other disasters expressive of the apocalyptic end of American exceptionalism.

Remapping the nation as the object of the Tocquevillean gaze restored its topography to what Benedict Anderson has described as the imagined national community. The experts that C-SPAN invited to comment on Tocqueville's travels attempted to link his observations about women, African slaves, and Indians to the changes in the United States produced by multiculturalism in particular. But in the very act of positioning these changes in the political landscape within Tocqueville's 1831 gaze, the tour also released what Lisa Lowe has called "national anxieties about maintaining U.S. hegemony in an age of rapidly changing boundaries and territories."[29]

In retracing Tocqueville's original travels through America, C-Span additionally reengaged the anxieties that informed the original expedition. In reprojecting his conceptual schema and national mythology onto the U.S. landscape through which Tocqueville had once traveled, the C-Span tour also acknowledged the fact that those places were now lacking that democratic topography.

Observing the importance of narratives to democratize places, Michel de Certeau has described the significance of their loss: "When stories disappear," de Certeau remarks, "there results a widespread loss of place. The individual or the group regresses" as a result "toward the disquieting experience of formless, indistinct, deconsecrated states."[30]

The Return of the Political

Earlier I proposed that Tocqueville's perception of their absence in America produced a desire to remove political antagonisms from French democracy. I have also claimed that C-Span's restaging of the Tocqueville tour was in part complicitous with Tocqueville's efforts to manage French democracy. But the C-Span tour also revealed within U.S. political culture a knowledge of the political antagonisms that the Tocqueville revival failed to cover over. In rendering visible these class hierarchies and racial and economic inequalities and political antagonisms, C-Span produced the occasion for figures like President Khatami to invoke the Tocqueville tour for a visual lexicon with which to address the complexities that had replaced the wished-for certainties of Tocqueville and the national aristocracy that would naturalize his gaze.

When Khatami cited Tocqueville to describe the resemblance between America's embrace of religious freedom and Iranian religious nationalism, he refused efforts to exclude him from the political terrain. Proposing that Tocqueville's devotion to liberty was itself cultivated in the rites and traditions of a national "civil religion," Khatami concluded that civil society could not be altogether distinguished from Iran's religious nationalism. In making this argument by way of the treatise that had been written to foreclose it, President Khatami introduced a conflict over the political significance of a democratic norm that Tocqueville had evacuated from his representation of U.S. democracy and that his heirs attempted to contain.

In concluding this discussion of the Tocqueville revival with an observation of the usage to which President Khatami has put *Democracy in America*, I do not wish to conclude that democracy constitutes a nonviolable form of politics. On the contrary, I wish to elucidate the "knowledge" that Khatami had erected at the site where the *New Republic*'s editors had declared "Tocqueville is not all you need to know." This "knowledge" would propose a mutual inherence in the relation between identity and otherness that resists the desire to suture an identity at the site of the Other's exclusion. If the condition governing the formation of democratic "identity" entails the affirmation of self-alterity, its constitution involves the pluralization of democratic allegiances with which one can identify. The desire to resolve or disavow the articulation of liberalism's logic of differences to democracy's logic of equivalences can only lead to the destruction of democracy. It is only in the tension between the logic of antagonistic differences that Tocqueville left France to disavow and the logic of equivalence that Tocqueville wrote *Democracy in America* to embrace that democracy can materialize.[31]

4

Patriot Acts:
The Southernification of America

Despite the Tocqueville revival, the antagonistic relationship between the two Americas intensified during the last two years of the Clinton presidency. The Monica Lewinsky scandal that broke out during his second term in office resulted in making Clinton answerable to a special prosecutor who represented the values spelled out in Newt Gingrich's Contract with America. Whereas Clinton had founded his New Covenant at the site where he foreclosed official recognition of the "murderous violence" he found evidenced in the "hate speech" broadcast there, talk radio harnessed its subscribers' accumulated resentment and invested those speech acts in impeachment proceedings that almost resulted in his removal from office. Clinton had recommended that his constituency publicly acknowledge its shame for the sins of their ancestors. But following his confession of guilt, President Clinton was himself made to feel shame for his violation of the nation's trust.

In his antiterror legislation, Clinton had correlated the internal acts of terrorism of the Christian fundamentalist and the militia movements with the acts of international terrorism of the Islamic fundamentalists as comparable threats to the national security. Clinton had intended for this legislation to produce a "liberal antiterrorism" after the model of "liberal anticommunism" and designed to represent Christian fundamentalist and paramilitary groups as the enemy within. But the targets of Clinton's legislation refused to assume these fantasmatic identifications. Rather than identifying with Clinton's demonology they represented themselves as American patriots who were comparable to those who emerged at the time of the American Revolution to fight British tyranny. In the summer of 2000, a film was released that endowed this fantasy with the authority of a full-length Hollywood feature.

During moments of historical transformation, government policymakers have often turned to scenarios produced by Hollywood directors to communicate and naturalize society-transforming fantasies. The cooperation between the society-transforming initiatives of governmental policymakers and the film scenarios through which they are naturalized has been frequently observed. Indeed since the Reagan presidency, Hollywood and Washington have collaborated in the production, distribution, and naturalization of state fantasies. Film's narrative emplotments and the characterization and stylized behavior of its heroes have been formalized into a system of visual representation that over the years has acquired the power to dramatize fundamental shifts in the society's self-representations. Because these collaborations produced the imaginary spaces through which alternative sociopolitical outcomes became imaginable, film scenarios have substituted for more politically elaborated rationalizations of policy. These cooperative efforts have resulted in the construction of the imaginary spaces through which these state fantasies have acquired symbolic efficacy. The screen's versions of the past have thereby been made to undergird the history of the present.

Throughout the cold war era, the cowboy western and the combat platoon film proved especially effective in their power to absorb political and social crises into the terms of a reigning consensus. Core metaphors and symbols like the western frontier and the patriotic soldier that were embedded within these film genres supplied the interpretive grid through which to come to terms with contemporary political crises and to manage the public's response to them. But *The Patriot*, a Roland Emmerich film, depicts the decision by Ben Martin, a hero from the French and Indian War, to return from retirement into his home. A widower and a single parent responsible for the security of seven children, Martin, who became notorious for the atrocious acts of violence he performed during the French and Indian War, does not decide to join the fight for the South Carolinian Homeland until after his son is murdered and his house destroyed by the head of the paramilitary wing of the British army. The film, which was released during the Southern phase of the 2000 presidential primaries, replaced these foundational metaphors with a series of substitutions—the Revolutionary South for the cowboy West, the Lost Cause for the frontier, and paramilitary terrorism for British (or Soviet) tyranny—that symptomatized a major reconfiguration of the sociopolitical order as well as the cinematic formulae through which it was naturalized.

At the time of its release, the film received little critical attention and was a disappointment at the box office. But in the wake of 9/11, the film has enjoyed a spectacular afterlife as a feature presentation on Home Box Office television and through its wide distribution at first as a videocassette and more recently a DVD extended its popularity into the juridico-political domain that was organized out of the emergency measures spelled out in John Ashcroft's Patriot Act. Since its release in 2000, the film has become part of the rituals of commemoration of seemingly every national holiday.

The time in which the film takes place mirrors the moment in which it was released—a historical moment when the political landscape was rapidly changing and the nature of domination was itself in ferment. The Patriot, which concluded with a filmic representation of the Battle of Cowpens when the South Carolina militia defeated the forces of General Cornwallis, appeared in the aftermath of the cold war when U.S. nationalism no longer needed to be endowed with ideological substance out of representations of the nation's opposition to a common enemy, when the private sector had become a replica of the market, and when the state had seemingly been reduced to its policing function. The Patriot's reconstellation of central themes and archetypal agents organizing the national mythology was also indicative of a fundamental shift in the dominant state fantasy, which the film at once reflected, shaped, and authorized.

During the nation's transition to the New World Order, a debate ensued among historians over whether national memories should be communicated from the perspective of the victims or the beneficiaries of the cold war. The context for The Patriot's public reception was informed by a debate over the appropriate attitude to assume with regard to the nation's past; specifically, whether discussion of shameful political events should overshadow pride in the nation's achievements. The

Smithsonian Institution set the terms for this debate in its 1991 installa-
tion of "The West in America: Reinterpreting Images of the Frontier,
1820–1920," which interpreted westward expansion from the perspective
of indigenous peoples it displaced and the immigrants it exploited. The
controversy reached a crescendo in the 1995 exhibition of the plane
Enola Gay, whose crew was assigned the duty to drop the atomic bomb
over Hiroshima in 1945. The debate between U.S. historians over the
historical significance of that event spilled over into the political domain.

The curators of both exhibits adopted a standpoint on World War II
that associated its culmination with the extermination of the Japanese
in Hiroshima and the incarceration of the Japanese in the West. Roland
Emmerich explained the cinematic effect of the cultural attitude the
curators had exhibited when he described the cold war and political
correctness as comparably responsible for having eliminated an entire
century of movie villains—Indians, Latinos, African Americans, Chi-
nese, and Russians. "Aliens are the best movie villains since the Nazis,"
Emmerich added. Emmerich's film *Independence Day* made such productive usage of this Hollywood villain that it received approbation
from both of the presidential candidates who were competing for office
during its release.[1] Bob Dole praised *Independence Day* for having returned to the moral logic forged by the allied forces during World War II.
After a private viewing of the film at the White House Bill Clinton ac-
claimed it for having imagined an event that resulted in a multicultural
reuniting of America.[2]

Independence Day may have been unambiguous in its praise of American patriotism as crucial to the global struggle against alien terrorism.
But *The Patriot* drew upon newfound ambivalence concerning the topic.
The film dealt with the crisis of values raised during the historians'
debate by restaging this conflict between national shame and national
pride within the mythic terrain of the nation's founding. The film's
stance toward these primordial national sentiments weirdly echoed
Richard Rorty's admonition in *Achieving Our Country: Leftist Thought in
Twentieth-Century America* that "as long as the American left remains
incapable of national pride, our country will only have a cultural left
and not a political one."[3]

When Rorty criticized the "antipatriotic" legacy of the New Left for
being too concerned with culture, he intended to contrast it with the
Old Left, which he characterized as primarily concerned with real or

electoral politics. We have a "spectatorial, disguised, mocking left rather
than a Left which dreams of achieving our country"(35), as Rorty elaborated on this insight. After explaining that an unpatriotic Left has
never achieved anything, Rorty concludes that a Left that fails to take
pride in our country cannot expect to have an impact on its politics,
because it will soon become an object of contempt rather than a beacon of hope.

Rorty's cautionary remarks reflected the commonsense belief that
just as too little self-respect makes it difficult for a person to display
moral courage, so insufficient national pride makes energetic participation in and effective debate about national policy unlikely. "Emotional
involvement with one's country—feelings of intense shame or glowing
pride aroused by various parts of its history, and by various present-day
national policies—is necessary if political deliberation is to be imaginative and productive. Such deliberation will probably not occur unless
pride outweighs shame" (3).

Throughout this meditation, Rorty draws upon the assumption that
the distinction between shame and pride can be firmly ascertained and
that shame should finally give way to pride in the nation if our politics
are not to be spectatorial but actual. Released two years after the publication of Rorty's *Achieving Our Country*, *The Patriot* would appear to
have elevated Rorty's formulation into its organizing coda. The film
tracks the ordeal of Ben Martin, a South Carolinian veteran of the
French and Indian War, as he confronts the difficult task of discovering
how to transform his shame over the atrocities he committed during
that campaign into the grounding motives for the acts of patriotism
required for the successful execution of the Southern phase of the Revolutionary War.

But the film is the more astonishing for the spectacular turn it gives
Rorty's admonition. For, after corroborating Rorty's assessment of shame
as an unpatriotic affective economy, *The Patriot* turned Rorty's analysis
on its head and recast patriotic pride as the effect of the representation
of historically shameful events as heroic deeds. After the disembodied
voice with which the film opens confesses that "I have long feared that
my sins would return to visit me and the cost is more than I can bear,"
Ben Martin, the subject of that confession, designates the horrific acts of
brutality he committed during the French and Indian War as the referents for the "sins" whose recurrence he fears.[4] As the film's plot unfolds,

the affective intensity of the shame that accompanies Ben Martin's testimony ceases after a certain point to remain connected solely with the crimes against humanity he committed at Fort Wilderness eighteen years earlier. They allude as well to the entirety of the South's discredited history of civic violence. By the time the film concludes, *The Patriot* represents Ben Martin's increasingly violent efforts to overcome his shame into the unregulatable force required to achieve the country.

The film's strategies of historical forgetting were not designed merely to assimilate the South within an encompassing national geography; they rehabilitated Southern history in its entirety. The film's retroactive transformation of the South into the region whose soldier-citizens had performed the acts of valor that resulted in the nation's independence from British rule elevated that region into the historical origin of the nationalizing sentiments of courage, patriotism, and pride. The film thereby transmuted the region whose history of slavery and secessionism had formerly aroused feelings of intense shame into the ideal representative of American nationalism.[5]

In the third chapter, I discussed the role that the cowboy western played in binding together the residual cold war fantasies of the Christian militia and the callers to talk radio. The shift in the setting for its action from the Western frontier towns of the nineteenth century to the South at the time of the American Revolution, and the substitution of the leader of a Southern militia group for the cowboy hero, authorized *The Patriot* to act out the Christian militia's fantasy of the U.S. place in the New World Order. The film turns its protagonist, Ben Martin, a hero in the South's defeat of the British occupying force at the Battle of Cowpens during the American Revolution, into an ancestor of contemporary members of the militia movement. Martin personifies this role when he refuses to be shamed for the extralegal violence he performs to defeat a terrorist enemy.

In *The Patriot*, the Revolutionary War that had not yet facilitated the founding of the United States of America became a screen memory for Ben Martin's traumatic experiences during the French and Indian War eighteen years earlier and for the Civil War that would not take place for another fourscore and five years. By describing the action that takes place in *The Patriot* as a screen memory for the French and Indian War that preceded it and the Civil War that took place after it, I mean to refer to the film's capacity to activate a spectral recollection of the historical events it has replaced. *The Patriot's* geographical setting is haunted by memories of Martin's extralegal violence during the French and Indian War as well as by intimations of the U.S. South's future history of civic violence, which the film renders more or less equivalent.

The film's ideological work turns on the equivalence it produces between two otherwise incompatible temporal registers: Ben Martin's efforts during the Revolutionary era to overcome Colonel Tavington's Green Dragoons on the one hand; and, on the other, the New South's efforts to dissever itself from the history of civic violence that had resulted in its discrediting. I intend to offer a brief explanation of the way in which the film inextricably intertwines these registers at the conclusion of these remarks. But the rationale for that operation requires that I analyze each of these dimensions of *The Patriot* separately.

The Force of Patriotism

The screen writer of *The Patriot*, Robert Rodat, had previously written the screenplay for *Saving Private Ryan*, a film that participated in the collective effort to celebrate the men who played a role in World War II as the members of America's "greatest generation." Rodat constructed the character of Ben Martin out of an amalgam of three legendary figures from the Revolutionary era: Thomas Sumter, whose exploits on the battlefield won him the nickname the "Carolina Gamecock"; Daniel Morgan, the rifleman who stated that he would risk everything for the American cause; and Francis Marion, who was popularly known as the "Swamp Fox" because of his ability to slip unnoticed into the Carolina swamps and gather together his hapless band of militia who mounted from there a series of successful guerilla raids against the British.[6] The film specified the difference between Ben Martin and the historical personages upon which his character was loosely based in a conversation between Colonel Tavington, Martin's antagonist, and one of the soldiers under his command who proposed the sobriquet the "Ghost" (rather than "Swamp Fox" or "Carolina Gamecock") to call attention to Ben Martin's ability to elude capture and to strike without warning. After Tavington enquired as to the reasons for the failure of his troops to defeat Martin's forces, the soldier complains "My Lord they're not like Regulars. We can't find them and we don't know where they're going to strike!" Tavington rebukes him for this explanation and sneeringly describes Martin and his followers as little more than "farmers with pitchforks," to which his soldier retorts that they're much more than that and that they were "made so by their commander, the 'Ghost.'"

The "Ghost" described the spectral apparition Ben Martin became when he moved in between the positions of the head of his family and the commander of a militia. Unlike the empirical embodiment of Ben Martin he parasitized, the "Ghost" was neither a father nor a colonel; it was an affective intensity that supported yet threatened both of these socially mandated roles. While Ben Martin may have provisionally identified with each of these roles, the figure that was mobilized into action under the name of the "Ghost" was reducible to neither. Inhabited by forces that cannot be identified with either the family or the military, Ben Martin passed through both of these domains as the spectral violence required to protect and sustain them. He was the terrible power whose enforcement of the paternalistic order was presupposed by the socially symbolic role of the father. As the personification of the excessive violence needed to achieve the emergent nation's patriotic ideals, the "Ghost" also haunted the patriotism Ben Martin was supposed to personify with fierce impulses that patriotic ideals could neither justify nor control. The uncanny violence through which he guaranteed the security of his home also revealed the militarized zones as the only spaces in which Ben Martin felt at home. The "Ghost" named the spectral, invisible violence required to secure the stable positioning of every other representation within the social spaces under Ben Martin's command.

Acts of reciprocal violence cannot be stably attached to the name of the subject through whom they are exercised. The subject through whom reciprocal violence takes place is perforce displaced by the violence that passes through this outlet—as it is projected onto the force facilitating its return. When violence appears, the subject through whom it is expended disappears into the enactments through which violence executes itself. It was this economy of reciprocal violence to which Martin's sentence "I have long feared that my sins would return to visit me, and the cost is more than I can bear" has reference. The "cost" of Martin's unregulatable violence is unbearable in that it is expended outside the restricted economy of calculable loss and gain and by way of an agency of reversibility that remains external to the subjectivity through which it is borne. It was because this violence could neither be lost nor gained that Martin described the enactments through which he expended it as "sins," and he discerned the "return" of this violence in the form of a specter that he has "long feared." As the excessive force needed to install and to defend every socially mandated position, the "Ghost" that thereafter took possession of him also dispossessed him of every quality except the power to arrive at his aim by whatever means necessary.

One of the film's organizing paradoxes turns on the fact that, although he was the father of two devoutly patriotic sons, Ben Martin never considered any of the activities he performed during combat as having been motivated by patriotism. Before he married and fathered seven children, Ben Martin participated in the ritual dismemberment and mass extermination of the French soldiers and the Cherokee warriors responsible for the murder of women and children at Fort Charles. After he married, Ben Martin became a slaveholding member of the Southern plantocracy and a potential secessionist who harbored serious questions about the political validity of the "causes" for which his sons Gabriel and Thomas were willing to risk their lives.

But it was precisely Ben Martin's ambivalent relationship with patriotism that enabled The Patriot to correlate the nation-founding violence of the colonists' struggle for independence from the British Empire with the state-preserving violence Colonel Ben Martin's "Irregulars" expended against British terrorists. The military formation against which Ben Martin's South Carolina militia was mounted in opposition was not General Cornwallis, who was rendered ineffectual out of his strict adherence to the rules of war, but Colonel Tavington, the commander of a paramilitary battalion known as the Green Dragoons, who did violence to those rules. Roland Emmerich based Tavington's character on Lieutenant Colonel Banastre Tarleton. British regulars referred to Tarleton as "Bloody Ban." The members of the Continental army troops called him "the Butcher." Colonel Banastre Tarleton gained notoriety during the Revolution for administering the "Tarleton Quarters." The phrase designated Colonel Tarleton's practice of killing all the members of the oppositional forces no matter whether they surrendered or not.[7]

Through his filmic representation of Colonel Tavington, Roland Emmerich added the following items to the "Butcher's" list of war crimes: the targeting of civilian populations, the mass conflagration of the inhabitants of Pembroke, South Carolina, and the hanging of envoys carrying marked parcels. Ben Martin regarded Tavington as the target for his

unregulatable violence after he murdered Thomas, Martin's second oldest son, and then ordered that Martin's house and property be destroyed
and that Martin's first son Gabriel be hanged as a spy.

In describing Ben Martin's violence as "state-preserving" rather than
"nation-making," I have drawn upon a distinction that Walter Benjamin had introduced to discriminate between separable iterations of
the law. In his essay "Critique of Violence" Walter Benjamin grapples
with the question of the sources of the authority of the law's force. He
asks more specifically whether there was a founding violence that was
responsible for the emergence of the law even as there was a violence
that assured the law's survival and its continued survivability. In answering these questions, Benjamin concludes that "the function of violence
in lawmaking is twofold, in the sense that lawmaking (as opposed to
the law-preserving work of regular policing) pursues as its ends, with violence as its means, what is to be established as law, but at the moment
of instantiation does not dismiss violence; rather, at this very moment
of lawmaking, it specifically establishes law as not an end unalloyed by
violence, but one necessarily bound to it, under the title of power. Law-
making is power making, and to that extent, an immediate manifestation of violence."[8] Benjamin established the distinction between these
two forms of violence in his discussion of the relationship between violence, law, and the State of Exception. The violence that is responsible
for making a law is comparable to the violence responsible for founding
a nation in that neither form of violence can be understood to belong
to an already constituted legal or political entity. Both founding acts
take place in the State of Exception that exists independent of any
already constituted order. When Martin and his band of militia exercised the force necessary to sustain the survivability of the Continental
army, they did so as part of the security state apparatus of the not yet
emergent nation.

The Patriot represented Ben Martin's Southern militia rather than
Colonel Burwell's Continental army as the military agency responsible
for the successful overthrow of General Cornwallis's troops at the Battle
of Cowpens. Martin's state-preserving violence was unlike the nation-
founding violence of Colonel Burwell, who led the Carolina contingent
of the Continental army, in that the forces Martin gathered to defeat
Colonel Tavington's brutality did not depend on soldiers who were willing to give up their lives for the "nation." Martin's irregular forces were

largely made up of men who, like Martin, were motivated to join in the fight because of the illegal acts of violence Tavington's forces had performed against their families and friends. In representing the members of Martin's militia as primarily motivated by their recollections of Tavington's savage violence, the film also explained why their counterviolence took place through paramilitary operations that lay outside the canons of war. The "counterterrorism" of Martin's militia was regulated solely by the excesses of an antagonist whose violence they preemptively mirrored in order to prevail.

If the act of signing the Declaration of Independence had retroactively produced "We the People," the film suggests that it was the "Ghost's" Irregulars who supplied the force necessary to guarantee the accomplishment of that activity. But when the film represented the militia's paramilitary violence as the foundational force necessary to give birth to the nation, it also established a spectral connection between the extralegal violence of Ben Martin's militia in 1775 and the contemporary militia movement. In forging this connection in the persona of a figure who did not know how to distinguish war crimes from acts of valor, the film was also introducing a linkage between Martin's militia and the Vietnam veterans who had inaugurated the militia movement.[9]

Before his forces could overpower Colonel Tavington, Ben Martin did not merely mirror Tavington's violations of the rules of war, he also enacted a violence that would preserve the laws of war against Colonel Tavington's efforts to violate them. In order to protect the State of Exception, which was the precondition for the making of the American nation, against Tavington's propagation of an alternative state apparatus, Martin was obliged to occupy a space within the law that was exempt from the law's regulations. For it was only by exercising powers that were not subject to the regulations of already existing laws that he was empowered to protect the entire order of law.

Martin's acts of law-preserving violence took place at a space where the law might be imagined as having arrogated to itself the power to declare the legitimacy of the law as such—in its totality. However, since the law could only declare its own legitimacy from an extralegal position, the position from which Ben Martin would preserve the law might also be described as inherently transgressive of the legal system as such, and transgressive as well of every particular law that he would preserve.

In his untimely meditation on what he calls the mystical foundations of the law, Jacques Derrida has described the paradoxical relation
to the law of war that Ben Martin occupies with exceptional lucidity:
"There is a law of war, a right to war.... Apparently subjects of law
declare war in order to sanction violence, the ends of which appear
natural (the other wants to lay hold of territory, goods, women; he
wants my death, I kill him). But this warlike violence that resembles
'predatory violence' outside the law is always deployed *within* the
sphere of the law. It is an anomaly *within* the legal system with which it
seems to break. Here the rupture of the relation is the relation. The
transgression is before the law."[10]

The fact that Martin enacted his law-preserving yet state-making
violence at the limit point that was internal to the law disclosed why
his violence had to remain exempt from the rules of war it would (trans-
gressively) enforce. Since this space from within which he would preserve already existing laws itself lacked any legal warrant, however, it
might be more accurate to describe this space as the locus for the State
of Exception in which Martin's violence founded the law he simultaneously aspired to preserve. The fact that the law Martin founded was as
yet devoid of a nation over which it could exercise its jurisdiction requires a description of Martin's violence as having founded the State of
Exception (in the restricted form of the militia and the extensive form
of the Continental army) as the precondition for the emergence of the
nation. Whereas the state normally required that the subjects under its
protection cede their right to violence as the precondition for the state's
monopoly over the legitimate use of violence, however, it was Ben
Martin's very refusal to surrender his violence that empowers him to
personify the state's monopoly.

Americans, like Ben Martin's sons, who declared the right to exercise
revolutionarily new yet universalizable principles of freedom and equality
produced a retroactive justification for the War of Independence. But
the revolutionary violence that was materially responsible for securing
these rights and for founding the Republic in fact took place in the
State of Exception. Understood as a prenational state of emergency,
the American Revolution constituted a form of nation-making violence
that facilitated the formation of a nation in whose name the war was
retroactively justified. Insofar as the American Revolution took place before the Constitution out of whose principles the nation was established,

the American Revolution turned the State of Exception into the sovereign constituting power responsible for the birth of the American
nation-state. Obeying the as yet unwritten, nation-constituting laws
that brought British juridical and political rule to their limits, the
American Revolution suspended British law as such in order to found a
new order of things. The Constitution fused the sovereign power at work
in the interaction between the exemplary national people and the state's
revolutionary violence into the political hypostasis called the American
nation-state.

   This Janus-face of American exceptionalism was also discernible in
the national and international reactions to the nation's founding. The
advocates of American exceptionalism who set Europe's feudal past
against America's democratic future typically invoked the moral exemplarity of the nation's civic nationalism to justify their description of
American democracy as the telos for the progressive movement of world
history. But it was the state's demonstrable military and economic power
that inspired international observers to recognize the United States as
a political model that constituted an alternative to Europe's.

   The Patriot established homologies between the patriotic violence
that gave rise to the nation-state in its struggle for independence from
the British Empire and the lust for vengeance of Ben Martin's militia.
The men's primary motivation for entering Martin's paramilitary force
was their need to be revenged against the British for the violence
Tavington had exerted against their homes and property. Haunted by the
unsanctioned violence against which it was mounted, Martin's counterviolence perforce operated outside the canons of war sanctioned by international treaties. Martin's embodiment of the nation's foundational violence rendered him unfit to become a member of the nation's "regular"
military. In exerting the extraneous force necessary to obtain the success
of the Revolution, Martin passed through the military ranks as a figure of
excessive violence exempt from military rules. Like Tavington, whose
violence he at once opposed yet mirrored, Martin found it necessary to
violate all the rules of war in order to let the law called war prevail.

   When Martin acted upon this exceptional force that secured the
distinction between the state and the nation, he personified the means of
transition from the founding (state) violence into the achieved (national) order. As the personification of the force that negotiated between the founding of the nation and the preservation of the State of

Exception, Martin did not represent the values of the nation. Those nation-making values would not emerge until Martin's sons suppressed their father's excess violence as the precondition for their giving expression to the patriotic values of self-sacrifice in the name of the "cause."

Martin put his ability to personify the state's monopoly of violence on display in an incident that took place at Fort Wilderness eighteen years earlier. Before decapitating them, Martin along with the soldiers he led to victory within that encampment first tore out the tongues of the French and Cherokee survivors. Then he gouged out their eyes, cut off their fingers, and flayed the skin from their faces. Next, Martin ordered his troops to sort these accumulated body parts into two piles and to address them to separate destinations. Specifically, Martin ordered that the decapitated heads be placed on plates and sent to the French military headquarters, and that the tongues, fingers, and eyes be arrayed on rafts and set adrift in the river that passed through Cherokee territory. After Fort Wilderness, the Cherokees broke their treaty with the French. "That's how they [the British settlers] justified it," Martin explained this matter to his son Gabriel.

Martin offered his son an account of this wartime atrocity as Gabriel and he sat around a campfire. Martin recounted this narrative after Gabriel had asked his father why their fellow South Carolinians had elevated him into a heroic legend in the wake of the Wilderness campaign. Throughout his recollection of the events that took place at Fort Wilderness, Martin appeared to wish to dissociate from these ghastly memories. But while he confessed these "sins" to his oldest son, the camera tracked Martin's engagement in quasi-ritualized activities that seemed weirdly continuous with his previous compulsive behavior. In the midst of attesting to these horrific deeds, Martin placed one of his dead son Thomas's toy soldiers on a spoon, then he inserted the spoon into the campfire. After the flames melted the metal into a liquid substance, Martin shaped the liquefaction into the bullet with which he intended to kill the man who had killed his son.

In his confession to his son, Ben ceases to be the father and turns into the specter, the thing in war that is more than himself, the figure from the French and Indian War who can be neither repatriated nor domesticated. Martin had only joined the Revolutionary army after Colonel Tavington's Green Dragoons had torched his home and murdered his son. Since Martin restricted the reach of his affective attachments to familial loyalties, he placed his family's security above the country's honor. After he underwent the transformation from identifying with the role of the head of the family to accepting a military commission in the Continental army, Ben Martin displayed so much undischargeable rage in the bloody acts of aggression that he performed to protect his family members that he became virtually unrecognizable to them. In one of the film's unforgettable scenes, Martin's two youngest sons look on in abject horror as their father hatchets one of the Green Dragoons Tavington had commissioned to hang his son Gabriel into what is quite literally a bloody pulp.

Martin's neighbors and the Carolinian legislators attributed patriotic motives to the unregulated violence he displayed at Fort Wilderness, but Martin's confession of his "sins" at the opening sequence of *The Patriot* bore witness to Martin's belief that his military exploits were part of a vicious cycle of violence. In choosing to become soldiers, Martin's sons Gabriel and Thomas remade themselves in the image of the principles— of loyalty, freedom, and honor—that repress and supplant the father's violence. Their willingness to sacrifice their lives for the sake of a nation-making cause was the agent responsible for their transformation into (citizen-)soldiers. Martin's sons considered the violence they performed for the sake of the country on the battlefield to be less important than the revolutionary values of freedom, property, and solidarity in whose name they undertook it. Martin's sons may have believed in the political ideals of liberty and representative government as the "cause" for which they gladly sacrificed their lives, but their father's actions placed these justifications of violence into crisis.

The U.S. citizens who came into existence in the wake of the Revolutionary War displaced the violent events that took place during the war with the revolutionary principles in whose name the war had been fought. Rather than the principles that would appear to have motivated his sons, who lost their lives in the name of the emergent nation, Benjamin Martin was motivated solely by the imperative of enraged revenge. Martin never fought for the patriotic principles that would achieve "our country"; he fought to avenge Tavington's murder of his sons and destruction of his property. In avenging these losses, Martin gave expression to an excess violence that his patriotic sons were required to disown as the precondition for their allegiance to the American cause.

Martin's work of mourning entailed the transformation of the relics of the dead sons from whom he could not part into the instruments for the absolute destruction of the persons he holds responsible for their deaths. When he transmuted these remnants of his dead sons—Thomas's toy soldiers but also the cloth flag Gabriel has been repairing throughout the course of the film—into the raw materials for the weaponry with which he would avenge their losses, Martin converted these signs of his sons' patriotism into expressions of his unappeasable violence, which is to say the "sins" that never stopped returning to visit him. Gabriel asked his father not to act upon his revenge because he feared that the indistinction it effected between the violence of Martin's militia and Tavington's Green Dragoons might undermine the noble aims of the Revolution. But Ben Martin's motives for military action—rage over the deaths of his sons and despair over the loss of his household—embroiled the principle of patriotism itself in an irresolvable contradiction. The affective intensities of rage and despair that traverse Ben Martin's military activities constituted the spectral violence that rendered his "patriotism" effective even as they left Martin at once ashamed and afraid of retribution against his family. As its "Ghost," Ben Martin haunted the revolutionary cause with an uncanny violence that patriotism could neither justify nor regulate.

Patriotism's Lost Cause

The cause Martin's son Gabriel repeatedly invoked was not unambiguously tethered to the American Revolution. At a crucial moment in *The Patriot*, the film produced a tacit correlation between the colonists' struggle for independence and the Lost Cause of the Southern Confederacy. In the scene to which I refer, a wounded soldier watched Benjamin Martin pick up a tattered piece of cloth from off the ground upon which it had been trampled.[11] After noticing that the cloth bore the imprint of the stars and stripes, the veteran announced to his interlocutor that both he and Gabriel were caught up in a "lost cause" for which there existed no hope for success. In associating the flag under whose authority the revolutionists sought to overthrow British rule with the Lost Cause, the scene encrypted the ideology of confederate nationalism onto a historical scene in which U.S. nationalism had not yet been achieved.[12]

But when *The Patriot* rendered the "cause" for which Gabriel and Tom Martin sacrificed their lives equivalent to the Southerners' Lost Cause, it encouraged its viewers to imagine the new American nation as having emerged at a site within which the Lost Cause was also redeemed. The anachronistic energies within the scene turned the secessionist South and Revolutionary America into mirror images. The film's anachronistic strategies did not merely assimilate the South within an encompassing national geography, they also ostensibly restaged the emergence of the American nation within a geographical region that had formerly been all but excluded from the national symbolic order.

The religion of the Lost Cause elevated the Civil War into a holy war, and it canonized the ancestral figures from that mythical time who sacrificed their lives for the Southern way of life. Antistatist in principle, Lost Causism became a cover story for members of the Ku Klux Klan, and during the civil rights movement it consolidated the resistance Southerners directed against the state in opposing the extension of civil rights to Southern blacks and against mass culture. It also became the banner under which the members of the contemporary militia movement convoked it members. In this scene *The Patriot* produced a homology between "Old Glory," the flag under whose banner the revolutionists overthrew British rule, and the Lost Cause, the flag of the Confederacy under whose aegis the South Carolinian Ben Martin achieved his revenge. The film thereby transformed the Lost Cause of the post–Civil War South into the object cause of the America that would refound itself in the aftermath of the cold war.

The political imperatives of the secessionist South and Revolutionary America became mirror images at the South Carolina Congressional Assembly in Charleston where Ben Martin was engaged in a debate with Colonel Burwell, the head of the Southern wing of the Continental army, over whether or not he should join the Revolution. Their debate took place at the session of the Provincial Congress in Charlestown that had been called to decide whether South Carolina should enter the war. During the debate, Ben Martin correctly predicted that the war would be fought neither on the frontier nor on distant battlefields but "among our homes. Our children will learn of it from their own eyes and the innocent will die with the rest of us." "And your principles?" Burwell asked. To which Ben Martin replied, "I'm a parent. I don't have the luxury of principles."

In the course of this debate, Ben Martin also declared immunity from his obligations to the military by describing his need to protect and defend his family as a more primordial loyalty. But Colonel Burwell did not recognize a father's moral obligation to protect his family as a rationale that takes moral precedence over the needs of the state. Because he would not fight, Martin also would not cast a vote that would send others to fight in his stead. After listening to his father's rationale for refusing to join the Revolutionary cause, his son Gabriel chastised his father with the rebuke, "Father, I did not know you had no principles." Martin responded that his son would understand when he became responsible for a family. Gabriel answered that he hoped that he would "not hide behind the family."

At the time of the American Revolution, the Continental army could not protect the households of the civilian population. Since Martin placed the family's security above devotion to country, Martin refused to surrender his surplus violence to the state. After expressing his shame at his father's declaration that his need to protect his family took precedence over the assembly's desire to liberate the colony from British rule, Gabriel decided to serve in his father's place. Gabriel quite literally joined the army in order to fill up the space his father had symbolically evacuated during the Congressional Assembly when he abstained from casting a vote in favor of (or against) the Revolution. In choosing to sign up for the Revolutionary cause, Martin's son thereby remade himself in the image of the principles—of loyalty, freedom, and honor—that his father had repudiated. Gabriel invoked these nation-making principles to supplant his father's family loyalties, which Martin had rendered more important than the patriotic cause to which Gabriel has pledged his allegiance.

Gabriel's decision to serve in the name of these principles added the elements that were missing from his father's decision. But when his father did finally decide to join the Revolutionary army, it was the unprincipled nature of his violence that proved responsible for his military successes. In adding the principles that conferred dignity and honor on his father's violence, Gabriel Martin has produced a salutary supplement that has "completed" the Revolution by including what it needs to appear just. But in adding the excess violence that the Revolution required to succeed, Ben Martin acted upon the dangerous supplement that must perforce be placed outside the national civil polity before that order could obtain its internal coherence.

When Gabriel Martin repudiated his father's wishes, the state absorbed Ben Martin's desire for his son yet disavowed it as the father's desire. As a realm of blood kinship rather than arms, the family occupied the space whose violent disruption the state has presupposed as the basis for its affiliations. Indeed the social basis for the successful inauguration of a state might be understood to transpire through the forcible supplanting of local kinship bonds with patriotic affiliations. Because the family alone could produce male warriors that the state required to advance its purpose, the state claimed the son that Martin's family has produced— but for the purpose of engendering the nation.

Martin's placing his loyalty to the family above his allegiance to the nation-state prefigured a crime against the United States that would subsequently assume the form of the South's secession. But in *The Patriot*, the South's threat to secede did not merely precede the founding of the nation. The threat of secession also opened up the space within the law in which the distinction between state-preserving violence and nation-making violence could be founded. Ben Martin embodied the force required to effect the transposition of the state's founding violence into the national symbolic order.

In *The Patriot*, Roland Emmerich produced a fantasy that was designed to transmute the South from a discredited region to an exemplary geographical space in which to commemorate the origin of the nation.[13] The film's plot elaborated an extensive analogy between the acts of nation-making violence that Ben Martin enacted during the Southern phase of the Revolutionary War and the state-preserving violence of the Civil War into the matrix for this fantasy. The symbolic efficacy of the fantasy depended upon the film's dislocating the historical events— lynchings, slavery, civic violence—for which the South had become a discredited geography and resituating them within the period of the nation's emergence. *The Patriot* then reassigned the historical agency responsible for their commission to the unlawful violence performed by the members of Colonel Tavington's Green Dragoons.

This temporal displacement and transference of the South's discredited history has literally unstitched the South from the ideological shames to which it had been sutured and recharacterized the South as the site for the rebirth of the nation. The substitutions through which the film replaced the South's history of disgrace with its representations of British terrorism generates a series that renders homologous the South's liberation from Britain and the slave's emancipation from slavery, the murderous fraternal battles that took place during the Civil War and Colonel Tavingon's slaughter of the brothers Thomas and Gabriel Martin, the South's history of civic violence and Colonel Tavington's targeting of civilian populations. This last substitution effected a slippage between the actual violence Southern slaveholders performed against blacks and the symbolic violence that the South reputedly suffered in its segregation from the national history. The film supplies a placeholder for the site of this slippage in the character of Occam, a slave whose owner has signed him over to the Continental army to fight for freedom in his stead. During the Revolution, the British had promised slaves their freedom in exchange for their willingness to fight for the crown. But according to the perverse logic of *The Patriot*, Occam would rather die for the man who owns him as a slave than fight for his liberation from the Southern plantocracy. Occam, the indivisible reminder of the history of civic violence that the film has erased, signifies what the film has excluded from its field of visibility when he signs an "x" in place of a signature. When he signs his "x," he signifies his lack of freedom out of whose absence American freedom was produced.

If the Revolutionary War worked as a receptacle in which to retrieve and act out the South's traumatizing historical past, the crucible for this remembering and forgetting is supplied by the psyche of Benjamin Martin. It was in this location that the nation's ambivalent relationship to its past got reduced to the internal struggle over the atrocities he had performed during the French and Indian War. Rather than describing them as discredited alternatives to patriotism, the film represented Ben Martin's expressions of disloyalty and treason as indicative of the self-division inherent to Ben Martin's subjectivity. He was torn between devotion to his family and his belief in America.

In the wake of the cold war, colonial South Carolina also supplied Roland Emmerich with a regional geography in which to represent talk radio's fantasy of the nation's rebirth into a different order of things. In describing the South as the historical location for the transition from one national order to another, Emmerich has represented its secessionist violence as the self-treason necessary to found the New World Order. The Patriot's nationalizing identifications were based upon the fantasy of alien terrorists who threaten to destroy the white southern male's whole way of life. In defending against this enemy, Ben Martin embodied antagonistic sites of violence: on the one hand he embodied the violence needed to protect and defend the family, and on the other hand he represented the excessive and illegal violence necessary for the birth of the nation. Both of these violent supplements—to the family and to the nation—cohered in the contemporary Southern militia movements that have emerged in the wake of the cold war to reaffirm identification with the security state in place of national loyalties.

The fantasy organizing this film has turned the white southern male into the representative victim of U.S. history. It has thereby supplied the core complaint of listeners across talk radio—that they have been either devalued or damaged by the transition into the New World Order—into the navel of the fantasy. After the film substituted Ben Martin's white injured body in place of the bodies of African-American slaves as the corpus requiring postwar restitution, it represented the reparation of that body as the symbolic action required to bring about the rebirth of the nation. As it restaged the origins of the national history from the perspective of a white southern male, it also turned the loss of white privilege into the chief historical wrong that was deserving of reparation. Insofar as it is structured in the image of the historical violence directed against the injured white male body, The Patriot's social imaginary forecloses recognition of guilt over the historical wrongs of slavery or the displacement of Indian tribes from the Carolinas. The film's inclusion of the South within the consecrated ground of the nation's founding might be understood as an imaginary restitution for the imagined history of wrongs perpetrated against Southern white males.

The composite result of The Patriot's serial substitutions and its symbolic act of restitution was the obliteration from memory of the entire history of Southern civic violence. But if the film affirms the history of Southern civic violence through the repetition of its denial, it must also be said that these repeated denegations provide the only "cause" for U.S. patriotism that The Patriot acknowledges. After it obliterates the history that had connected the South to these ideological significations, The Patriot proceeds to designate the South's state-founding violence as the occult foundation of the national order. More specifically, the film proposed that the South's actual effort to secede from the union be imagined as having opened up the aforementioned space in which Ben Martin's violence founded the State of Exception that preserved the law in its entirety.

It was the South's very failure to accomplish this secession that rendered its transgression of the U.S. Constitution a ruptural event that took place within the law. Rather than founding an alternative order of legality, the South's unsuccessful effort to found an alternative American nation enabled the Emergency State to reoccupy the space hollowed out by the South's attempt to secede. The State of Exception designated the place from which the law exempted itself from its own rules so as to overcome the secessionist threat to the legal order as if it were an event formative of the law-preserving transgression internal to the legal order itself. When the state suspended Southerners' civil rights in the aftermath of the Civil War, it turned the South's former violation of the law into the authority for this suspension. For in attempting to found a new nation, the South had also perforce transformed the North's law-preserving violence into the grounds upon which the Emergency State was founded. When the Emergency State declared the South's effort to secede illegitimate, the law grounded its own legitimacy upon and by way of the Emergency State's declaration of the illegitimacy of Southern secession. The law, that is to say, turned the War of Secession into the occasion to prove that it was the state of emergency rather than the nation (or the people) that exercised a monopoly over power.

Now in proposing that the law derived the power to legitimate itself from the South's attempt to secede, I do not mean that the law identified with the substantive cause of the secessionists. I mean to propose instead that the law reentered the position that the secessionists had opened up when they posited alternatives to the articles of constitution, and with the obliteration of each and every individual alternative, the law produced an external legal authority that operated within the law as the law's power to regulate itself.

As the representative of a (lost) cause that the state was required to disown, the secessionist South became the ideal space in which to restage the origins of the United States—as the rebirth of the National Security State. Unlike the American nation, the security state does not require an ideological cause to justify its pronouncements—it invokes instead the reason of state. By deriving the legitimacy of Ben Martin's

state-founding violence from the disavowed civic violence of the secessionist South, *The Patriot* has emptied the South's lost causism of its
ideological substance so that it might serve as the object cause of U.S.
patriotism under a state of emergency.

The Emergency State's Family Values

Because I have mentioned John Ashcroft's Patriot (Proved Appropriate
Tools to Intercept and Obstruct Terrorism) Act as one of the contemporary contexts for the film's reception, I should also observe that
The Patriot already supplied a representation of the space within which
Attorney General Ashcroft enunciated the state's emergency measures.
But the film associates this space with the place of internal transgression formerly occupied by the Southern Secessionists. When the measures enumerated within the Ashcroft Act legally violated the civil liberties specified within the Constitution, they enabled the Patriot Act
to demonstrate the State of Exception's power to protect the Constitution as a whole from the threat it understands to have been posed by an
alien system of legality. It is in order to protect the Constitution as a
whole that Ashcroft declares his suspension (or attenuation) of civil
rights and liberties to lie beyond the regulative reach of any of the particular articles of the Constitution. But in legally violating the civil
rights that the Constitution was designed to guarantee, Ashcroft's Patriot Act might also be understood to have reenacted the civic violence
of the secessionist South, but voided its (lost) cause of the secessionist
rationale.

Throughout this discussion, I have argued that Ben Martin personified the Emergency State's monopoly of violence. I have additionally
maintained that, as the conduit through which the state effected the
transposition of a settler colony into an emergent nation, Ben Martin
was not motivated by patriotism. But I have also claimed that, insofar
as the family replaced the nation as the value system in whose name he
fought, Ben Martin placed his loyalties to his family's home and property above his allegiance to the nation. Having suggested that Martin's
family values comprise for him a "cause" that would appear to substitute
for patriotic pride, however, I am obliged to explain the relationship
between Martin's devotion to family and his personification of state
violence.

After he transforms the home into a militarized zone, Martin's "pa-triotism" sanctions the return of his sins of unregulated violence as symbolic compensation for the loss of his sons. Martin has not surren-dered his surplus violence to the state. He has aligned his aggression with the violence required to insure domestic security as a desideratum that he places above the founding of the nation. As the ghostly embodi-ment of the unregulatable violence through which the state secures the survivability of the nation, Ben Martin does not require the mediation of a nationalist ideology. And his motives for action cannot be reduced to a "cause." If Martin experiences his relation to the state through his need to protect and defend his family (rather than his country), he expe-riences his relation to the state as the need to introduce the Martin fam-ily's values into the state military apparatus.

His oscillation between state violence and family security transforms Martin into the meeting point through which these otherwise incom-parable value systems become inextricably intertwined. The violence with which Martin achieved his family's security resulted in the trans-formation of his home into a militarized zone. His original motives for entering the military, moreover, involved the extension of Martin's zone of domestic protection to the defense of his son Gabriel, who, un-like his father, had signed up for the cause of liberty. Because he believes that Gabriel's adherence to the rules of war have rendered him vulner-able to Tavington's illegal violence, Martin founds a paramilitary organi-zation within the Continental army through which he would insure Gabriel's safety. The core family value of domestic security that Martin formed the militia to propagate has thereby rendered the domestication of the military sphere virtually indistinguishable from the militarization of the domestic sphere. Which is to say that *The Patriot* has represented the Martin family's values (rather than say patriotism) as the means necessary for the National Security State to reproduce itself. In rendering family security and national security interchangeable zones, *The Patriot* has bypassed national principles as either a mediator or justification for the exercise of (patriotic) violence.

5

From Virgin Land to Ground Zero: Mythological Foundations of the Homeland Security State

The catastrophic events that took place at the Branch Davidian compound on April 19, 1993, and in Oklahoma City on April 19, 1995, emerged in the place of the absent conclusion to the cold war. Both events were embedded in the apocalyptic dimension of the state fantasy of American exceptionalism, but the disparate governmental responses to these events resulted in incommensurate national compacts (Newt Gingrich's Contract with America and Bill Clinton's New Covenant) that represented separate and utterly incompatible national peoples. Both of these events were embedded in the apocalyptic dimension of state fantasy of American exceptionalism, but after the cold war American exceptionalism had ceased representing all the people. The Contract with America represented the national people who believed that the state had itself become a terrorizing power in ordering the attack against the Christian fundamentalists at Waco; the New Covenant represented U.S. citizens who believed that the Christian militia responsible for destroying the Alfred P. Murrah Federal Building in Oklahoma City were terrorizing enemies of the people who deserved the state's capital punishment.

The events that took place on September 11, 2001, supplied the state with a traumatizing event out of which it constructed a spectacle that accomplished several interrelated aims. September 11 supplied a conclusive ending to the cold war even as it permitted the state to inaugurate an utterly different social configuration. The description of the site of the attack on the World Trade Center as "Ground Zero" supplied this scene with a representation that the bombing of Hiroshima had installed in the national psyche as one of the terrifying images with which to imagine the conclusion of the cold war. The Shock and Awe campaign with which the Bush administration inaugurated its response to these attacks became the first event in a total war—the Global War on Terror—whose powers of governance surpassed even the reach of the cold war.

In declaring a Global War on Terror, George W. Bush accomplished what his father had not. This apocalyptic event enabled him to bring closure to one epoch and to install a very different order of things. President George Herbert Walker Bush had attempted to inaugurate a New World Order in the form of a restricted war with Iraq. But at the conclusion to that war, U.S. citizens were still lacking the imagined presence of an internal enemy who could reinstate the dynamic structure of American exceptionalism as a collectively shared state fantasy. All that changed after 9/11. The buildings that were the targets of the attacks—the World Trade Center and the Pentagon Building—were icons that represented the people of both covenants.

The Clinton administration had correlated the international war against Islamic extremists with the Christian fundamentalist and militia movements, which it represented as the seedbeds for domestic terrorism. But the Bush administration recruited the apocalyptic imagination of the Christian fundamentalist to supply higher authority for the state's war against Muslim extremists. The administration then hired paramilitary forces from the Blackwater Corporation to carry out special military operations under banners like Operation Infinite Justice and Operation Enduring Freedom that turned foundational tenets of scriptural belief into the authorization for the use of deadly force. If Christian fundamentalism was made to represent the superiority of U.S. political theology to Islamic fundamentalism, the members of the Blackwater militia turned that surplus righteousness into the legitimation for the extralegal violence they directed against Islamic extremists. Having transformed Christian fundamentalism into the theological dimension of the reason of state and having incorporated the militia movement into a legitimate expression of state force, the Bush administration went on to represent the nation in whose name it fought as a multiculture whose members were united through their collective participation in the newly declared Global War on Terror.

But in subsuming the constituent national communities of both the Contract with America and the New Covenant, the Bush administration also depended upon the work of an alternative state fantasy to accomplish its reuniting of America. This chapter constitutes an attempt to interpret the state fantasy that has emerged in the wake of the events that took place on September 11, 2001, through a discussion of the consensual fictions it has displaced. Each of the keywords in its title—"Virgin Land," "Ground Zero," and "Homeland"—refers to a governing metaphor that has anchored the people to a relationship to the national territory.

The terms Virgin Land and Ground Zero are freighted with metaphorical significance and performative force. Virgin Land refers to a space that coincided with the nation's prerevolutionary origins wherein European settlers' grounding assumptions about America were inscribed. Ground Zero designates the site that emerged into visibility on September 11, 2001, whereon those grounding assumptions were drastically transformed. Whereas the collective representation Virgin Land emerged out of scholarship in the field of American studies, Ground Zero was a term of art devised within the realm of statecraft. Throughout the cold war, government policymakers invoked a national narrative that was organized out of these primal metaphors. The Virgin Land metaphor associated U.S. peoples with the National Security State, and it entailed their collective wish to disavow the historical fact of the U.S. forcible dispossession of indigenous peoples from their homelands. But after 9/11, the state reentered what might be described as the primal scene at which the nation's founding took place so as to replace Virgin Land with Ground Zero as the foundational trope of a different iteration of the constitutive relationship between the people and the state. The official narrative accompanying Ground Zero has linked the people traumatized by the events that took place on 9/11 with a Homeland Security State that emerged with the loss of the belief in the inviolability of the Virgin Land.

In what follows, I shall sketch the genealogy of each of these narrative formations and interrogate the political and cultural implications of this master fiction that has reorganized the U.S. citizenry's relationship with the land. I shall also briefly speculate on the role that American studies might play in interrogating this reconfiguration.

The Inauguration of the Global War on Terror

This analysis begins with the assumption that historical and political crises of the magnitude of 9/11 are always accompanied by mythologies that attempt to reconfigure them within frames of reference that would generate imaginary resolutions to these crises. The myths that accompany historical crises only become historically real when historical actors supply the hypotheses they project about contingent events with cultural significance. As the preserve of the discursive spaces wherein the conflicting claims of the imaginary and the historically factual are mediated and resolved, myths give closure to traumatizing historical events by endowing them with a moral significance.

National cultures conserve images of themselves across time by constructing such larger-than-life myths and transmitting them from one generation to the next. As the structural metaphors containing all the essential elements of a culture's worldview, myths empower writers and policymakers to position historically contingent events within preconstituted frames of reference that would control the public's understanding of their significance.[1] Richard Slotkin has explained how national myths accomplish this reconfiguration in terms of their power to assimilate historical contingencies to "archetypal patterns of growth and decay, salvation and damnation, death and rebirth."[2] As the structural metaphors containing the essential elements of a culture's habits of mind, myths take place in the gap in between a culture's perception of contingent historical events and their assimilation into the nation's collective memory. In supplying the events they retell with timeless cultural value, myths incorporate these events within the precincts of a national tradition the national mythology was created to transmit. Following their integration within the nation's core myths, these events are endowed with a time immemorial quality that renders them essential components of the culture that they thereafter reproduce. It was through their correlation with processes responsible for producing and conserving national tradition that core myths like Virgin Land acquired their powers of cultural persuasion. Their control of the keys to cultural persuasion enables national myths and symbols to function as the unacknowledged legislators that regulate a people's thought and behavior.

As the harbinger for the invariant core beliefs prerequisite to the reordering of reality, the national mythology supplied the master fictions to which Bush appealed to authorize the state's actions. The mythological tropes—"Virgin Land," "Redeemer Nation," "American Adam," "Nature's Nation," "Errand into the Wilderness"—sedimented within the nation's master narratives supplied the transformational grammar through which state policymakers have shaped and reshaped the national peoples' understanding of political and historical events. The state's powers of governance have depended in part upon its recourse to these master fictions that transmit a normative system of values and beliefs from generation to generation. After they subordinated historical events to these mythological themes, government's policymakers were empowered to fashion imaginary resolutions of actual historical dilemmas.

But the catastrophic events that took place at the World Trade Center and the Pentagon on September 11, 2001, precipitated a "reality" that the national mythology could neither comprehend nor master. In his September 20, 2001, address to the nation, President George W. Bush provided a reply that inaugurated a symbolic drama that was partly autonomous of the events that called it forth. The address to the nation was designed to lessen the events' traumatizing power through the provision of an imaginary response to a disaster that could not otherwise be assimilated to the preexisting order of things:

> On September 11, enemies of freedom committed an act of war against our country. Americans have known wars, but for the past 136 years they have been wars on foreign soil, except for one Sunday in 1941. Americans have known the casualties of war, but not at the center of a great city on a peaceful morning.... Americans have known surprise attacks, but never before on thousands of civilians.... All of this was brought upon us in a single day, and night fell on a different world.... I will not forget the wound to our country and those who inflicted it.... Our grief has turned to anger and anger to resolution. Whether we bring our enemies to justice or bring justice to our enemies, justice will be done.[3]

The executive phrases in Bush's address alluded to the foundational myths embedded within the national narrative. These phrases also inaugurated a symbolic drama that would transform the primary integers in the narrative the nation had formerly told itself into terms—Ground Zero, Homeland, Operation Enduring Freedom, Operation Iraqi Freedom—that authorized the Bush administration's state of emergency. Specifically, the state's symbolic response to 9/11 replaced Virgin Land ("Americans have known wars, but for the past 136 years they have been wars on foreign soil") with Ground Zero ("Americans have known the casualties of war, but not at the center of a great city on a peaceful morning") and the Homeland ("Americans have known surprise attacks, but never before on thousands of civilians") as the governing metaphors through which to come to terms with the attack. The spectacular military campaigns in Afghanistan and Iraq that followed Bush's September 20 address were in part designed to accomplish the conversion of these metaphors into historical facts.[4]

When George Bush cited the historically accurate fact that, "with the exception of a Sunday in 1941," the United States had not been subject to foreign invasion, he linked the public's belief in the myth of Virgin Land with the historical record.[5] But when he did so, Bush did not supply U.S. publics with historical grounds for the collective belief in Virgin Land. The myth that America was a Virgin Land endowed the historical fact that U.S. soil had never before been subjected to foreign violation with a moral rationale: Virgin Land was inviolate because the American people were innocent. In describing the surprise attack as a "wound to our country," Bush interpreted this violation on mythological as well as historical registers.

The wound was directed against the Virgin Land as well as the U.S. people's myth of themselves as radically innocent. The state of emergency Bush erected at Ground Zero was thereafter endowed with the responsibility to defend the Homeland because the foreign violation of Virgin Land had alienated the national people from their imaginary way of inhabiting the nation. This substitution anchored the people to a very different state formation. It also drastically altered the national people's foundational fantasy about their relationship to the national territory, redefining it in terms of the longing of a dislocated population for their lost homeland.

The myth of Virgin Land enabled the American people to believe in their radical innocence because it permitted them to disavow knowledge of the historical fact that the national people took possession of their native land through the forcible dispossession of native peoples from their homeland. Bush's speech possessed narrative and performative dimensions that reinterpreted 9/11 as an act of violence directed against these powers of disavowal. The state's response to the crisis emptied it of its reality and reorganized the master fiction productive of the national peoples' imaginary relations to actual events. The symbolic reply to this catastrophe supplanted it with a symbolic drama that was autonomous of the events that called it forth. After describing how the citizenry had been alienated from the mythology productive of their imaginary relation to the state, Bush linked their generalized sense of alienation with the vulnerability of the Homeland that became the protectorate of the security apparatus.

When Bush declared the country "wounded," he interpreted the violation on mythological as well as historical registers. The wound was directed against the Virgin Land as well as U.S. people's fantasy of itself as radically innocent. The Homeland Security State that Bush erected at Ground Zero was endowed with the responsibility to defend the Homeland because the foreign violation of their Virgin Land had alienated the national people from their imaginary way of inhabiting their native land. While the Homeland was associated with the geographical dimensions of the nation-state, its security required the state to extend its policing authority to the dimension of the globe. Moreover, the violation of the land's "virginity" required that Bush bring the event that the public had formerly disavowed—the forcible dispossession of an entire national people from their homeland—into spectacular visibility.

9/11: Virgin Land at Ground Zero

The metaphor of Virgin Land condensed a broad range of historically distinct actions—the uprooting, immigration, and resettlement of European exiles on a newly "discovered" territorial landmass—and the frame narrative of American exceptionalism regulated the meanings that should and that should not be assigned to these actions. At its core, the metaphor of Virgin Land was designed to fulfill Europe's wish to start life afresh by relinquishing history on behalf of the secular dream of the construction of a new Eden. The metaphor gratified European emigrants' need to believe that America was an unpopulated space. The belief that the new world was discovered and settled by the Europeans who emigrated there resulted from the coupling of a shared fantasy with historical amnesia.

If the fantasy of American exceptionalism enabled U.S. citizens to construe imperial events—the forcible resettlement of indigenous populations, the imperial annexation of Mexican territory—as exceptions to the nation's ruling norms, the myth of Virgin Land redescribed these exceptions as lacking a foundation in U.S. history. "Virgin Land" depopulated the landscape in the imaginary register so that it might be perceived as an unoccupied territory in actuality. The metaphor turned the landscape into a blank page, understood to be the ideal surface onto which to inscribe the history of the nation's Manifest Destiny. Virgin Land narratives placed the movement of the national people across the continent in opposition to the savagery attributed to the wilderness as well as the native peoples who figured as indistinguishable from the wilderness, and, later, it fostered an understanding of the campaign of Indian removal as nature's beneficent choice of the Anglo-American settlers over the native inhabitants for its cultivation.

Overall Virgin Land enabled the American people to replace the fact that the land was already settled by a vast native population with the belief that it was unoccupied. And the substitution of the belief for the historical reality enabled Americans to disavow the resettlement and in some instances the extermination of entire populations. In displacing historical events with the representations through which they became recognizably "American," Virgin Land narratives produced reality as an effect of the imaginary. The fact that this reality could be exposed as unreal did not diminish the control that the national imaginary exerted over the symbolic order; it worked instead to underscore the logic of fetishism as the decisive aspect of its mode of persuasion. U.S. citizens may have known very well that the historical record would not warrant the belief that the colonists who emigrated to America discovered a Virgin Land, but they nevertheless found it necessary to embrace the belief over the historical record. They found it so because the belief that America was a Virgin Land fostered the complementary belief in the radical innocence of the American people.

The belief as well as the disavowal were linked to the historical fact that U.S. civilian populations had not been subject to foreign attack since the War of 1812. The historical fact of the nation's inviolability associated the belief in a Virgin Land with the desire that U.S. soil would remain forever unviolated by foreign aggression. When this fact was conjoined with the belief that the violation of a native people's homeland took place on foreign soil rather than Virgin Land, the composite named what determined the United States' uniqueness.

But the catastrophic events that took place at Ground Zero on September 11, 2001, actualized both of the scenarios that the belief in Virgin Land had been designed to ward off. At Ground Zero, U.S. Virgin Land had not merely been violated by foreign invaders; this violation assumed the form of the forcible dislocation of a settled population. The buildings that had been erected to symbolize the U.S. rise to world dominance were turned into horrific spectacles of the violent removal of occupants from their site of residence.

The transformation of Virgin Land into Ground Zero brought into visibility an inhuman terrain that the national imaginary had been constructed to conceal. While the term Ground Zero was chosen to describe the unimaginable nature of the events that took place on September 11, 2001, the state's association of them with the demand for the securing of the Homeland invested them with an uncanny effect. For when it displaced the metaphor of the Virgin Land, the term Homeland rendered the devastation precipitated at Ground Zero at once utterly unexpected yet weirdly familiar.

After they were figured in relation to the Homeland Security Act, the unprecedented events that took place on 9/11 seemed familiar because they recalled the suppressed historical knowledge of the United States' origins in the devastation of native peoples' homelands. The sites of residence of the Paiutes and the Shoshones had more recently been destroyed as a result of the state's decision to turn their tribal lands into toxic dumps for the disposal of nuclear waste. The events also appeared familiar, as the signifier Ground Zero attests, because the unimaginable sight of the crumbling Twin Towers recovered memories of the fire bombings of civilian populations over Dresden and Tokyo as well as the unspeakable aftereffects of the atomic fallout on the inhabitants of Hiroshima and Nagasaki.

With the destruction of the fantasy that the nation was founded on Virgin Land, the violence that it covered over swallowed up the entire field of visibility. Ground Zero evoked the specter of the nation-founding violence out of whose exclusion the fantasy of the Virgin Land had been organized. At Ground Zero the fantasy of radical innocence upon which the nation was founded encountered the violence it had formerly concealed.

But according to what myth-logic were the American peoples constrained either to forget or suspend belief in the Indian removal policies that had effected the violent dispossession of indigenous tribes throughout the preceding two hundred years of the nation's history? And how did the myth of Virgin Land connect the belief in the state's power to secure the national peoples against foreign aggression with belief in their radical innocence?

A Brief Genealogy of the Rise and Fall of the Myth of Virgin Land

While the connection between the disavowal of state violence and the construction of the national mythology might seem remote at best, the facilitation of just such a connection was nevertheless a central concern of the founders of the Myth and Symbol school of American studies. With the notable exception of Henry Nash Smith, the founders of the Myth and Symbol school of American literary studies—R. W. B. Lewis, Leslie Fiedler, Leo Marx—were veterans of the Second World War. After the war's conclusion, these soldier-critics produced the patriotic fictions in whose name they could retroactively claim to have fought the war. The national myth they created linked their need for an idealized national heritage with the epic narrative through which that idealization was imagined, symbolized, and supplied with characters and events. The myths about the nation the founders of the Myth and Symbol school invented was at once a narrative about the national heritage in whose name these soldier-critics had fought the war and a screen memory through which they supplanted the recollections of the violent military campaign in which they had participated with the idealized representations of the nation to which they desired to return. But if the Myth and Symbol school originated out of their need to remove representations of violence from the nation's past, it lost its monopoly at the time of the War in Vietnam when the nation's myths and symbols encountered a historical violence it could neither foreclose from recognition nor deny.

The symbolic national tradition that Myth and Symbol scholars invented enabled the symbolic engineers responsible for the forging of the nation's foreign policy to fashion imaginary resolutions for the seemingly intractable political dilemmas that confronted Americans throughout the cold war. The Virgin Land upon which Myth and Symbol scholars emplotted historical events supplied the public screen onto which they projected the national culture's guilts as well as its fears and desires. Positioned outside the normative control of the social order, this spectacular counterworld replaced the vexing facts of the real world with invented characters and events that were compatible with collective social hopes and prejudices.

The idealized representations invented by the founders of the Myth and Symbol school of interpretation came to name, that is, entitle, the mastertexts of the field of American literary studies. These masterworks engaged a prototypical American self (*American Adam*) in an epic quest (*Errand into the Wilderness*) to liberate our native land (*Virgin Land*) from foreign encroachments (*The Machine in the Garden*).[6] While each of these foundational texts provided a slightly different account of the metanarrative that defined the practices of Americanists, all of them presupposed a utopian space of pure possibility where a whole self internalized this epic myth in a language and a series of actions that corroborated the encompassing state fantasy of American exceptionalism.

Scholars working within the Myth and Symbol school correlated the scholarly prerogatives of American studies with the formative values of U.S. society. In combining rigorous research with patriotic sentiment, the members of this scholarly community turned nation-centeredness into a professional ideal. As prevalued representations of reality, the myths that they interpreted within this school did not merely codify national metanarrative. The superstructural pressure of this national metanarrative transmitted an implied regulating intertext. This intertext works at the level of the discourse in the same way that grammar operates at the level of the sentence. In achieving its effects, this regulatory intertext eliminated any distinction between what the metanarrative meant to say and what it was constrained to mean.

As coherent structures of belief, these myths and symbols constituted what might be described as objective imperatives that brought historical events into conformity with the nation's preexisting self-representations. Their myths and symbols measured events against their

impact on the cohesion of the national community and created iden-
tifiable enemy images against whom to rally. Finally they suggested a
range of moral lessons, derived from past disasters, about how to act in
the present so as to safeguard a future. In so doing they also supplied
policymakers and speechwriters with the rhetoric and the grammar
through which they forged the addresses that won the people's consent. Following its deployment as the grounding mythos for pedagogy
in American studies, the U.S. metanarrative these critics invented
thereafter solidified into a relatively autonomous system of meaning
production that resulted in a semantic field by which individuals were
persuaded to live demonstrably imaginary relations to their real conditions of existence. Each of the foundational signifiers—Virgin Land,
American Adam, Errand into the Wilderness—sedimented within the
national metanarrative possessed a performative dimension empowered
to bring about belief in the truth of the state of affairs they represented.

Because it involved a universal subject in a transhistorical action,
Kenneth Burke has characterized the national metanarrative as the
"justifying myth" for the material history of the cold war. "An explanatory narrative that achieves the status of perfecting myth serves to rec-
oncile discrepancies and irrationalities while appearing to obviate public
or official scrutiny of actual circumstances. Such a narrative becomes
effectively monolithic and saturating, demonizing its opposite and can-
celing or absorbing all mediatory and intermediate terms and kinds of
activity."[7] At once a mode of inquiry, an object of knowledge, and an
ideological rationale, the Myth and Symbol school of American literary studies facilitated an interdisciplinary formation that empowered
Americanist scholars within the disciplines of literature, history, politics, sociology, and government to interpret and regulate the United
States' geopolitical order. Through this interdisciplinary approach, the
field of American studies collaborated with the press, university system, publishing industry, and other aspects of the cultural apparatus
that managed the semantic field and policed the significance of such
value-laden terms as the nation and the people.[8]

In *Virgin Land: The American West as Symbol and Myth*, Henry Nash
Smith analyzed the myths that were generated by the European settlers
in their historical encounter with the American West. After comparing
these myths with collective representations of the New World that were
formulated at the time of the Discovery of America, Smith explained

how this primary metaphor provided a means of spiritual, economic, and masculine renewal for the "sons of Cooper's Leatherstocking" who embraced the myth. In 1950, the year of the book's publication, the United States was engaged in a struggle with Russian communism over the political disposition of peoples across the globe. Because it was understood to be an expression of the sovereign will of the people that it was also understood to represent, the myth of Virgin Land was invoked by policymakers as indicative of the public's approval of the state's policy of rebuilding and developing nations across the planet. After the architects of the Marshall Plan under Truman's administration and the New Frontier under John F. Kennedy's deployed concepts and themes from this metanarrative to secure spontaneous consent for state policies, the myth of Virgin Land enabled them to legitimate the United States' place as the subject and telos of universal history.

Throughout the cold war, U.S. legislators required the silent partnership of the state fantasy of American exceptionalism to solicit U.S. citizens' belief in the United States as a unique political formation. The cold war state was grounded in a political metaphysics that elevated national security into the foundational national predicate. The metanarrative underpinning the myth of Virgin Land transmitted a national tradition in support of this predication. And during the first two decades of the cold war, Henry Nash Smith's *Virgin Land* hypothesis supplied the cultural code through which normative Americanist behavior was communicated and regulated. When Smith defined Virgin Land as open national landscape that fostered the construction and realization of self-reliant individualists, he supplied the terrain upon which state policymakers displaced actually existing social and political crises onto a strictly imaginary site where they underwent symbolic resolution. The rugged individualists who populated this transhistorical terrain subjectivized the codes regulating appropriate American behavior, and they thereby legitimated the norms suturing U.S. citizens to the patterns of domination, subjectification, and governmentality that the National Security State propagated across the globe.

However, the events that took place during the Vietnam War radically disrupted the historical effectiveness of the metanarrative of Virgin Land that had formerly endowed historical events with their intelligibility. Opponents to the War in Vietnam correlated the state's policy of Indian removal in the nineteenth century with the foreign policy that resulted in the massacres at My Lai. In so doing antiwar activists exposed the myth of Virgin Land as one of the ideological forms through which state historians and policymakers had covered up the nation's shameful history of colonial violence. The war effected what John Hellmann has described as a radical disruption in the nation's self-representations:

> When the story of America in Vietnam turned into something un-expected, the nature of the larger story of America itself became the subject of intense cultural dispute. On the deepest level, the legacy of Vietnam is the disruption of our story of our explanation of the past and vision of the future.[9]

In the wake of the Vietnam War, Americanist scholars desacralized the myths of the United States as a Virgin Land and the myth of the national history as a providential errand into the wilderness. They fostered new paradigm communities that replaced essentializing national myths with cultural constructivist models, that undermined the aesthetic authority of the national landscape, and that subverted the literary canon as an instrument of Americanization, and they imagined forms of citizenship that were not subject to the imperatives of the security apparatus.[10]

The Return of the National Mythology and the Emergence of the Global Homeland State

War might be said to begin when a country becomes a patriotic fiction for its population. A nation is not only a piece of land but a narration about the people's relation to the land.[11] And after 9/11, the national myths that had undergone wholesale debunking in the post-Vietnam era underwent remarkable regeneration. Around the time that the U.S. war machine was rolling into the area some biblical scholars have designated as the location of the Garden of Eden, Alan Wolfe published a lengthy review essay in *The New Republic* in which he argued that it was the ethical responsibility of Americanist scholars to rehabilitate the narrative of Virgin Land that had been fostered by the scholars in the Myth and Symbol school of American studies. In the opening paragraphs of his article, Wolfe invoked Marx's *Machine in the Garden* as an authorization for the following characterization of the deleterious consequences of revisionist Americanists' loss of belief in these core narratives: "It does not occur to these revolutionaries that the groups they hope will conquer America cannot do so if there is no America to conquer. Let America die, and all who aspire to its perfection will die with it."[12]

If one of the primary aims of war involves destroying the way an enemy perceives itself, Alan Wolfe represented 9/11 as an act of war in the sense that it brought about the destruction of the national people's foundational fantasy concerning their relation to the land. The foundational fantasy of the United States was organized around a traumatic element that could not be symbolized within the terms of the national narrative. In the United States, the fantasy of the Virgin Land covered over the shameful history of internal violence directed against the native populations. But as we have seen, this historical fact was not utterly effaced. It functioned as an occluded but obscene supplement to the nation's view of itself as a Redeemer Nation whose Manifest Destiny entailed the commission to undertake a providential errand into the wilderness. The disavowed knowledge of the barbarous violence that accompanied this civilizing mission was the unwritten basis for Alan Wolfe's need to embrace Virgin Land as a representative national metaphor.

But George W. Bush differed from Alan Wolfe in that he turned the enemy's violation of the nation's foundational fantasy into the occasion to fashion exceptions to the rules of law and war, which formally inaugurated a state of emergency. In his September 20 address, Bush designated the "enemies of freedom" as the historical agency responsible for this generalized unsettlement of the national people. But neither Osama bin Laden nor Saddam Hussein was the causative agent responsible for the forcible separation of the national people from their way of life. It was the state of emergency that ensued in the wake of the Homeland Security Act that required the people to depart from the norms and values to which they had become habituated and that tore to the ground the democratic institutions—freedom of speech, religious tolerance, formal equality, uniform juridical procedures, universal suffrage— that had formerly nurtured and sustained the national people.[13]

With the enemy's violation of the rules of war as rationale, the state suspended the rules to which it was otherwise subject and violated its own rules in the name of protecting them against a force that operated according to different rules. In order to protect the rule of law as such from this illegality, the state declared itself the occupant of a position that was not subject to the rules it must protect. Congress's passage of the U.S. Patriot Act into law effected the most dramatic abridgment of civil liberties in the nation's history. This emergency legislation subordinated all concerns of ethics, of human rights, of due process, of constitutional hierarchies, and of the division of power to the state's monopoly over the exception.

The Emergency State is marked by absolute independence from any juridical control and any reference to the normal political order. It is empowered to suspend the articles of the Constitution protective of personal liberty, freedom of speech and assembly, the inviolability of the home, and postal and telephone and Internet privacy. In designating Afghanistan and Iraq as endangering the Homeland, Operations Infinite Justice and Enduring Freedom simply extended the imperatives of the domestic emergency state across the globe.

Following 9/11 the state effected the transition from a normalized political order to a state of emergency through its spectacular enactments of the violence that Virgin Land had normatively covered over. Whereas 9/11 dislocated the national people from the mythology productive of their imaginary relation to the state, Bush linked their generalized dislocation with the vulnerability of the Homeland, which thereafter became the target of the security apparatus. Bush endowed the state of emergency that he erected at Ground Zero with the responsibility to defend the Homeland because foreign aggressors had violated Virgin Land.

Bush exiled the people from their normative nationality so as to intensify their need for home. Amy Kaplan has described the possessive investment of white American nationals in what President Bush called the "ownership society" as a reaffirmation of the distinction between the foreign and the domestic. In "Manifest Domesticity" Amy Kaplan has explained that within the U.S. structures of feeling the domestic has a double meaning. It not only links the familial household to the nation but also imagines both in opposition to everything outside the geographical and conceptual borders of the home: "the idea of the foreign policy depends on the sense of the nation as a domestic space imbued with a sense of at-homeness, in contrast to the external world perceived as alien and threatening. Reciprocally a sense of the foreign is necessary to erect the boundaries that enclose the nation at home."[14]

The violation of the land's inviolability had not only disinhibited the state of its need to mask its history of violence; this act of aggression required the state to bring the event that the public had formerly disavowed—the forcible dispossession of national peoples from their homelands—into the quasi-apocalyptic visibility of its Shock and Awe military demonstration in Iraq.

But the Homeland that emerged as the justification for the state's exercise of excessive violence was not identical with the land mass of the continental United States. The Homeland Bush invoked to "authorize" these emergency actions did not designate either an enclosed territory or an imaginable home. The Homeland secured by the Emergency State instead referred to the unlocatable order that emerged *through and by way of the people's generalized dislocation from the nation as a shared form of life*. The Homeland Security Act inaugurated a State of Exception that positioned the people in a space that was included in the Homeland through its exclusion from the normal political order.

The historical precedent for the Homeland was the legal fiction of the domestic dependent nation that Chief Justice Marshall invented as rationale of the state's right to dispossess the Cherokees of their land. In relegating U.S. citizens to a Homeland that it secured and defended against terrorist attacks, Bush's State of Exception relocated the national community within the equivalent to that exceptional space that Justice Marshall had called a "domestic dependent nation" in his 1831 ruling on the rights of the Cherokees. Rather than sharing sovereignty with the state, U.S. citizens were treated as denizens of a protectorate that the State of Exception defended rather than answered to. This new protectorate or consumer compound was composed of passive consumers who understood good citizenship to entail the practice and consumption of the America way of life.[15]

As the relationship between the state and the population that comes into existence when the state declares a state of emergency, the Homeland names a form of governmentality without a recognizable location. As the unlocalizable space the population is ordered to occupy when the state enters the site of the exception to the normative order, the Homeland names the structure through which the state of emergency is realized normally.

As we have seen, the national mythology turned the nation into a stage for the enactment of particular forms of life. But if the nation designates the arena in which the national peoples enacted these ways of life, the Homeland named the space that emerged when these peoples were dissociated from their ways of life. The introduction of the signifier of the Homeland to capture this experience of generalized dislocation recalled themes from the national narrative that it significantly altered. But insofar as these themes were antithetical to the range of connotations sedimented within Virgin Land, the historical antecedents for the Homeland surely must give pause.

The Homeland named the site that the colonial settlers had abandoned in their quest for a newly found land. The Homeland also named the country to which the settlers might one day return. In its reference to an archaic land that the colonial settlers either voluntarily departed from or were forced to abandon, the Homeland represented a prehistoric pastness prior to the founding of the United States. Following 9/11, the Homeland named the space in which the people were included after acts of terrorism had violently dislocated them from their ways of life. The metaphor of the Homeland thereafter evoked the image of a vulnerable population that had become internally estranged from its "country of origin" and dependent on the protection of the state. The Homeland found historical precedent for this sequestration of the national peoples in the protectorates it established in the territories the United States colonized—Guam, the Philippines, the Virgin Islands—as well as in the juridical category of the domestic dependent nation that Justice Marshall had invented to describe the juridical status of Indian reservations.

When it was figured within the Homeland Security Act, the Homeland engendered an imaginary scenario wherein the national people were encouraged to consider themselves dislocated from their country of origin by foreign aggressors so that they might experience their return from exile in the displaced form of the spectacular unsettling of homelands elsewhere. This imaginary scenario and the spectacles through which it was communicated sustained the dissociation of the people from recognizably "American" ways of life. Insofar as the Homeland named what emerged when the population became dislocated from the conditions of belonging to a territorialized nation, its security required the domestic emergency state to extend its sovereign policing authority over every territory across the planet.

Virgin Land as Ground Zero

The Homeland Security Act regressed the population to a minority condition of dependency upon the state for its biopolitical welfare. But the state thereafter correlated this regression in political standing with the reenactment of a formerly suppressed historical event. After the people were regressed to the condition of a political minority, the state produced a series of spectacles that returned the population to the historical moment in which colonial settlers had deployed the illicit use of force against native populations.[16] With the invasion of Afghanistan and Iraq, the figurative meanings associated with Virgin Land were demetaphorized into the actuality of the state's violence. The state's spectacular violation of the rights of the "enemies of freedom" was thereby made to coincide with the Emergency State's radical abridgment of the domestic people's civil rights.

The putative insecurity of the homeland's civilian population and the threat of terrorist attack were coconstituting aspects of the Homeland Security State. The state's representation of a vulnerable civilian population in need of the protection of the state was fashioned in a relation of opposition to the captured Taliban and Iraqis who were subjected to the power of the state yet lacked the protection of their rights or liberties.

This new settlement required the public to sacrifice their civil liberties in exchange for the enjoyment of the state's spectacular violations of the rights of other sovereign states. The Bush administration did not exactly represent the military operations that took place in Afghanistan and Iraq as wars conducted between civilized states that respected one another's sovereignty. It constructed them as confrontations between the emergency state apparatus and terrorizing powers that posed a threat to the Homeland. If the modern state is construed as the embodiment of Enlightenment reason, and the neoliberal principles of market democracy comprise the means whereby this rationality becomes universalized, neither the Taliban regime in Afghanistan nor the Baathist regime in Iraq could be construed either as modern states or as rational actors in the global economy. In their military operations in Afghanistan and Iraq, the U.S. emergency state apparatus imposed this modern state formation and that market logic on the Afghani and the Iraqi peoples. As a result of these acts of "defensive aggression," Iraq and Afghanistan were relocated within the global order of the Homeland Security State.

The spectators' enjoyment of them derived from the spectacles' violation of the normative assumptions—that the United States was a redeemer nation rather than an aggressor state, whose manifest errand was civilizing rather than brutalizing—sedimented within the national imaginary. Because the spectators could not enjoy the state's spectacles without disassociating from the assumptions that would have rendered them unimaginable as *American* spectacles, these spectacles enforced the separation of the state's spectatorial publics from their national forms of life. After these spectacles intermediated between the people and their forms of life, they substituted the lateral linkages with the emergency state apparatus for the people's vertical integration with a democratic way of life.

In Iraq and Afghanistan the emergency forces of the state openly reperformed the acts of violence that the myth of Virgin Land had formerly covered up. Operation Infinite Justice quite literally depopulated the Afghani landscape so that it might be perceived as a blank page onto which to inscribe a different political order. Operation Iraqi Freedom fostered an understanding of "regime change" as the Iraqi people's beneficent choice of the political exemplars of its Anglo-American occupiers for the institutions of its new political order. As witnesses to the state's colonization of Afghanistan and Iraq, the United States' spectatorial publics were returned to the prehistoric time of the colonial settlers who had formerly spoliated Indian homelands. By way of Operation Infinite Justice and Operation Iraqi Freedom the Homeland Security State restaged the colonial settlers' conquest of Indians and the acquisition of their homelands. The terror and the killing became the Homeland Security State's means of accomplishing anew the already known telos of U.S. history as the inaugural event of America's global rule in the twenty-first century.

These spectacles redescribed imperial conquest as a form of domestic defense in a manner that reversed the relationship between the aggressor and the victim. The Homeland Security State constructed the preemptive strikes against others' homelands as a spectacular form of domestic defense against foreign aggression. Both spectacles invited their audiences to take scopic pleasure in the return of the traumatic memory of the unprovoked aggression that the colonial settlers had previously exerted against native populations. These massacres, which could not be authorized or legitimated by the Virgin Land narrative, became the foundational acts that inaugurated the Global Homeland as a realm outside the law.

Whereas the myth of Virgin Land produced historical continuity by suppressing the traumatic memory of lawless violence, the events of 9/11 demanded the recovery of this traumatic memory so as to reverse the national people's relation to violence, and to inaugurate a new global order. The spectacles that unfolded in the deserts of Afghanistan and Iraq transformed the U.S. spectatorial population into the perpetrators rather than the victims of foreign aggression. The state's literal recovery of the traumatic memory of barbarous aggression against native peoples thereby overcame the traumatizing experience of aggression at the hands of "foreign" terrorists.

These spectacles of violence encouraged the public's belief that it participated in the state's power because it shared in the spectacle through which the state gave expression to its power. But the people were also the potential targets of the shows of force they witnessed. In transforming the citizens into spectators, the state interposed a disjunction between the people and the ways of life that the state protected through its exercises of retributive violence. After this new settlement induced the people to suspend their civil liberties in exchange for the enjoyment of the state's spectacular violations of the rights of its enemies, the Emergency State transposed the nation and the citizen into dispensable predicates of global rule.

Homeland Security as a Global Biopolitical Settlement

As we have seen, the Homeland enacted into law by the Homeland Security Act did not have reference to an enclosed territory. And it was not exactly a political order. The Homeland Security Act was the political instrument on whose authority the state transformed a temporary suspension of order erected on the basis of factual danger into a quasi-permanent biopolitical arrangement that as such remained outside the normal order. After the passage of the Homeland Security Act, the State of Exception no longer referred to an external state of factual danger. It was instead identified with the juridico-political order itself. This juridical-political apparatus thereafter authorized a biopolitical settlement that inscribed the body of the people into an order of state power that endowed the state with power over the life and death of the population.[17]

This biopolitical sphere emerged with the state's decision to construe the populations it governed as indistinguishable from unprotected biological life. The body of the people as a free and equal citizenry that was endowed with the capacity to reconstitute itself through recourse to historically venerated social significations was thereby replaced by a biologized population that the state protected from biological terrorism. The biopolitical sphere constructed by the provisions of the Homeland Security Act first subtracted the population from the forms of civic and political life through which they recognized themselves as a national people and then positioned these life forms—the people, their way of life—into nonsynchronous zones of protection with the promise that their future synchronization would resuscitate the nation-state.

After undergoing a generalized dislocation from the national imaginary through which their everyday practices were lived as recognizably "American" forms of life, the national peoples were reconstituted as biological life forms. Their dislocation from the national imaginary resulted in their mass denationalization. As naked biological life under the state's protection, the biopoliticized population also could play no active political role in the Homeland Security State's reordering of things. The Homeland Security State thereafter represented the population as an unprotected biological formation whose collective vitality must be administered and safeguarded against weapons of biological terrorism. But insofar as the Homeland state's biopolitical imperative to regulate the life and death of the population that it governed was irreducible to the denizens of the nation-state, the Homeland Security State's biopolitical regime became potentially global in its extensibility.

It was the state's description of the weapons that endangered the aggregated population as "biological" that in part authorized the state's biopolitical settlement. In representing its biopolitical imperatives in terms of a defense against weapons of biological destruction, the state also produced an indistinction between politics and the war against terrorism. This redescription produced two interrelated effects: it transformed the population's political and civil liberties into life forms that were to be safeguarded rather than acted upon; more importantly, it turned political opponents of this biopolitical settlement into potential enemies of the ways of life that the state safeguards.[18]

Detainees: The State's Injured

The detention camps were in a realm beyond good and evil where abduction and execution were naturalized by a mythology that rendered them exempt from tests of reality. Mythological structures of exceptions to legal categories doubled back tautologically to reinforce the state's adoption of an unprecedented power as the exception to its own rules. And the public entered this realm beyond good and evil when they were bound as witnesses to the formation of persons outside the existing juridical categories and refused the basic dignities of legal process. The people ratified the power of the state to declare itself an exception to its own rule by participating visually in the construction of persons who were construed as exceptions to the human condition.

The fact that the spectacle of the "justice" "we" brought to our enemies took place on Guantánamo Bay requires some brief explanation. Bush anticipated the state's usage of this space as the staging ground for the state's violation of the Geneva Conventions with the phrase "except for one Sunday in 1941" as the historical location to the sole exception to the United States' exemption from foreign attack. But this attack did not exactly take place on U.S. soil. On December 7, 1941, Hawaii was not a state and Pearl Harbor was officially designated, like Guantánamo Bay, Cuba, as an unincorporated territory.

The exceptional nature of the attacks that took place on this unintegrated territory of Pearl Harbor on December 7, 1941, supplied the state with a metaphoric precedent for its choice of a comparable space to produce its exceptions to the rules of law and war. The Justice Department referred to Guantánamo Bay's exceptional status as an unincorporated territorial possession of the United States to justify its contention that as a "foreign territory" it lay outside the jurisdiction of any U.S. court. It was the extraterritorial status of Guantánamo Bay, its exemption from the juridical reach of any state or nation, that enabled the Emergency State to demonstrate its monopoly over the exception there.

But the act of transferring these "enemies" to Guantánamo brought about the magical transformation in the condition of the persons interned there. By rendering them at once stateless and countryless, the act of transporting them to Guantánamo Bay set the internees beyond the pale of humanity. The very same gesture that placed them outside the condition of territorial belonging provided the tautological rationale for the deprivation of their human rights. They were interned on Guantánamo Bay because they lacked the protection of human rights, and they lacked human rights because they were displaced onto Guantánamo Bay. The transfer of these "unlawful combatants" from Afghanistan to Guantánamo Bay rendered what was undecidable in Bush's musing over whether "we bring our enemies to justice or bring justice to our enemies" juridically practicable.

On Guantánamo Bay the state produced persons who were exceptions to the laws that protected the due process rights of citizens and exceptions as well to the Geneva Conventions that endowed prisoners of war with the right to refuse to respond to interrogation. Stripped of the rights of citizens *and* prisoners of war, these persons were reduced to the status of unprotected carnality. As the embodiments of animated flesh whose lives the state could terminate according to decisions that were outside juridical regulation, these unlawful combatants were invoked by the state to justify its positioning of itself as an exception to the rule of law. The Emergency State arrogated to itself its power to operate beyond the jurisdiction of the laws that regulated the World of Nations through this production of persons it could hold without due process and that it could kill without being accused of murder.[19]

The detention camps erected in Guantánamo Bay by the Halliburton Company occupied a realm outside the law in which the Emergency State's practices were naturalized by a mythology that rendered them exempt from critical scrutiny. The mythological structures that accompanied the state's fashioning of exceptions to legal categories triggered a recursive operation that reinforced the state's exercise of the power to fashion exceptions to its own rules. The people ratified the power of the state to declare itself an exception to its own rule by participating visually in the construction of persons who were construed as exceptions to the human condition.

The Emergency State invoked the terrorists' recourse to unlawful combat as the pretext for the state's violation of the laws regulating due process and the rules regulating the conduct of war. The state violated its own rules, that is to say, in the name of protecting them against a force that was said to operate according to different rules. In order to protect the rule of law as such from this alien legality, the state declared itself the occupant of a position that was not subject to the rules it must protect. As Attorney General John Ashcroft explained, in order to protect the entirety of the law against attack, the state transgressed its own laws. All concerns of ethics, of human rights, of due process, of constitutional hierarchies, and of the division of governmental power were subordinated to this urgent eschatological mission.

The vacuum opened up by the vanishing of objective reality into the singularity of Ground Zero was thereby filled in by the mythologized reality in which the Emergency State erected its eschatological version of Realpolitik and the forcible detention of unlawful combatants made complementary sense. With its undisclosed abductions of persons within the territorial nation-state, the Bush administration shifted its war on terrorism from the Afghani desert to the bodies of persons it suspected of domestic terrorism. Ignoring the time-consuming details of due process, the state condensed the juridical-penal process into the moment of abduction wherein accusation, judgment, and punishment coincided. The terrorist may have supplied its official rationale, but the detainee was in fact the cause and effect of the state of emergency. The state, which had victimized these detainees through the removal of all of their legal rights, magically transformed itself into the potential target of its victims when it constructed them as the unlawful enemies of the state.

Because the Emergency State was not subject to the rules of law that it enforced, it inhabited a realm that was quite literally beyond good and evil. After September 11, civil rights groups estimated that more than eleven hundred terrorist suspects were disappeared into a juridical maze where they were denied lawyers, beaten by guards and fellow inmates, subjected to sensory deprivation, and forced to take lie detector tests. Current immigration laws permit indefinite detainment laws, so no criminal charges were required to warrant the abductees' internment. Their guilt could not be proven, so this "transfer" of detainees to Camp X-Ray was a euphemism for extrajudicial measures.

The spectacle of detainees disappearing into the maze of an unaccountable juridical system and into the cages on Guantánamo did not

impose a mythology on the public so much as it encouraged the formation of a society of captivated spectators who agreed to the abridgment
of their civil liberties in exchange for the spectacle of persons utterly
stripped of all rights and liberties and rendered subject to the full power
of the law. Guantánamo Bay did not constitute a contradiction but an
exception to the national mythopoesis. The public in its role as audience
for these productions implicitly endorsed such rites of passage through
the acceptance of a discourse of legalized illegality crystallized in phrases
like "enemy combatants," "material witness," and "persons of interest."

Afterword: The Part of No Part

Overall, 9/11 brought to the light of day the Other to the normative
representation of the United States. It positioned *unheimlich* dislocatees
within the homeland in place of the citizens who exercised rights and
liberties on the basis of these normalizations. When the signifier of the
Homeland substituted for the Virgin Land, the National Security State
was supplanted by the Emergency State. Whereas Virgin Land enforced
the disavowal of the state's destruction of indigenous populations'
homelands, Ground Zero demanded that spectacle of the destruction of
a homeland as compensation for the loss of the land's "virginity."

In tracking the radical shift in the governing frames of reference, I
have indicated the ways in which the state coordinated the signifiers
9/11, Ground Zero, and Homeland into a relay of significations undergirding the biopolitical settlement of the Global Homeland State. But
in recollecting the radical shift in the nation's relationship to its master
fictions that took place during the Vietnam War, I have also alluded to
the inherent instability of the nodal points that have been constructed
to coordinate these newly invented governing representations.

When he inaugurated the prerogatives of the Emergency State at
Ground Zero, Bush conscripted the traumatic power of the events that
took place there to offer preemptive strikes as compensation for the
loss. But the events that took place on September 11, 2001, fractured
the nation-state's continuist time. As the locus for events lacking a
preexisting signification in the social order, 9/11 exists as a sign of what
cannot take place within the order of signification. But if it marks the
rupture of the time kept by the nation-state, 9/11 is no less discordant

with the mode of historical eventuation the Bush administration has inaugurated in its name. Inherently nonsynchronous, 9/11 calls for a time to come.

The Bush administration has attempted to supplant the loss of the belief in Virgin Land that underwrote the myth of U.S. exceptionalism with the arrogation of the power to occupy the position of the exception to the laws of the World of Nations. But insofar as the Homeland Security State's exceptions to the rules of law and war are themselves instantiations of force that lack the grounding support of norms or rules, they resemble the traumatic events upon which they depend for their power to rule. As such, these exceptions will maintain their power to rule only as long as U.S. publics remain captivated by the spectacles of violence the state has erected at the site of Ground Zero.

If the global Homeland has erected an order in which the people have no part, that order has positioned the people in a place that lacks a part in the global order. As the surplus element in the Global Homeland, the people also occupy the place of an empty universal.[20] This place may presently lack any part to play in the Homeland's Global Order. But the very emptiness of this space, the fact that it demarcates the peoples of the Global Homeland included but with no part to play in the existing order, simultaneously empowers the people to play the part of articulating an alternative to the existing order. Because the people are without a part in the order in which the people are nevertheless included, they also constitute a part in an alternative to that order. The part without a part in the given global order constitutes an empty universal in an order to come that the global peoples can particularize differently.[21] That order to come will not begin until the global state of emergency is itself exposed as the cause of the traumas it purports to oppose.

6

Antigone's Kin:
From Abu Ghraib to Barack Obama

Given the preceding account of the relationship between the state's exceptions and American exceptionalism, how was it possible that the Bush administration instituted an imperial state formation that did not require the structure of disavowal at work in the discourse of American exceptionalism? Bush's State of Exception did not require this structure of disavowal because it was its construction of itself as The Exception to the discursive norms of American exceptionalism that constituted the grounding authority of its power to rule. After the attacks on the Twin Towers on September 11, 2001, Bush inaugurated a State of Exception that did not just change the rules and norms informing the United States' domestic and foreign policy, it also changed the interpretive framework through which those rules and norms could be understood. As The Exception to the exceptionalist norms that it propagated and enforced across the planet, Bush's State of Exception did not depend for its legitimation on the hegemony of exceptionalist norms, and it did not require the fantasy of American exceptionalism to disavow its status as The Exception. Bush's State of Exception instituted a version of American exceptionalism that was voided of the need for American exceptionalists.

Bush had instituted this State of Exception in a world in which two of the constitutive norms of American exceptionalism—rule of law, free markets—had become the planetary norm. In order to see to it that they remained the norm, Bush's State of Exception enforced the planetary conditions that rendered them normal. But in instituting exceptions to the norms of U.S. political governance, Bush's State of Exception had also suspended the U.S. Constitution that had defined the terms of the state's relationship with U.S. citizens in terms of shared sovereignty.

The State of Exception operated in a sphere that was separable from the logics of the nation and that was irreducible to its terms. Bush's State of Exception suspended the laws that protected civil liberties and the metanarrative frameworks through which citizens internalized these laws as ruling norms. Bush's State of Exception in effect placed the state and the nation into two separate and mutually exclusive spheres. In relegating U.S. citizens to a Homeland that it secured and defended against terrorist attacks, Bush's State of Exception repositioned the national community within the equivalent to that exceptional space that Justice Marshall had called a "domestic dependent nation" in his 1831 ruling on the rights of the Cherokees. Rather than sharing sovereignty with the state, U.S. citizens were treated as denizens of a protectorate that the State of Exception defended rather than answered to.

Bush disassociated the State of Exception from the normalizing powers of the discourse of American exceptionalism because he wanted to render the state exempt from answering to its norms. In declaring the United States The Exception to the rules and treaties governing other nations, the Bush administration redefined sovereignty as predicated less upon national control over territorial borders than upon the state's exercising control over global networks. The United States did not want territory. It wanted to exercise authoritative control over the global commons—the sea and the air—in the interests of guaranteeing the free movement of capital, commodities, and peoples. It was the putative threats that terrorism and rogue states posed to global interconnectivities that supplied the United States with the planetary enemy that it required to justify its positioning of itself as The Exception to the rules that it enforced across the planet. In justifying the U.S. monopoly over all the processes of global interconnectivity, the war on terrorism enabled the Bush administration to arrogate to itself the right to traverse every national boundary in its effort to uproot international terrorist networks and to defend the Homeland against incursions of Islamic extremists.

From the eighteenth century through the cold war epoch, nationalism and imperialism contributed to global capitalism by dividing the globe into national and colonial enclaves. International capitalism appealed to the nation-state's powers of regulation and distribution. However, the economic demands of the global marketplace have redefined the state's mission, requiring that it downplay its obligations to the constituencies within a bounded national territory so as to meet the extranational needs and demands of global capital. The unruly capitalism that globalization has sponsored would strip nation-states of their regulatory powers and reinstate an earlier alliance between capital and the state that restricted the states to the role of protecting the newly emerging regions and local outposts of the global economy.

In an era when market priorities have reshaped sociopolitical agendas, the nation-state's social and political commitments are perceived as impediments to the efficient functioning of the global marketplace. The state has aspired to exempt itself from its contractual obligations to the national community and to dissever its ties with every constituency except the entrepreneurial capitalists responsible for managing the global economy. Rather than representing the interests of the entire nation, the selective interests of this managerial elite has bifurcated nation-states into capitalist sectors that are integrated into the global capitalist order and regions whose premodern economic practices are subjected to the exploitative forces of the capitalist sector.[1]

Describing it as a justification of America's having taken up the task of policing the globe, President George W. Bush turned 9/11 into the opportunity to reshape the configuration of global power relations. Bush associated America's monopoly on the legal use of global violence with the intervention in human time of a higher law (what he called his "higher father"). He thereby endowed the doctrine of American exceptionalism with a metaphysical supplement that enjoined the belief that the preemptive violence through which the United States would defend the globe against the threat of Islamic terrorism was metaphysically superior to that of other nation-states. The apocalyptic register of Bush's invocation of this higher law was not intended to reestablish America's claim to historical uniqueness, however. This higher law had positioned the United States outside the World of Nations as The Exception.

In what follows, I will discuss Bush's State of Exception and the Homeland fantasy through which it was hegemonized in the context of the extraneous elements that unsettled its jurisdiction and the state fantasy that has emerged to supplant the Homeland.

Abu Ghraib: The Biopolitical Unconscious of the Injuring State

The detainees who disappeared into the maze of an unaccountable juridical system and into the cages on Guantánamo Bay represented the Other to and within "We the People." The state proffered this spectacle of sublegal persons being stripped of all rights and liberties as symbolic compensation for the Patriot Act's drastic abridgment of civil liberties. "We the People" indirectly authorized the state's detainment policies in their dual offices as (1) secondary witnesses to the legality of the governmental operations that accomplished these infernal rites of passage and as (2) informal signatories to the discourse of legalized illegality crystallized in phrases like "enemy combatants," "material witness," and "persons of interest."

After 9/11, Bush made reference to the vulnerability rather than the sovereignty of the people. Representing the U.S. peoples as exposed to a biopolitical threat, Bush represented "We the People" in the image of vulnerable biological bodies in need of the protection of the Homeland Security State's emergency workers Bush had designated as the people's representatives. In celebrating emergency workers as the representatives of the Homeland Security State, President Bush produced an equivalence between the nation and the Emergency State.

The Emergency State expropriated sovereignty from the Homeland people so as to establish sovereignty as the rationale for the state's construction of the category of this Other to the people. Bush's declaration of a "War on Terror" disrupted the entire social edifice by undermining the mores that regulated the intersubjective relations of the polity. The people were asked to identify with the urgency that expropriated "We the People" from their rights. Lacking the ground from which "we" might respond, "We the People" were made to identify with the security priorities of the Emergency State.

But the denizens of the Homeland Security State withdrew their indirect authorization for what went on inside the state's security en-
campments on April 28, 2004. On that date *Sixty Minutes* broadcast a
series of photographs that displayed an orgy of penal violence perpetrated by military police guards at Abu Ghraib prison in Iraq. The photographs depicted male and female American soldiers playing various
roles in a theater of cruelty that was designed to make the prisoners under
their charge feel as if they were extraneous to the human condition. In
one of the photographs a female guard was depicted holding a leash
tethered to a dog collar that had been placed around the neck of an un-
clothed Iraqi man groveling at her feet; another snapshot represented
the same woman locked in melodramatic embrace with a grinning male
MP standing behind the naked bodies of Iraqi male prisoners who had
been stacked on top of one other; another pictured a guard forcing a
hooded prisoner to simulate oral sex with another prisoner; still another
Polaroid represented an Iraqi prisoner precariously perched on a chair
with a sandbag over his head and electrical wires attached to his hands.

After they were transmitted globally, the photographs of the abuse
at Abu Ghraib prison became the space in which the spectatorial public
refused the complicities that the security state had solicited. Whereas
Bush's biopolitical settlement had set the populations it secured and
defended in a relation of opposition to the Muslim extremists imprisoned at Abu Ghraib, the photographs of these vulnerable, unprotected
bodies evoked in their viewers the collective desire to shield this unprotected population from continued brutality. Rather than lending
the actions represented in these photographs their visual approval, the
viewers of these images galvanized a morally authorized, global opposition to the war. World opinion condemned the Bush administration for
arrogating to the Homeland Security State the power to violate internationally agreed upon rules of engagement with prisoners of war.[2]

In remakng the internees at Abu Ghraib in the image of what Giorgio
Agamben has called *homo sacer* (persons who could be killed without the
accusation of murder), the guards had set the images of persons whose
lives were not worth living in a relation of opposition to the images of the
peoples whose lives must be defended. Through their staging of scenarios
designed to terrorize their Iraqi prisoners, the military police at the Abu
Ghraib prison exacted revenge for the thousands who had lost their
lives in the Twin Towers. In revealing the biopolitical imperatives that

informed the guards' optical unconscious, the photographs reproduced Bush's biopolitical settlement reduced to its simplest visual terms. As we have seen, the Bush administration had defined the Homeland Security State as populated by a vulnerable people whose biopolitical security depended upon the state's defending them against a people that was negatively represented as posing a biopolitical threat. But the Abu Ghraib photographs renegotiated the relationship between these two biologized populations. The photographs represented a way of looking at the prisoners that the guards had staged for the visual pleasure of the members of the Homeland society as well as one another. The photographs depicted Iraqi prisoners visually cast into subjective positions that the guards had constructed to do violence to their Muslim identities. Their digital cameras transmitted the gaze through which the guards aspired to propagate their extravagant enjoyment of this violation.

The photographs depicted the soldiers deriving spectatorial pleasure from quite literally stripping their prisoners of their human rights as well as their right to be human. In deriving pleasure from these scenarios of retributive violence the guards represented the gaze of the spectatorial public for whom the Bush administration had staged its military operations. But instead of identifying with the guards' visual perspective, upon bearing witness to the prisoners' suffering, the spectatorial public protested against these obscene acts of state violence. "How can someone grin at the sufferings and humiliations of another human being?" Susan Sontag asked representatively in "Regarding the Torture of Others," an essay she published for *The New York Times Magazine* on May 23, 2004: "is the real issue not the photographs themselves but what the photographs reveal to have happened to 'suspects' in American custody? No," Sontag responded. "The horror of what is shown in the photographs cannot be separated from the horror that the photographs were taken—with the perpetrators posing, gloating, over their helpless captives."[3]

If the Abu Ghraib photographs represented the guards exacting retributive violence against the enemies of American freedom, however, why did not the Homeland population, on whose behalf the guards reputedly acted, share their visual pleasure in these photographs? The military prison guards at Abu Ghraib had not in fact acted against orders, and Abu Ghraib prison was not an anomaly. Abu Ghraib was one of the manifestations of a distinction the Bush administration had introduced between two different biopoliticized populations—a Homeland population that was comprised of citizens who were represented as temporarily dissociated from their civil and political rights and the "subhumans" that constituted the prison population at Abu Ghraib who were represented as permanently lacking the right to have human rights. The military prison guards' intercultural relations with their Iraqi prisoners at Abu Ghraib followed the regulations spelled out in Bush's biopolitical settlement. The guards' treatment of the Iraqi prisoners at Abu Ghraib established and policed the disjunction between the embodiments of bare life populations imprisoned at Abu Ghraib and the Homeland people.

But the photographs of the horrific means whereby the guards regulated the distinction between these two populations instead opened a space in between the war on terrorism and the inhuman violence it legitimated. The photographs that drew the most notice from the international press were the six photographs taken of a figure that Pentagon officials designated as "Detainee Number 15." These photographs depicted a hooded man who was made to stand precariously on the edge of a box, sprouting wires from his hands and from under the poncho that covered his torso.[4]

The voluminous commentary on this hypercanonized photograph positioned the "Man on the Box" within a series of preexisting images from religious and political typologies that memorialized socially sacralized acts of martyrdom. The photographic memories that the "Man on the Box" recalled—of African-Americans lynched during the era of Jim Crow, of Jesus Christ crucified—reactivated traumatic memories of slavery, the violent history of the civil rights movement, and a scene of venerated self-sacrifice. The historical personages with whom the "Man on the Box" solicited comparison would most likely have been unimaginable to the Abu Ghraib guards who took the photographs. But in discussing the family resemblance between the guards' photographs of their victims at Abu Ghraib prison and the photographs of the victims of lynching taken between the 1880s and 1930s, Susan Sontag characterized both sets of images as "the souvenirs of a collective action whose participants felt perfectly justified in what they had done."[5]

In a lecture that he delivered at Dartmouth on July 21, 2004, the iconologist W. J. T. Mitchell interpreted the "Man on the Box" in terms of religious rather than political typology. Mitchell described the theatricalization of pain common to both image repertoires as the basis for the comparison he adduced between the guards' photographs of this figure and Christian iconography. Mitchell elaborated upon the implications of these shared traits when he interpreted the hooded figure in terms of artistic representations of a devotional image of Christ as he was stationed in between the crucifixion and the resurrection. The box on which the man in the photograph stood resembled the pedestal upon which Christ was placed in that both pediments at once mocked yet elevated the figures standing upon them, and like the "Man on the Box," the devotional image of the "Man of Sorrows" too was either hooded or blindfolded so as to ensure the invisibility of his torturers.[6]

The power of Christian iconography may explain why this photograph was reappropriated by western commentators to fashion their political condemnation of torture. But in turning the hooded Iraqi prisoner into the double of the tortured and sacrificed Christ, these western commentators utterly ignored the perspective of the Iraqi Muslims who regarded these worshipful comparisons with the Christian "Man of Sorrows" as culturally demeaning. The photograph's significance to the Iraqis' lived history was brought to an apocalyptic pitch by an Iraqi street artist who placed the photograph of the "Man on the Box" next to his sketch of the Statue of Liberty caught in the act of pulling the lever that would send a fatal electrical charge coursing through the hooded man's body. To make certain that this pictorial irony was not lost on the viewer, the Iraqi artist added a caption to his portrait that read "That Freedom for Bush."[7]

When they superimposed this representation of an "enemy of American freedom" upon the photographic memories of persons who had died in their effort to achieve the freedom of the West, the western commentators on "Man on the Box" reconstituted it as the limit figure in the Homeland Security State's visual imaginary. Insofar as it brought the United States' official policy of delivering freedom to the Iraqi people into proximity with its unacknowledged technologies of torture, this limit figure brought the spectacle of socially gratifying acts of violence to an abrupt conclusion. They also quite literally short-circuited the media relays through which the Pentagon conducted its war of images. At the site of this short-circuit a very different attitude toward the photographs emerged.

But if the image of the "Man on the Box" recalled images from Christian iconography as well as from the fraught history of the civil rights movement in America, what about the other photographs? Were the images of the Iraqi prisoners who were forced to masturbate publicly or simulate oral sex with one another solely informed by the information about Muslim phobias that the guards had learned in their one-week crash course on the culture and history of Iraqi Muslims.[8] The phobias—bodily nudity, homosexual touching of male genitals, appearing naked before a woman—conventionally attributed to Muslim men may have informed some of the staged settings in which the guards conducted their photo shoots. But these scenarios have solicited political decodings in which the guards were accused of having drawn from the image repertoires of feminist and gay liberation for the props and behaviors through which the guards terrorized these suspected Muslim terrorists.

Some of the poses that the guards forced their captors to assume mirrored sexual practices that have in other contexts been represented as possessing an emancipatory social value. Indeed if they were recontextualized within the manifestos of these social movements, some of these photographs could have been interpreted as expressive of demands for liberation from the recalcitrant order of the male patriarchate, or from the imperatives of heteronormative social order.[9] The emancipatory value of these alternative sexual practices was premised on the right to self-fashioning and the autonomy of individual choice. Upon imposing the bodily practice of gays, feminists, and lesbians on Iraqi prisoners who experienced them as painful impositions rather than liberating rights, the guards turned these emancipatory practices into a means of annulling the Iraqis' way of life. But why did they turn these sexual practices into weapons of biopolitical warfare?

Gayatri Spivak has suggested a possible basis for the guards' having correlated the image repertoires of contemporary social movements with their theater of cruelty when she remarked that "it has seemed increasingly clear to me, that 'terror' is the name loosely assigned to the flip side of social movements—extra-state social action—when such movements use physical violence. (When a state is named a 'terrorist state,' the intent implicit in the naming is to withhold state status from it, so that, technically, it enters the category of *extra*-state collective action.) 'Terror' is also, of course, the name of an affect. In the policymaking arena, terror as social movement and terror as social affect come together to provide a plausible field for group psychological speculation. The social movement is declared to have psychological identity. In other words, making terror both civil and natural provides a rationale for exercising psychological diagnostics, the most malign ingredient of racism."[10]

With Spivak's observation as warrant, the prison guards in the *theatrum politicum* of Abu Ghraib might be described as having conducted a war of images on two fronts—against Islamic terrorists abroad and against emancipatory social movements at home. After they harnessed the practices and behaviors associated with feminist and gay liberation movements into the instrumentalities of sexual and cultural abuse, the Abu Ghraib photographs voided them of their emancipatory potential.

The guards who took these photographs effaced any distinction between the technologies of self-production within emancipatory social movements and the techniques through which they annulled the social ontologies of their Iraqi prisoners. Upon reversing liberationist technologies of emancipatory social movements into the machines with which they tortured and abused prisoners, the guards turned the prison into an extralegal sphere maintained by the indistinction between law and violence. Moreover, when they directed the terrorism ascribed to these social movements against suspected Muslim terrorists, the military guards intended the annihilation of both forms of terrorism.

The military guards at the Abu Ghraib prison distilled the liberation technologies of the various social movements into biopowers that they then turned into biologized weaponry they used against their prisoners. Then they deployed those technologies to terrorize Muslim extremists. After they detached these sexual behaviors from the gay and lesbian bodies through which they were normatively subjectivized as emancipatory legal rights and forcibly imposed them onto Iraqi prisoners, the guards voided these practices of their normativity. But when they alienated these sexual and gendered practices from the human bodies through whom these biopowers had been legalized as civil and human rights, the guards had practiced a form of symbolic violence on the civil rights of the persons from whose bodies they had alienated these rights. In reducing gay and feminist rights into the means of stripping Iraqi prisoners of the right to have rights, the guards also practiced a form of symbolic violence on these rights.

The photographs taken by the guards at Abu Ghraib prison recorded forms of violence that were untethered to law and acknowledged no conventions concerning the rights of prisoners. But the viewers of these photographs interpreted these representations as further evidence of the ways in which the technologies of American freedom had become indistiguishable from American oppression.[11] The images mobilized opposition to the occupation in the name of the Abu Ghraib prisoners who had been victimized by this oppression. The viewers who posed this spontaneous global demonstration on behalf of the human rights of the prisoners at Abu Ghraib transformed their right to human rights into the representative demand of the peoples of the Global Homeland State.

Awakening the Interrogator Within

Abu Ghraib's significance resided in its restoration of the memory of a history of national shames that met with the disapproval or condemnation of the entire political spectrum. The restoration of this memory laid the groundwork for a possible hegemony that perceived the welfare of the vulnerable, the homeless, the unprotected as the principal cause of the antagonism in the social order.

I concluded the preceding chapter with the observation that, insofar as the Homeland Security State's exceptions to the rules of law and war were themselves based upon a force that lacked the grounding support of norms or rules, they resemble the traumatic events upon which they depended for their power to rule. Such exceptions could maintain their power to rule only as long as U.S. publics remain captivated by the spectacles of violence the state had erected at the site of Ground Zero.

The people of the Global Homeland may have lacked a part to play in the governance of the Homeland Security State, but after the photographs of the prison abuse at Abu Ghraib circulated worldwide, they did what the photographs of Rodney King had done earlier. Insofar as these extraneous elements could not be included within Bush's biopolitical settlement, the Abu Ghraib photographs exposed the Homeland Security State as the cause of the traumas it purported to oppose, and rendered the Global Homeland State indistinguishable from the punctum out of which it had emerged.

After 9/11, the state was involved in a battle for the hearts that preoccupied the minds of the American people. When President Bush invested the American people's collective feelings of grief and rage in a Global War on Terror, he delegated the emotional authority to act out their grief and rage to the state's acts of revenge. In enlisting the U.S. public's collective work of mourning into this alternative mode of affective expressivity, he intended to supply the war with moral clarity. After 9/11, many U.S. citizens felt all right about going to war. But the pictures of these repugnant forms of violence severely complicated the terms of this emotional compact and threatened to shift the balance of emotional authority away from revenge and onto compassion. Through its photographic representations of the victims of the guards' torture, Abu Ghraib seemingly included these figures among the community of the 9/11 aggrieved.

The interpretive commentary on these photographs marked Abu Ghraib as the site that facilitated the return of national shame from within the very gaze that was designed to ward it off. Instead of captivating its viewers as subjects who were supposed to enjoy the torture and destruction of the terrorist enemy's way of life, the Abu Ghraib photographs turned the gaze of the spectatorial public inward. The state's response was to change the perspective on this crime scene by representing it as a restricted aberration as opposed to a generalized violation of the law. After describing the photographs as evidence of prisoner abuse, the state reduced its legal status to that of a correctible violation of prison rules.

By turning them into instruments of prison torture, the Abu Ghraib guards were acting out their moral panic about the sexual dimension of emancipatory social movements. At first they displaced this panic into the technology of torture. Then they communicated it to their Muslim prisoners. The spectators who condemned the actions that took place within Abu Ghraib were in a sense identified with the political unconscious of the guards' behavior. As long as they remained tethered to the emotional contract Bush had forged after 9/11, U.S. citizens would remain fascinated with these repugnant spectacles to which they were ostensibly opposed. While their condemnation was consciously directed against the guards' brutality, it also included the rejection of these "terrorizing" instruments within its ambit. By restricting his attention to their means of torture, President Bush turned this aspect of the photographs into the basis for his description of the guards' behavior as "un-American."

The U.S. public's opposition to the guards' acts of torture presupposed the war in Iraq as its spectral term of comparison. Through their continued support of the war in Iraq, U.S. citizens acquiesced to the belief that the war in Iraq constituted the legitimate form of state punishment in contrast to which the despicable scenes depicted in the Abu Ghraib photographs were describable as serious transgressions. Indeed the public's spontaneous collective condemnation of the illegality of the guards' actions tacitly produced a legitimation for the continuation of the Iraq War. The photographs turned Abu Ghraib into an obscene supplement to the war in Iraq, in the sense that it recorded the extralegal violence that supplemented U.S. soldiers' legal violence on the battlefield. The revelation of the excess violence there established a strong contrast with the legitimate forms of state violence that the state exercised in the war effort. The fact that the photographs called attention to the failure of even those horrific acts of brutality to break the enemy's will tacitly corroborated the state's explanation for the longevity of the war. If U.S. enemies were so "barbaric" that they would not surrender even in the face of these acts of degradation, U.S. troops were in it for a very long haul.

The Abu Ghraib images underwent a related transformation during the presidential campaign of 2004 when the Swift Boaters resurrected the memories of POWs and MIAs from the Vietnam era to discredit John Kerry's opposition to the War in Iraq. John Kerry, who had received the Medal of Honor for his display of valor during the Vietnam War, was reconstructed as a traitor by the Vietnam veterans who retrieved the memories of the prisoners of war and the mythology of the MIAs to propose that America had once again become hostage to the Vietnam Syndrome. Their recollections of the Viet Cong's brutal treatment of the POWs were designed to erase, if not justify, what had taken place at Abu Ghraib. But like the Abu Ghraib photographs, the Swift Boat war of images also split their spectators into surrogate interrogators of the guards' brutality and interrogators as well of their own reaction to these images.[12]

Cindy Sheehan: Devastating the Fantasy of the Homeland at Its Limits

Symbolic death usually comes after real death—with the burial of the dead. But the symbolic death of the state fantasy of the Homeland took place when Cindy Sheehan, the mother of a soldier killed in Iraq, protested against the war by publicly refusing to mourn in the terms of the state discourse that justified the continuation of the violence. Cindy

Sheehan's son Casey had been killed while on a mission in Sadr City on April 4, 2004. When she traveled to Crawford, Texas, on August 6, 2005, to set up a camp memorializing the death of her son, Sheehan turned the U.S. public's internal interrogator into the juridical instrument with which she connected the state's official act of mourning with the 9/11 crime scene it was supposed to avenge.[13]

After 9/11, the Bush administration drew upon the generalized anxiety and panic generated by this historic catastrophe to declare a state of permanent emergency domestically through the initiation of a Global War on Terror. The Bush compact was designed to establish an alliance between national security and the aggressive drives of the U.S. people so as to incriminate dissent as a minor form of treason and to eliminate any loyalty that was more cosmopolitan than the defense of the homeland.[14]

The Bush administration forged a justificatory discourse to legitimate the Global War on Terror. The grounds for its new compact with U.S. populations required the invention of a series of novel symbolic representations (Ground Zero, Homeland, Enemy Combatants, etc.) to accomplish a reorientation of the perspectives through which U.S. citizens were supposed to make sense of the events taking place within the newly organized geopolitical situation. The administration's efforts to solicit the U.S. people's consent to this new compact was accompanied by legislation (the USA Patriot Act, Campus Watch, revisions to the Higher Education Title VI legislation) that regulate the knowledges produced about this new form of governmentality. The legislation that the Bush administration installed to propagate its policies characterized anyone who questioned either this form of governmentality or the discourse that justified it as posing threats to homeland security.

The introduction of the signifier of the Homeland to capture this experience of generalized trauma recalled events from the historical archive that it significantly altered. The Bush doctrine of preemption can be traced to the colonial adventures of Anglo-American colonial settlers and the forms of warfare in which they were engaged. Whereas the myth of Virgin Land produced historical continuity by suppressing the traumatic memory of the lawless violence that colonial settlers had perpetrated against indigenous populations, the Bush administration recovered the memory of colonial aggression so as to reverse the national people's relation to the history of colonialism and imperialism. The National Security State required that the state dissociate from the history of U.S. imperialism so as to oppose the ambitions of the imperial Soviet, but the Homeland Security State's forcible depopulation of peoples from their homelands in Afghanistan and Iraq recovered memories of settler violence as the appropriate forms through which U.S. freedom could now be practiced.

The state fantasy of the Homeland took hold by rendering the U.S. people a captive audience to the spectacular shows of force through which the state violently changed regimes in Afghanistan and Iraq. The people's consent to the new symbolic dispensation assumed the form of their participation in the state's power to impose this newly forged symbolic order upon the populations of Afghanistan and Iraq.

The term Homeland was the keystone that anchored all of the other terms in the Bush administration's new symbolic arrangement insofar as it performed the double function of structuring the placement of all the other terms (Ground Zero, Enemy Combatants) within the new com-pact, and of serving as the object cause of the Homeland Security State. The Homeland named the locale the security apparatus was pledged to protect and defend against terrorist attack.

The Homeland did not name a place within the social order so much as the condition produced through the violent desymbolization of the order of things. It was the efficacy of its absence from any locat-able place within the symbolic order that enabled the Homeland to determine the entire structure of assigned places. The placeholder for a place that was produced out of violent subtraction from all locatable places, the Homeland exercised a structural causality for all of the other terms within the newly symbolized order.

Because this compact with the Homeland was about who would make the rules and who would enforce them, it could not warrant criticism of the ethical or juridical values of those rules. Despite the state's efforts to discredit them, however, increasing numbers of citizens criticized the state's policies. But rather than taking such critiques of its policies and discourses that would justify them seriously, the Bush administra-tion characterized any criticisms directed against its terms either as anti-American or as guilty of violating the memory of the soldiers who had "paid the ultimate price" in their loyalty to the country.[15]

Despite numerous exposés of the administraton's rationale as well as its conduct of the war—the revelation of prisoner abuse in Guantá-namo and the Abu Ghraib scandal, the discovery that Saddam Hussein possessed neither weapons of biological destruction nor nuclear devices, the exposure of the fact that the Bush administration had distorted or manufactured evidence to garner public support for the war, the growing numbers of military and civilian casualties in Iraq, the publication of the Downing Street memo—and despite the fact that more than 60 percent of those surveyed by the Pew Center endorsed the belief that President Bush lacked a clear plan to bring the war to a successful conclusion, as of August 3, 2005, over 50 percent of the American public continued to support the decision to use military force against Iraq. Three of the misrepresentations fostered by the Bush administration— that Saddam Hussein conspired with Al-Qaeda in the 9/11 bombings, that he trained and harbored Al-Qaeda terrorists in Iraq, and that he had weapons of mass destruction—were believed to be true by comparably large percentages of the U.S. population.[16]

However, after Cindy Sheehan traveled to President Bush's home in Crawford, Texas, on August 3, 2005, she set up a camp site on which she staged a scene that radically challenged the Homeland's legislative authority. Crawford, Texas, was itself founded by Texas settlers in their prolonged frontier campaign against native tribes. After opening up Camp Casey within the precincts of the *terra nullius* that the myth of Virgin Land had covered over, she installed a necropolis there in which she kept public track of the numbers of U.S. troops who had died in Iraq. As she did so, she represented herself to President Bush and to the U.S. public as a mother whom the Bush Settlement had forcibly dissevered from her home and land.

When she opened up Camp Casey, Sheehan suspended her bonds with the Homeland compact and inaugurated an alternative fantasy. Camp Casey instituted a different representation of the meaning of the people's relationship to the state and to the dead. It restaged emancipation from the Homeland in the space where U.S. civil liberties had been disallowed. In pronouncing the terms of her resistance to the Bush Settlement, Cindy Sheehan spoke in the name of the global homeland peoples who had been left insecure at home and abroad.

Cindy Sheehan's protests against the state assumed the form of a series of open letters. She published the first open letter to President Bush entitled "What Noble Cause?" on August 6, 2005. The letter began with two acknowledgements: that she was furious about the horrible loss of life and that she felt heartbroken for the families whose homes

had been wrongfully devastated. She located the source of her indignation in the language George Bush used to justify the death of her son:
"The families of the fallen can rest assured that your loved ones died
for a noble cause," and "We have to honor the sacrifices of the fallen
by completing the mission."[17] Sheehan found this last phrase especially
offensive.

The key phrase in the state's emotional contract with the American
people—"We have to honor the sacrifices of the fallen by completing
the mission"—demanded that the American people give the military
branch of the government the monopoly over the public expression of
grief. But Cindy Sheehan refused to obey President Bush's demand that
she justify the death of her own son by honoring the nobility of the
"cause" for which he died. Rather than accepting the terms of this contract and mourning her son's death by authorizing the continuation of
the war in Iraq, Cindy Sheehan formulated the following series of responses to President Bush:

> First of all what is the noble cause? The cause changes at will when the
> previous cause has been proven a lie. . . . What did Casey and over
> 100,000 wonderful human beings die for? What exactly is, George, the
> "noble cause"? And I demand that you stop using my son's name and
> my family's sacrifice to continue your illegal and immoral occupation
> in Iraq.[18]

Cindy Sheehan's letter to the president upset the balance of emotional
power that the Bush administration had introduced in relation to the
public's attitude toward the war. If politics can be described as in part a
battle to change the public's feeling about a political question, Cindy
Sheehan turned Camp Casey into a scene of emotional contestation.
In undertaking this struggle, Cindy Sheehan did three things: she refused
to grieve through revenge, she turned the state's acts of revenge into
the target of her grievance, and she thereafter included the soldiers and
civilians who were killed in Iraq, the Abu Ghraib prisoners, and the 9/11
dead as intertwined effects of the state's aggression. In so doing, Sheehan
revalorized critique and dissent as patriotic forms of grieving.

The state's imperative to "support our troops" had constituted the
limit to freedom of expression beyond which opposition to the war
could not tread. The figure that the administration had erected to protect this borderline was fashioned in the image of a grieving mother,
who represented the unappeaseable losses that the families of soldiers

killed in Iraq had suffered. To secure the symbolic value of this figure of the grieving Mother of the Homeland, the administration fostered the inauguration of the Gold Star Mothers, an association comprised of mothers whose sons and daughters had been killed in Iraq or Afghanistan. Bush's Homeland Security State depended upon their public demonstrations of maternal grief as the emotional legitimation of its campaign of vengeance.

Cindy Sheehan's identification with the maternal role did not merely enable her to confront President George W. Bush with the recognition of the outcome of the state's shameless acts of violence. When she publicly condemned the war in Iraq, condemning it as the cause of her son Casey's death, she did not merely violate the state's prohibition against protesting the war. She enunciated her repudiation of the state's "cause" as a Gold Star Mother and in the name of honoring her son.

When President Bush declared war on Iraq, he enlisted the family in the service of the state's militarization. The state normally receives its army from the family, which encounters the limits to its continuation in the state. The young men and women families furnish for war become the patriots who define the values of the nation by sacrificing their lives for them. The family structure figures the mother as the basis for the reproduction of this kinship system. Since the state is dependent upon this kinship structure for its emergence and maintenance, the state must expropriate the maternal function and reproduce itself through the acquisition of her kin. After the state substitutes itself for the mother it sublates the maternal imago within the security aspect of the state. The mother is supposed to show her love for the nation-state by sacrificing her progeny to the state for the purpose of its reproduction. But after the state separates her from her children, the mother is supplanted by the homosociality of the state's desire.[19] Luce Irigaray has aptly described the state's violent foreclosure of the maternal bond as the act that inaugurates the basis of its masculine authority.[20]

After 9/11 the state doubled itself. In one of its aspects it wore the face of a grieving mother that the Homeland symbolized. In its other face, the state bore the terrifying countenance of the patriot who would avenge the mother's losses. At Camp Casey, Cindy Sheehan assumed the persona of a grieving mother within the Homeland. But she then dissociated her grief from the militarism through which the state enacted its official work of mourning. In refusing to surrender her feelings of grief to the state's terrorism-security complex, she contested the emotional legitimacy of the war in Iraq. After she refused to cede the state the authority of her sorrow in the name of a child whose death the state had identified as an emotional warrant for war, Cindy Sheehan characterized her grief as ungrievable in the terms of a militancy that turned grief into a motive for war.

By refusing to submit to the official rites of mourning, Cindy Sheehan had placed her grief outside the borders of the aggrieved Homeland community. She articulated what she found affectively unintelligible in the state's demand that she surrender her relations of kinship for the sake of a war by explaining that it had made her life unlivable. In deforming and displacing the norms of emotional intelligibility of the state of the Homeland she brought its emotional compact into crisis.

This enactment confounded the symbolic position that mothers were compelled to represent and refused to authorize the transition from the order of kinship to the order of the state. Rather than aligning her work of mourning with President Bush's justification for the compulsive cycle of state violence, Cindy Sheehan's articulation of her maternal grief within the idiom of political dissent introduced an alternative emotional compact.[21] After Cindy Sheehan treated the body of her dead son as the occasion for dissolving her bonds with the Bush Homeland Security State, she also transformed Camp Casey into the site for an alternative juridical-political order.

Antigone in Crawford, Texas: Changing the State Fantasy

Analysis of the juridical and political dimensions of Cindy Sheehan's confrontation with George W. Bush at Crawford, Texas, requires a return to the logic of the primal scene—in which the founding words of the culture had themselves become stakes of the encounter—for its comprehension.[22] To facilitate an understanding of the stakes of their encounter, I would propose that Cindy Sheehan's encounter with Bush be imagined as a reenactment of Antigone's with Creon.

President Bush explained his actions in terms of the reason of the Emergency State. In the letters she adddresed to the president from Camp Casey, Cindy Sheehan opened up the limit site to the provenance of his rule. The statements she published there and the site from which they were enunciated, in lacking a position within the existing symbolic field, demanded the formation of an alternative.

When it is not overridden with crises, the symbolic order forms an implicit backdrop to an individual's embeddedness in socially mediated reality. It tacitly informs everyday behavior and understanding. But during times of crisis, inconsistencies within the symbolic order open up opportunities for momentary breaks with its overdeterminations and introduce occasions to separate from its foundational fantasies. Jacques Lacan has described the outcome of this separation as an example of what he calls "traversing the fantasy," which he has defined as becoming "destitute" to the subject positions the fantasy authorizes. Lacan has also explained the infrequency of this event by correlating it with the death drive.[23]

According to Lacan, to desire something other than the continued existence of the social order is to fall into a kind of death. But to risk this desire, by means of which death is courted, also constitutes the elementary precondition for a truly ethical act. Lacan maintains that there can be no ethical act that does not entail the momentary suspension of the sociosymbolic network of intersubjective relationships that guarantees the subject's identity. This means that an authentic ethical act can only take place if its subject is willing to risk the gesture that suspends the authority of the symbolic order.[24]

Lacan made these observations in the course of his commentary on Sophocles' Antigone. By defying Creon's edict, Antigone also repudiated the symbolic order of the city that Creon personified. Following her decision to disobey Creon, Antigone was excluded from the social symbolic order, and she found herself in a realm in between two deaths: the death of her mandated social position and the death of the symbolic order that had guaranteed its continuation.

Slavoj Žižek returned to Lacan's discussion of Antigone to spell out a crucial distinction between the radical aspect of Antigone's ethical act and a merely performative reconfiguration of one's symbolic condition.[25] In conducting a war of positions that would turn the terms of the hegemonic field against itself, Žižek explained, such a marginal reconfiguration of the predominant discourse would nevertheless remain within the social order that it would simply reorganize. But Antigone's more radical act involved a thoroughgoing transformation of the entire field in that it redefined the very conditions of socially sustained perfomativity.[26]

I have invoked Lacan's and Žižek's discussions of *Antigone* as an interpretive context for Cindy Sheehan's actions at Camp Casey in order to draw attention to the radical dimension of Sheehan's ethical actions. Although she was embroiled in a conflict with the state over how to mourn a son rather than a brother, Sheehan resembles Antigone in that she encountered a comparable deadlock in the surrounding symbolic order. This deadlock assumed the form of a forced choice that compelled her to decide between the state's demand that she bury her dead son in terms that ratified the war in Iraq (as the state's work of national mourning) and her felt obligation to grieve him in terms that refused to cede the power to kill her child to the state. Sheehan's way out of this deadlock inspired her to constitute an alternative to the state's juridical and political order.

Sheehan's experience of this rupture in between her child's death and the demands of the state interpellated her to the traumatic foreclosed dimension of the Homeland, the disallowed knowledge of the history of violence condensed within its "fatal environment." The state fantasy of the Homeland was founded upon this foreclosure. Her experience of being hailed by this foreclosed dimension of the Homeland opened a primal scene that might be described as the underside of an Althusserian interpellation. According to Althusser, interpellation designated a process wherein the positive functional dimension of the state's ideology imprinted itself on an individual so as to subjugate her to the preconstituted order of things. But Cindy Sheehan had undergone a process of interpellation wherein an extraneous object within the order—the gap between the Homeland and the traumatic element that located what structurally decompleted the order—has hailed her. The demand that she herself subjectivize this Thing that lacked a recognizable position within the symbolic order plunged her into an abyss of ethical freedom devoid of the solid ground of the social norms and directives that the Homeland Security State had taken for granted.[27]

Cindy Sheehan placed the edge of President Bush's Crawford estate under the shadows of the Valley of Death. While sojourning through this domain, she represented her relation to her son as a primordial attachment that exceeded the reason of state. In refusing to take up her "proper" maternal position within the state fantasy, Cindy Sheehan lived the equivocation that unraveled the figure of grieving Mother of the Homeland.[28] As we have seen, this maternal figure had been assigned the quasi-military responsibility to enforce President Bush's edict setting the limits to dissent: "Do not mourn the deaths of the sons of the Homeland in ways that undermine the memory of their sacrifice." By drawing the Mother of the Homeland Security State into crisis, Cindy Sheehan undermined this foundational prohibition of the Homeland Security State.

Her performance of this act of refusal voided her relationship with Casey of the condition of the mother–son kinship bond that the state had consecrated in its representations of the war effort. By standing in the place of her dead son's unexpressed opposition to the war, she protested in his stead. Her extrication of her son from Bush's "cause" did not merely result in the dissolution of his and her bonds with the Homeland Security State; it also invoked a juridical realm beyond the Homeland's jurisdiction. Like Antigone's, Cindy Sheehan's kin emerged at the juncture where her biological blood relations encountered the state's imagined kinship community so as to detach the one from the other around the more primordial question of the law that can bind persons to one another.

Her speech acts might be described as having emanated from another order of legal rationality that the public reality of her speech acts had presupposed.[29] Although the higher law Sheehan invoked did not have the power to rewrite public law, the incommensurability between the two spheres of law transformed her scene of address into a tribunal of justice. In struggling to give expression to a law of a different order, she grounded her acts in a law that the juridical order did not yet count as law. Speaking in the name of this future juridical order, she performed the legality of what did not legally exist in the form of a law to come whose claims to justice marked the limit condition of the Homeland's jurisdiction.[30]

Members of the Bush administration represented her actions in Crawford, Texas, as a degradation of her son's valor and as the violation of his memory.[31] But to whom does the memory of her dead son belong? The war in Iraq redefined maternity as sacrifice for the cause of the nation. But since she refused to sacrifice her bond with Casey to that cause,

Sheehan's act of refusal brought the sacrificial order to its limits. In
place of sacrificing him to the state, she spoke in the name of a grievance directed against the complex interdependency of law, militarism,
and grief upon which the Bush Homeland Security State was founded.

Hurricane Katrina and the Exodus from the Homeland

In breaking the emotional compact with the Homeland Security State,
Cindy Sheehan effected a turning point in the public's support of the
war. When she began her "peaceful occupation" of Crawford, over 50
percent of the public surveyed continued to express their belief in the
legitimacy of the war (a comparable percentage expressed their dissat-
isfaction with Bush's handling of the war). By August 15, more than 50
percent of the U.S. citizens surveyed expressed their opposition to the
war.[32] During her stay in Crawford, Texas, she turned grief into an emo-
tionally legitimate resource for giving expression to grievances against
the state. The camp that Cindy Sheehan erected at Crawford, Texas,
represented the shift from the nation to the Homeland in terms of
the state's abandonment of the welfare of the people. By speaking
on behalf of the figures who had been left behind by the Homeland Security State, Cindy Sheehan gave expression to the emotions it disallowed. But it took the landfall of Hurricane Katrina on the city of
New Orleans on August 29, 2005, to produce unforgettable representations of the vulnerable and homeless persons that the Homeland had
abandoned.

If the Global Homeland has erected an order in which the people
played no part, the people who lacked a part in the New World Order
came into stark visbility on August 30, 2005, when photographs of the
disastrous effects of Hurricane Katrina on the Gulf Coast flashed into
view. The desolation that overtook the city of New Orleans when the
levees broke supplied the ideological representation of a terrified Homeland population with an all too literal referent.

The Bush administration delayed sending assistance and emergency
supplies for weeks after the event. In the days after Hurricane Katrina,
the government declared martial law but had no effective police presence to enforce it, and the people of New Orleans whom the storm had
forcibly removed from their homes and lands were ignored rather than
protected by the Homeland Security State. As people ran out of food

and water, they entered flooded stores and markets for provisions to survive. Described as looters by the National Guardsmen who occupied the city, most of New Orleans's residents were forced to gather up what was left of their belongings, evacuate their homes, and move into the Superdome for temporary shelter.

Bush sent in a military force to protect private property and to arrest and shoot the survivors who were struggling to find food and shelter there. As an increasingly large military force moved in to forcibly depopulate the residents of their Homeland, it appeared to these observers that New Orleans in the wake of Hurricane Katrina bore an uncanny resemblance to the city of Baghdad after the U.S. invasion. After the state placed it under the rule of martial law, New Orleans had itself become a space whose inhabitants lived under the imagined conditions of death. New Orleans also "proved" the accusation that Cindy Sheehan had directed against the Bush administration: the state had indeed produced the traumatic site against which it purported to defend the Homeland.

In making the state feel shame at the abandonment of its people, Hurricane Katrina transformed the homeless people in New Orleans into the transitional objects who changed the dominant structure of feeling from vengeful aggression to profound compassion. Hurricane Katrina had disseevered the U.S. people's bond with Bush's Homeland Security State by revealing how the administration had reneged on the core promise that was crucial to the continuation of the compact—to secure the U.S. domestic population through the forcible depopulation of Homelands *elsewhere*. Photographs that circulated worldwide in the wake of Hurricane Katrina brought with them unforgettable images of a vulnerable domestic population whose members had been forcibly separated from their homes and of a Homeland within the territorial United States that had quite literally been devastated. These images meant that the state fantasy of the Homeland Security State had been drowned in the same waters as the city of New Orleans. After the New Orleans streets and neighborhoods were deluged, the utter emptiness of this space produced representations of peoples of the Global Homeland included but with no part to play in the existing order yet empowered to demand an alternative to it.

Despite the ethical work she had accomplished in exposing the devastating consequences of Bush's policies for the national population,

Cindy Sheehan was not in a political position to replace his regime with an alternative configuration. Her refusal to take up any of the mandated positions within the Homeland had enabled her to traverse Bush's state fantasy, but it took a young African-American senator from Chicago to put an alternative fantasy in its place.

Changing the State of Fantasy

Throughout this book, I have explained the legislative work state fantasies perform in terms of the identifications those fantasies enable their addressees to take up in the symbolic order. I have directed most of my attention to the difficulty in completing the transition from the cold war's state fantasy to a New World Order. Although it has had the most disastrous consequences, it was actually George W. Bush's inauguration of the Homeland Security State that was most successful in establishing a state fantasy that was as encompassing and inclusive as the cold war state fantasy. Rather than restricting it to the dimensions of the Persian Gulf, as his father did, George W. Bush's declaration of a Global War on Terror had extended the reach of the U.S. war mentality across the globe. It conscripted the Christian fundamentalists and the national militia to its war effort, and it incorporated what one Bush official described as the victim mentality of the Democratic Party within the emotional logic of the state.

Bush's Homeland fantasy depended on U.S. citizens' acquiescence to their places within the reconfigured Homeland for the continuation of its cultural dreamwork. But Hurricane Katrina had not merely denaturalized the power of Homeland Security to acquire the people's consent to President Bush's policies. This traumatizing event also brought this national compact to the limits of its provenance.

After President Bush declared a Global War on Terror, he turned the State of Exception into the Other to the nation that the state must enter to exercise the extralegal powers necessary to defend the people against terror. In executing this war, the state was neither within the constitutional order nor altogether outside of it. But while the war supplied the occasion for the state to enact extraconstitutional, illegal violence, it also rendered the sites at which the state exercised this violence vulnerable to being declared an illegal usurpation of the people's sovereignty. The State of Exception imposed limitations on the people's

rights. However, at the site of those imposed limits the people could inaugurate a praxis that declared their right to question the state's right
to inaugurate a State of Exception. But the people who declared the
right to question the state's arrogation of the power to speak and to act
in their name could no longer be described as a people whose sovereignty was represented by the existing state.

By claiming the right to say and do what the state would not, this
people would question the legitimacy of the state's extralegal violence.
Indeed this inaugurative practice would produce a people who, in lacking any part in the order over which the Homeland Security State
ruled, could not demand the state's sovereign power as the guarantor of
their right to question the state's violence. Insofar as they have questioned the state's sovereign powers, the people could not represent
their demands within the context of the sovereign rights authorized by
the state. As a people who have added a right that the Homeland's
people are lacking, this singular people's infinite demand for rights
could not be met within a nationalist provenance. This other to the
national heritage could only be met through and as the emergence of
the political formation of an America that is to come.

As we have seen, the state attributed the sovereign power through
which it regulated them to the people so that the people would construe
their authorization of the state's actions as the precondition for the
state's enactments. In questioning the state's right to introduce exceptions to such authorizations, the people inaugurated an utterly different
sovereign right—the right to question the state's sovereignty. Because
this right was claimed at the moment at which the state has exercised
extraconstitutional power, the people's claiming of it would constitute
legal grounds to call for an alternative constitutional congress in which
the people could reconstitute themselves.

In the preceding chapters of this book, I attempted to explain how
one state of fantasy was dismantled and to demonstrate how it was supplanted by antagonistic state fantasies. I have also analyzed the ways in
which President George W. Bush established a new state of fantasy by
subsuming these antagonistic state fantasies. But I have not yet described
how a state fantasy can undo another and then replace it.

In taking up this task, I want to turn to two of the interlocutors
whose work has proven crucial to my understanding of the relationship
between the State of Exception and the law as well as the legislative

powers of state fantasy. When Carl Schmitt argued that the law would never tolerate the existence of a violence that lay outside of the law's jurisdiction, he was constructiong a response to Walter Benjamin's notion of pure violence. Benjamin arrived at the notion of pure violence within the same set of reflections that led him to install a distinction between law-making and law-preserving violence. He defined pure violence as a violence that "lies abolutely outside and beyond the law and that as such could shatter the distinction between law-preserving and law-making violence."[33] This definition also enabled Benjamin to imagine a violence that inhabited a zone of pure anomie that not only lay apart from the jurisdiction of the State of Exception, but that possessed the potential to create an utterly different form of legality from that which was already constituted and that the State of Exception claimed to defend. If violence was assured "an existence outside the law as pure immediate violence, this furnished proof that revolutionary violence— which is the name for the highest manifestation of pure violence by man—is also possible."[34]

Schmitt found these speculations repugnant to his conceptualization of the law's sovereignty, and he reiterated his conviction that the law could tolerate no violence outside the law's monopoly. In his response to Schmitt, Benjamin invoked the State of Exception as the appropriate context for understanding the stakes of their dispute. Observing that "the tradition of the oppressed teaches us that the state of the exception in which we live is the rule. We must attain to a concept of history that accords with this fact. Then we will see that it is our task to bring about the real state of exception and this will improve our position in the struggle against fascism."[35]

With this observation Benjamin has also produced an utterly factual account of the existing state of affairs: "Now that any possibility of a fictitious state of exception—in which exception and normal conditions are temporally and locally distinct—has collapsed, the state of exception in which we live is real and cannot be distinguished from the rule."[36] Since the State of Exception has effaced any possibility of a correlation between existing constitutional law and the violence it would either regulate or redeploy, "there is nothing but a zone of anomie, in which violence without any juridical form acts." With this sentence, Benjamin has unmasked any attempt by the state to annex anomie through the State of Exception as a sheer fiction. As the generalized suspension of the law, the State of Exception itself constitutes a form of anomie rather than a form of law that is capable of regulating another form of anomie that Benjamin calls pure violence. What now takes the place of already constituted law, Benjamin concludes this line of legal reasoning, "are civil war and revolutionary violence, that is human action that has shed every relation to law."[37]

In rendering Benjamin's argument with Schmitt applicable to Barack Obama's "movement," I wish to substitute what Antonio Negri calls "constituent power" in place of what Benjamin terms "anomie." Negri invented the concept of constituent power to allow us "to think political freedom in terms of its separation from the social and in terms of its rejection of synthesis with the political for the power to constitute or to begin anew *ex nihilo* a new state of affairs is grasped in its nonsynthetic character—this new state cannot be acquired by its social basis, but comes about through a cutting off from that basis, a loss of ground which bespeaks the fact that political freedom is also an abyss. While at the same time this constitutent power does not stand in a synthetic relation to what is constituted by or through it: political freedom is the ungrounded ground of every constituted power."[38]

In the first chapter of this book, I proposed that the extralegal power of the State of Exception could only be unsettled through the incitement of a movement to reconvene the constitutional convention and recontract the people's relation to their constitutive agreements. Such a movement would act upon what Negri calls constituent power by calling attention to the permanent crisis to the Constitution that the State of Exception has effected.

Barack Obama inaugurated a presidential campaign that possessed the symbolic force of a constitutional movement and the political force of an antiwar movement. At the level of the law, Obama incited the constituent power of "We the People" to animate the constitutional power of a movement that would succeed in overthrowing Bush's State of Exception by redefining it as the permanent crisis of the state of constituted power.

Obama inaugurated this movement at the very site where Bush's fantasy was washed away. His movement opened up a symbolic site in which the constituent powers of the peoples of the New Covenant and the peoples of the Contract with America could reunite America by reconstituting its bases.

In *The Audacity of Hope*, Barack Obama wrote an account of the origins of his movement at the moment of his spontaneous recollection of post-Katrina New Orleans at a memorial service President George H. W. Bush led to commemorate Rosa Parks. While listening to President Bush's father celebrate her memory, Barack Obama recalled images of the abandoned and homeless people of New Orleans after Katrina as the sites of memory that this memorial service had foreclosed from recognition.

> As I sat and listened to the former President, my mind kept wandering back to the scenes of devastation when Hurricane Katrina struck the Gulf Coast and New Orleans was submerged. I recalled images of teenage mothers weeping or cursing in front of the New Orleans Superdome, their listless infants hoisted to their hips. And old women in wheelchairs, heads rolled back, the withered legs exposed under soiled dresses. I thought about a solitary body someone had laid against a wall, motionless beside the flimsy dignity of a blanket, and the scenes of shirtless men in sagging pants, their legs churning through the dark waters, their arms draped with whatever goods that they had managed to grab from nearby stores, the spark of chaos in their eyes.
>
> Listening to their stories it was clear that many of Katrina's survivors had been abandoned before the hurricane struck. They were the faces of any inner-city neighborhood in any American city, the faces of black poverty—the jobless and almost jobless, the sick and soon to be sick, the frail and the elderly. A young mother talked about handing her children to a bus full of strangers. Old men quietly described the houses they had lost and the absence of any insurance or family to fall back on. A group of young men insisted that thieves had been blown up by those who wished to rid New Orleans of black people. One tall, gaunt woman, looking haggard in an Astros tee shirt two sizes too big, clutched my arm and pulled me toward her. "We didn't have nothing before the storm," she whispered, "now we got less than nothing." Stories drifted back from the Gulf that big contractors were landing hundreds of millions of dollars worth of contracts, circumventing prevailing wage and affirmative action laws, hiring illegal immigrants to keep their costs down. The sense that the nation had reached a transformative moment—that it had had its conscience stirred out of a long slumber—this could not die away.[39]

In this passage, Obama has identified himself with the Homeland people who quite literally had no part in the New World Order, and he has transformed their dream for a different America into the object cause of his presidential campaign. While President Bush was paying lip service to the memory of Rosa Parks, Obama's memories of the living dead were returning from New Orleans.

These spontaneous recollections reversed the effects of the state's commemorative ritual. President Bush assumed reconciliation between the memory of Rosa Parks and the official state symbols through which she was memorialized. But the undead images that flooded into Obama's consciousness could not find their proper places in existing historical symbolizations. Like the image of Rodney King during the Persian Gulf War, these images performed the dialectical work of inciting a whole series of associated images—of the Middle Passage, the Great Migration, the Trail of Tears, the Iraqis and Afghanis in flight from their homelands—that inflooded Obama's consciousness, and continue to haunt us still.[40]

Obama seized the revolutionary moment that surged up in this space when he linked the images of Katrina with this montage of associated images to position this "moment of danger" as the origin of his movement. At the level of the law, Obama personified sheer anomic or constituent force—neither constituted not constituting power—of what Benjamin referred to as pure, revolutionary violence. This revolutionary violence undermined Bush's State of Exception. But Obama also worked with and through the fantasy of American exceptionalism.

Obama aspired to change America through a radical transformation of three of the grand themes of American exceptionalism—the American dream, the perfectible Union, the land of promise—organizing the "positionality" of the nation's citizens. In undertaking this transformation, Obama identified with figures who were excepted from this state of fantasy rather than the state doing the excepting.

Throughout the discussion of the mythological foundations of Bush's Homeland, I called attention to its anomalous relation to the national myth of the Virgin Land. The Homeland named the place either from which the colonial settlers and slaves and immigrants and indigenous populations emigrated or from which they were involuntarily uprooted in moving into "America." The fantasy Barack Obama has installed through his oratory and his actions is directed to the people who have become stranded within the Homeland Security State. In claiming the power to lead the people out of the Homeland protectorate, Obama has drawn upon multiple and contradictory American fantasies and offered his movement as the site at which they could converge.

After identifying with the figures who had been structurally excluded, he produced subject positions for the addressees of his discourse to establish symbolic identifications with blacks, gays, the disabled, minoritized ethnics, and other members of the internally excluded population. The tidal shift in the national self-regard that Barack Obama's fantasy engendered was not the result of the restriction of his identification to the homeless peoples of New Orleans. His "movement" was grounded in a much more pervasive fantasy of dispossession—of citizens stripped of their constitutional rights by the Patriot Act, of parents separated from their children by war, of families forced from their homes by the subprime mortgage crisis—that was already inscribed and awaiting enactment in the script responsible for the production of the Bush Homeland Security State.

Obama stood in the place of all of the figures who, in having been dispossessed of their positions within the social order, now lacked a place. As the placeholder for all who could not be constitutively included within the social order, Obama became the originative lack out of which our individual desires arise, as well as the object cause of the missing America through which we grasp our desires. Desire takes off when its object cause embodies or gives positive existence to the void that animates desire, and Obama, the odd man in, is the embodiment of the void introduced by desire into objective reality. As the placeholder for all who could not be included within the social order, Obama embodied the object cause of the missing America through which "we" grasped those desires.

If the psychic reality of America comes into consciousness through the American Dream, the figures through whom we become conscious of that dream can only be apprehended through the heterogeneous desires that have been caused by the dream's anamorphoses. Barack Obama holds the position of the figure onto whom those anamorphotic desires got projected.

Born two years before Martin Luther King Jr. delivered his "I have a dream" speech, in *Dreams from My Father*, Obama represented his life as itself the outcome of the confluence of three heterogeneous American lineages—the immigrant's dream of escape from economic poverty and political persecution, the minoritized American's endlessly deferred dream of "one day" being included within the American dream, and the white middle-class Americans' dream of future prosperity—and he promised to open up a future for all three of them.[41] The son of a black African father and a white American mother, Barack Obama was raised by his mother's parents in the American heartland state of Kansas. In identifying himself as the inheritor of the dream of his father who emigrated to America from his African homeland in the tiny African village of Alego, Barack Obama has also opened up a fantasy space for nonblack subjects to imagine their own resilience in the face of impossible global conditions and to hope that things will get better through their hard work and resolve.

Navigating in between the Scylla of U.S. identity politics and the Charybdis of state fantasies of colorblindness, Obama's constituent movement started from the ground up. In his autobiography, Obama identified with his Kenyan father's race, but in his movement he turned this identification into the precondition for building cross-racial relationships by passing them *through* the complexitites of U.S. race politics. He then connected the consciousness of the realities of racial inequality to class and gender issues as the critical precondition for realizing democracy. Rather than either excluding whites or validating the entrenched distinction between white Americans' governmental belonging and the passive belonging of minoritized populations, Obama situated himself in the rift in between these constituencies. He did so to enable those who are raced white to enter into solidarity with people of color in a constituent movement that disrupted previous assumptions about social change.

In the Introduction, I described the figure that underwent the metamorphoses within the American Dream as a transgenerational trauma. Transgenerational haunting would also be the appropriate term to describe the strand of fantasy that coursed through Obama's contest with Hillary Clinton during Democratic primaries as well as during the campaign he waged against John McCain for the presidency. This fantasy resembled a family secret in that it hovered in the space in between social shame and psychic disavowal.

During the primaries a history that was not of the candidates' choosing unfolded in the deepest recesses of the minds of its viewers. After the airing of the advertisement that represented a white woman rushing into the bedroom of her sleeping daughter after a 3 a.m. emergency call, political commentators accused Hillary Clinton of retrieving a racist representation of black men—as terrorizing night-time intruders—that had historically resulted in lynching. Her husband Bill Clinton's comparison of Obama's presidential run with that of Jesse Jackson during the 1980s was likewise condemned for its racist subtext. Jesse Jackson subsequently received public rebuke for failing to recognize the difference between Obama's movement and the Civil Rights movements of the 1960s and 1970s. When she needed to justify the continuation of her campaign long after it was clear that she lacked the votes to win, Hillary Clinton delivered a speech in which she impersonated Harriet Tubman admonishing fugitive slaves to "keep running."

Obama's candidacy aroused memories of the assassinations of revered leaders—Lincoln, Martin Luther King, the Kennedys—even as Obama was associated with assassins and terrorists like Osama bin Laden and William Ayers. Gary Wills compared Obama's relationship with his black separatist minister Jeremiah Wright to Lincoln's with the violent abolitionist John Brown.

John McCain ended his speech at the Republican convention by recalling his experiences as a prisoner of the Viet Cong during the Vietnam War. His campaign was premised on a "Country First" platform that was designed to draw correlations between Obama and leftwing extremists who resembled the Viet Cong and Muslim terrorists in their hatred of America. His running mate Sarah Palin personified the ethos of a pioneer woman from the western frontier. Her self-reliance was expected to appeal to Hillary Clinton's disgruntled supporters. Representations of her willingness to sacrifice her children for her country were designed to render her the antithesis of Cindy Sheehan.

But Obama's campaign successfully laid the transhistorical ghosts haunting the relations between generations to rest. Hillary Clinton's prolonged competition with Obama enabled her supporters to work through the issues that separated them from Obama's post-1968 generation. Although McCain recalled the memories of POWs and MIAs from the time of the Vietnam War, his campaign provided him with the opportunity to work through his wartime trauma. McCain publicly accomplished this working through by discovering (in his "my fellow prisoners" parapraxis) that the "message" his handlers imposed upon him during his campaign was comparable in its impeding his "straight talk" to the false confessions he was compelled to deliver during his imprisonment in North Vietnam.

The turning point in the campaign took place when the subprime crisis enabled the U.S. public to reinvest the credibility they had withdrawn from the economy onto the wish for a transgenerational dream to come true. The need for this fantasy became starkly evident after Bill Clinton described Obama's campaign as "nothing but a fairy tale." The public outcry that arose in the wake of this dismissal faulted Clinton for having deprived the country of the empty space of fantasy where U.S. citizens could project their desires and enter into the consciousness of their dreams.

The mirrors that Obama had added to the U.S. political culture did not merely reconfigure the existing field. They also took the ground out from under the already positioned field, and they brought an entirely different field into view. The acceptance speech that Obama delivered at the Democratic National Convention on August 29, 2008, the third anniversary of Hurricane Katrina, associated his presidential campaign with the audacious hope for this alternative future. In his victory address at Grant Park, he associated that hope with the nonsynchronous aspirations from 1968.

Obama's hope was audacious because it was virtually impossible to say ahead of time what the outcome of this hope might be. The speech inspired the courage to act in the face of all the uncertainty that results from not being able to ascertain the shape of the order such hope might bring about. Obama urged the multiple constituencies he has addressed to gather up their resolve and prepare to emigrate from their involuntary exile within an intolerable Homeland and to migrate to a new as yet unimagined America that he described as rising up again in the West. Whether that state of fantasy is a sign of the audacity of hope or a symptom of cultural despair is a question that remains to be answered.

Notes

Introduction

1. Jacqueline Rose, *States of Fantasy* (Oxford: Clarendon Press, 1996) has broken ground in explaining the significance of state fantasies to the political culture of the modern nation-state: "It is the central argument of her book that there is no way of understanding political identities and destinies without letting fantasies into the frame" (4).

2. Ibid., 8.

3. Ibid., 6–7.

4. Ibid., 6–7.

5. In *Spectral Nationality: Passages of Freedom from Kant to Postcolonial Literatures of Liberation* (New York: Columbia University Press, 2003), Pheng Cheah has written about the mutual contamination of national and state fantasies with great insight and nuance. He specifically tracked the itinerary of a series of core concepts and metaphors—freedom, culture, organism, nature, *bildung*, artifice—as they underwent translation from Kant, Fichte, Hegel, and other canonical texts in eighteenth- and nineteenth-century German idealism into twentieth-century postcolonial literatures. Cheah was more specifically preoccupied with the ways in which contemporary theories of freedom at work within accounts of postcolonial nationalisms were underwritten by the aporias that continued to accompany the metaphor of the organic body.

According to Cheah, the organismic metaphor emerged as a concept metaphor through which it became possible to articulate and to resolve the paradoxical relationship between freedom as an auto-causality within the intelligible realm

215

and freedom as a moral practice to be incarnated within a sensible realm regulated by efficient causality. If freedom was incapable of completion in the intelligible realm of the state, it was also incapable of incarnation in the sensible realm of the nation. In order to resolve these dual incapacities, the state became entwined with the *Bildung* associated with national culture so as to disassociate from representations of its operations as that of an artificial machine imposed upon the people. But if culture constituted the national medium through which the state dissociated from mechanistic descriptions of its workings, culture also supplied the nation with the statist means of withstanding the very technologies that produced its organismic appearance (Enlightenment knowledge, print technology, and literary culture). Overall culture turned the nation-state into "a self-organizing whole imbued with organismic causality... and suitable for the realization of human freedom and the historical incarnation of the moral law" (94).

After reconceptualizing both the nation and the state in terms of an organismic natural body in which to incarnate and to practice the promise of freedom, however, Cheah concluded that the organismic body of this nation-state must itself be construed as spectral—neither living nor dead—rather than organic. In elucidating the figure of "spectral nationalism" that replaced the organic type, Cheah underscored the uncanny intertwinings it effected when he wrote that "the state is an incontrollable specter that the national organism must welcome within itself, and direct at once, for itself and against itself... and the nation too must be seen as a specter haunted by and haunting the state" (390, 395).

6. In *Legislators and Interpreters: On Modernity, Post-modernity, and Intellectuals* (Ithaca, N.Y.: Cornell University Press, 1987), Zygmunt Bauman has explained the difference between modern and postmodern attitudes towards knowledge production in terms of a profound change in the self-representation of intellectuals—from legislators who established the authority of the law to interpreters of already written laws. Bauman's explanation of the legislator's role in authorizing the law has influenced my thinking about the legislative powers of state fantasy.

7. I have composed a more comprehensive rationale for the emergence of what Frederick Crews called "national shames" in an essay that I published in 1990 entitled "New Americanists: Revisionist Interventions into the Canon," *boundary 2* 17, no. 1 (Spring 1990): 1–38.

8. Of the numerous overviews of the subject of America exceptionalism, the following have been especially useful to my thinking: Michael Kammen, "The Problem of *American Exceptionalism*: A Reconsideration," *American Quarterly* 45, no. 1 (1993): 1–43; Deborah L. Madsen, *American Exceptionalism* (Jackson: University of Mississsippi Press, 1998); Jack P. Greene, *The Intellectual Construction of American Exceptionalism and Identity from 1493 to 1800* (Chapel Hill: University of North Carolina Press, 1993).

9. Recent reassessments of American exceptionalism have led to useful accounts of its purposes. I recommend the following as especially insightful: David Keith Adams and Cornelius A. van Minnen, eds., *Reflections on American Excep-*

tionalism (Staffordshire: Keene University Press, 1994); Daniel T. Rodgers, "American Exceptionalism Revisited," *Raritan* 24, no. 2 (2004): 21–47; Dorothy Ross, "Liberalism and American Exceptionalism," *Intellectual History Newsletter* 24 (2002): 72–83; and Byron E. Shafer, ed., *Is America Different: A New Look at American Exceptionalism* (Oxford: Oxford University Press, 1991).

10. In *The Right Opposition: The Lovestoneites and the International Communist Opposition of the 1930's* (Westport, Conn.: Greenwood, 1981), J. Robert Alexander has explained that the Lovestoneites drew Stalin's condemnation for having claimed that economic developments in the United States differed from those in Europe and that these differences explained why the United States had not yet arrived at the point of economic collapse that then plagued the countries of Europe.

11. Daniel T. Rodgers, "Exceptionalism," in *Imagined Histories: American Historians Interpret the Past* (Princeton: Princeton University Press, 1998), has explained the historical rationale for this appropriation with characteristic clarity: "Extracting 'exceptionalism' from Communist party jargon, scholars moving centerward from the anti-Stalinist left injected it into the central vocabulary of American social and political science. An absence—the relative failure of socialism in the United States—became the defining point of the nation's history, a ratification of the special dispensation of the United States in a revolutionary world where Marx still tempted" (28).

12. For an analysis of these interdependent imaginaries, see Rodgers, "Exceptionalism," 22–39, and Ian Tyrrell, "American Exceptionalism in an Age of International History," *American Historical Review* 96 (1991): 1031–55.

13. See Daniel Bell, *The End of Ideology: On the Exhaustion of Political Ideas in the Fifties* (Glencoe, Ill.: Free Press, 1960) and Louis Hartz, *The Liberal Tradition in America: An Interpretation of American Political Thought Since the Revolution* (New York: Harcourt Brace, 1955).

14. For an elaboration of this dynamic, see Donald E. Pease, "Imperial Discourse," *Diplomatic History* 22 (1998): 605–15.

15. William Appleman Williams, *Empire as a Way of Life* (New York: Dell, 1980), 380.

16. Rose, *States of Fantasy*, 11–25.

17. Slavoj Žižek, *Tarrying with the Negative: Kant, Hegel and the Critique of Ideology* (Durham: Duke University Press, 1992), 201–2.

18. Ibid., 6.

19. Ibid.

20. Renata Salecl, *The Spoils of Freedom: Psychoanalysis and Feminism after the Fall of Socialism* (London: Routledge, 1994), 50. But at the same time as it relies on the production of a scapegoat to be stigmatized as the one who is to blame for our lack, this fantasmatic identification with the enemy also enables subjects to get back the enjoyment that they sacrificed in entering the symbolic order.

21. For an elaborated analysis of the Gaze, see Slavoj Žižek, *Looking Awry: An Introduction to Jacques Lacan through Popular Culture* (Cambridge, Mass.: MIT Press, 1991), esp. 1–25.

22. I am indebted to Giorgio Agamben for my understanding of the State of Exception: Giorgio Agamben, *The State of Exception* (Palo Alto: Stanford University Press, 2006).

23. In order to understand why American leaders were willing to accept such an aggressive strategy to undermine Soviet communism, we need to look at President Truman's March 1947 speech before Congress. In this speech Truman describes the emerging cold war as a global conflict between two "alternative ways of life": "Whereas 'our' way of life is based on the will of the majority, and is distinguished by free institutions, representative government, free elections, guarantees of individual liberty, freedom of speech and religion, and freedom from political repression, [their] way of life is based upon the will of a minority forcibly imposed upon the majority. It relies upon terror and oppression, a controlled press and radio, fixed elections, and the suppression of personal freedoms." Declaring what has become known as "the Truman Doctrine," President Truman argued that the United States must become the "global policemen," responsible for protecting and securing freedom and democracy in the "free world," which he defined as all countries not presently controlled or dominated by Soviet communism.

On September 30, 1950, President Truman officially approved National Security Council Report 68. NSC 68 was a fifty-eight-page classified report issued on April 14, 1950. NSC 68 would shape government actions in the cold war for the next forty years and has been described as the blueprint of the national security strategy to undermine Soviet influence. NSC 68 begins by noting that the conclusion to World War II witnessed the defeat of the German and Japanese Empires, and the decline of the French and British Empires, leaving two major global powers competing for global leadership and dominance, the United States and the Soviet Union. Describing the Soviet Empire as motivated by the desire to expand their control over the Eurasian land mass so as to eventually dominate the world, the document concluded that the United States was faced with a threat that could lead to the "destruction not only of the Republic but of civilization itself."

Following the observation that "unwillingly our free society finds itself mortally challenged by the Soviet system," NSC 68 endorsed the U.S. commitment to create "a military shield under which . . . [the peoples of the free world] can develop," a military shield strong enough "to deter, if possible, Soviet expansion, and to defeat, if necessary, aggressive Soviet or Soviet-directed actions of a limited or total character." But NSC 68 also described the cold war struggle between the United States and the Soviet Union as, in fact, a "real war": "The whole success of the proposed program hangs ultimately on the recognition by this Government, the American people, and all free peoples, that the cold war is in fact a real war in which the survival of the free world is at stake."

NSC 68 also laid out the terms of the United States' third world strategy with the assertion that the nation was obliged to use covert means to wage "economic warfare and political and psychological warfare with a view to fomenting and supporting unrest and revolt in selected strategic satellite countries." Finally,

NSC 68 called for the construction of "internal security and civilian defense programs" in order to prepare the American people to accept the cold war and the need to be prepared to fight and win global nuclear wars.

On December 16, 1950, Truman issued Proclamation 2914: Proclaiming the Existence of a National Emergency: "WHEREAS world conquest by communist imperialism is the goal of the forces of aggression that have been loosed upon the world, Now, THEREFORE, I, HARRY S. TRUMAN, president of the United States of America, do proclaim the existence of a national emergency, which requires that the military, naval, air, and civilian defenses of this country be strengthened as speedily as possible to the end that we may be able to repel any and all threats against our national security and to fulfill our responsibilities in the efforts being made through the United Nations and otherwise to bring about lasting peace. I summon all citizens to make a united effort for the security and well-being of our beloved country and to place its needs foremost in thought and action that the full moral and material strength of the Nation may be readied for the dangers which threaten us." For the complete transcripts of these documents, see J. M. Hanhimaki and O. A. Westad, *The Cold War: A History in Documents and Accounts* (New York: Oxford University Press, 2003).

24. Carl Schmitt, *The Concept of the Political,* translation, introduction, and notes by George Schwab; with Leo Strauss's notes on Schmitt's essay, translated by J. Harvey Lomax; foreword by Tracy B. Strong (Chicago: University of Chicago Press, 1996). My understanding of Schmitt's critique of liberalism draws upon Chantal Mouffe's "Carl Schmitt and the Paradox of Liberal Democracy," in *The Challenge of Carl Schmitt,* ed. Chantal Mouffe (New York: Verso, 1999), 38–53.

25. Ghassan Hage, *White Nation: Fantasies of White Supremacy in a Multicultural Society* (Sydney: Pluto Press, 1998), 45.

26. Ibid., 46.

27. Ibid., 45.

28. Ibid., 46.

29. Renata Salecl has found the work of Oscar Ducrot especially helpful in explaining how a state fantasy achieves this quasi-permanent status. In *Spoils of Freedom,* Salecl selects two notions from Ducrot's conceptual apparatus to explain how a political discourse can produce positions wherein political subjects can recognize themselves as its addressee over a *longue durée.* Ducrot's theory of the speech act described the addressees of political discourses as inherently split or divided. After the speech act opens up a certain intersubjective space, it is up to the empirical hearer either to recognize himself or herself as the figure called to occupy this position or to ignore it.

Ducrot introduced this account of the split within the addressee to corroborate the distinction between the figure who takes up the place created by the discourse and the empirical receiver of the address. In her effort to explain how addressees of a political discourse can felicitously determine whether or not they feel obliged to take up this position, Salecl takes up Ducrot's concept of the "later discourse."

According to Salecl, the later discourse refers to the encompassing socio-symbolic "network by means of which the present discourse self-referentially establishes the link between itself and what is to follow" (32). Any given utterance must always be taken up from the point of view of its "ideal continuation (i.e., it always constructs an ideal space of its possible continuation, which retroactively confers on it its signification)" (32). The most accessible way to understand how the later discourse accomplishes the expectation of its ideal continuation involves recognizing how it works when a political discourse addresses a question. The discourse in which the question is asked "delineates in advance the ideal, fictional space of the response to come. . . . If I ask somebody a question, I not only determine the type of speech I expect from the addressee at the same time I establish a certain discursive relationship between myself and the other, I locate my own discourse in relation to the other" (32). It is the expectation that the discourse of American exceptionalism will not only be continued, but that it will situate its addressees in positions in which they believe themselves able to produce the responses that the discourse expects them to enunciate that explains the semiotic basis for its *longue durée*.

30. Although Jacqueline Rose does not take up the differences between their differing accounts of its consequences, in *Eros and Civilization: A Philosophical Inquiry into Freud* (Boston: Beacon, 1966), Herbert Marcuse anticipates Jacqueline Rose's claim that fantasy constituted an essential mediation between the demands of the individual subject and the state in that it facilitated the internalization of social laws. But unlike Rose, Marcuse ascribed an emancipatory potential to fantasy, which he found inherent to its critical and counterfactual quality. According to Marcuse, fantasy's liberatory potential resided in the fact that it was primarily governed by unorganized processes associated with the pleasure principle. Like Rose, Marcuse described fantasy as possessing a truth value of its own. But unlike Rose, Marcuse claimed that the truth value of fantasy could not be disassociated from its counterfactual aspect. Indeed it was fantasy's capacity to engender a counterfactual world that enabled it to overcome social antagonisms.

In giving expression to a language of pleasure free from the constraints of the reality principle, fantasy could accomplish the reconciliation between the individual's desire for a fully gratified society and the existing state of things. While political theorists who pledged allegiance to the reality principle repudiated fantasy as in the service of an impossible unreality, Marcuse argued that fantasy is not to be correlated with what is not real but with a reality "of socially gratified desire" that, although it has not yet been realized can and indeed must become real.

Lauren Berlant has supplemented the link Marcuse has established between fantasy and utopianism in her brilliantly argued *Anatomy of National Fantasy: Hawthorne, Utopia, and Everyday Life* (Chicago: University of Chicago Press, 1991): "By passing into the citizenhood through inscription in the National Symbolic of the body politic that expresses her/him, the citizen reaches another plane of existence, a whole, unassailable body, whose translation into totality mimics the nation's permeable yet impervious spaces. According to this logic, disruptions in the realm of the National Symbolic creates a collective sensation of almost physical vulnerability: the subject without a nation experiences her/his own mortality and vulnerability because s/he has lost control over physical space and the historical time that marks that space as part of her/his inheritance" (24).

But there is no reason why fantasy should bring about a better society or more contented subject. State fantasies have promoted racism, nationalism, and ethnic hatred at least as frequently as they have fostered belief in a harmonious and conflict-free society. And the vulnerability of the utopian national fantasy of an "ideal nation" to the usages of the State of Exception discloses one of the limitations of this account.

31. John Rawls, *Political Liberalism* (New York: Columbia University Press, 1993), addressed Schmitt's critique of the liberal political sphere by claiming that political liberalism promoted civic harmony by encouraging the pluralism that Schmitt described as a threat to its viability. But Rawls also took Schmitt's criticism into account by observing that such civic harmony could only be attained by removing or bypassing the most divisive political issues. This insight led Rawls to introduce an exception of his own to the rules of liberal pluralism and inclusion.

According to Rawls, the liberal political sphere fostered deliberative understanding through the exchange of conflicting opinions among individuals who have also presupposed a shared and overlapping consensus about the nature of political liberalism. Persons who presented their positions within the liberal political sphere were required to remain neutral and disinterested in their evaluation of the plurality of political positions enunciated there. Without that requirement, the liberal sphere would be unable to foster the formation of a robust overlapping consensus. Political liberalism could not acknowledge the absolute truth value of a position, but only the relative values of positions to which it is reasonable either to assent or to dissent.

This meant that persons whose political positions were founded upon absolute truth claims that were not subject to refutation or counterargument could not be included within the liberal political sphere. Political liberalism could not admit a political position that was founded upon an absolute truth claim into the political realm without violating the rules of the political sphere as such. Insofar as the individuals who engaged in political discussions within the liberal political sphere presupposed a shared and overlapping consensus about the nature of political debate in order to gain entry, liberal political culture could not admit absolute truth claims without violating its founding preconditions. The only absolute truth claim that political liberalism recognized pertained to the truth of its description of the political realm. The National Security State secured the realm by turning itself into the guarantor of the liberalism its citizens practiced. My understanding of the limits of political liberalism draws upon Chantal Mouffe's analysis of Rawls in "Carl Schmitt and the Para-dox of Liberal Democracy," 46–53.

1. Staging the New World Order

1. Lynn Spigel, *Make Room for TV: Television and the Family Ideal in Post-war America* (Chicago: University of Chicago Press, 1992).

2. The best available critique of official coverage of the war can be found in Douglas Kellner's *The Persian Gulf TV War* (Boulder: Westview Press, 1992).

3. Dick Hebdige, "Bombing Logic," *Marxism Today*, March 1991, 46. For an example of a thoroughly postmodernist reading of the Persian Gulf War, see Jean Baudrillard's "La Guerre du Golfe n'a pas eu Lieu," *Liberation*, 29 March 1991.

4. This documentary accord appears in Christopher Norris's *Uncritical Theory: Postmodernism, Intellectuals and the Gulf War* (Amherst: University of Massachusetts Press, 1992), 110–11.

5. The cover story for the 18 May 1992, *U.S. News and World Report* "Special Report: Iraqgate—How the Bush Administration Helped Finance Saddam Hussein's War Machine with American Tax Dollars" is a fine sample of the delayed response to the Gulf War.

6. Cal Thomas, "Time to Think Nuclear," *Boston Globe*, 7 February 1991, op-ed.

7. Doug Lummis, "The United States, Japan, and the Gulf War: An Inter-view with Mojtaba Sadria," *Monthly Review* 43, no. 11 (April 1992): 9–10.

8. Douglas Kellner has documented the linkages the Bush administration adduced between the Persian Gulf War and the SDI in *Persian Gulf TV War*, 176–85.

9. State of the Union address before a Joint Session of the Congress, Janu-ary 28, 1992.

10. Ibid.

11. Dean MacCannell, "Baltimore in the Morning . . . After: On the Forces of Post-Nuclear Leadership," *Diacritics* 14, no. 2 (1984): 41.

12. George Mariscal, "In the Wake of the Gulf War: Untying the Yellow Ribbon," *Cultural Critique* 19 (Fall 1991): 114.

13. In note 29 of the "Introduction," I explained the usage to which Renata Salecl, in *Spoils of Freedom*, had put Oswald Ducrot's notion of the "later dis-course" to explain the longevity of the discourse of American exceptionalism. But an understanding of the efficacy of the fantasy of exceptionalism requires an understanding of the distinction that Salecl adduces between a presupposi-tion and a surmise. Before it can be an effective fantasy, a political discourse must construct the later discourse in a way that leaves a space open to be filled out by images of the addressee's ideal ego. Successful political discourse does not simply respond to needs; it isn't the needs but the position from which their meaning gets perceived by the addressee that is crucial to the uptake of

the discourse. This symbolic space can be construed as a site of symbolic identification, "a point of view from which we could appear likeable to ourselves" (33). This positioning was always accompanied by an unspoken fantasy frame. Whereas the later discourse constructs the place of the subject's identification, the surmise functions as a place for fantasy.

Renata Salecl does not locate the fantasy within the precincts of the later discourse. She locates it in the following distinction she adduces between presupposition and a surmise. "By pronouncing a certain proposition, a speaker also guarantees its presupposition. For example, if I say 'I promise to revenge your father's death,' I assume thereby a whole network of intersubjective relationships and my place within it is to accept as a fact that the father's death was the result of an injustice, I assume that I am in a position to compensate for it, and so forth. The surmise is on the other hand the place of the inscription of the addressee in the enunciation; it is the addressee who assumes responsibility for the surmise, who has to derive it from what it said" (35). The surmise emerges as an answer to the question what did the speaker mean by saying that. The "split between a proposition and surmise assumes the form of the necessary distance between the field of meaning of an ideological discourse and the level of fantasy functioning as its surmise" (35).

14. Jacques Derrida, "No Apocalypse, Not Now (full speed ahead, seven missiles, seven missives)," *Diacritics* 14, no. 2 (1984): 23.

15. George Bush, January 28, 1992, State of the Union address.

16. Guy Debord, *The Society of the Spectacle* (Detroit: Black and Red Unauthorized Translation, 1970).

17. Michael Paul Rogin, "'Make My Day': Spectacle as Amnesia in Imperial Politics," *Representations* 29 (Winter 1990): 116–17.

18. Paul Virilio, *Nuclear Democracies* (New York: Semiotexte, 1991), 77.

19. For a somewhat different account of the way in which this understanding of the cold war narrative functioned in the construction of the Americanist canon, see Donald E. Pease, "Moby Dick and the Cold War," in *The American Renaissance Reconsidered*, ed. Walter Michaels and Donald E. Pease (Baltimore: Johns Hopkins University Press, 1985), 115–17.

20. Marita Sturken, "The Wall, the Screen and the Image: The Vietnam Veteran's Memorial," *Representations* 35 (Summer 1991): 137–38. Marita Sturken expands this argument in *Tangled Memories: The Vietnam War, the AIDS Epidemic, and the Politics of Remembering* (Berkeley: University of California Press, 1997), 44–85.

21. Sturken, "The Wall, the Screen and the Image," 137.

22. W. J. T. Mitchell, "The Violence of Public Art: Do the Right Thing," *Critical Inquiry* 16 (Summer 1990): 888.

23. John Hellmann, *American Myth and the Legacy of Vietnam* (New York: Columbia University Press, 1986), 153.

24. Noam Chomsky, "On War Crimes," in *At War with Asia* (New York: Pantheon, 1970), 298–99.

25. Jean-Paul Sartre, *On Genocide* (Boston: Beacon, 1968), 81–82.
26. Robert Jay Lifton, *The Future of Immortality and Other Essays for a Nuclear Age* (New York: Basic Books, 1987), 58, 71, 72.
27. See ibid., 31–73.
28. For an elaboration of this myth, see H. Bruce Franklin, *M.I.A., or, Mythmaking in America* (New Brunswick, N.J.: Rutgers University Press, 1993).
29. Ibid., 145.
30. Department of State, Current Policy, No. 869.
31. Mike Davis, *L.A. Was Just the Beginning: Urban Revolt in the United States: A Thousand Points of Light* (Westfield: Open Magazine, Pamphlet #20, 1992), 5 and 7.

2. America of the Two Covenants

1. See Hayden White, "The Value of Narrativity in the Representation of Reality," *Critical Inquiry* 7 (1980): 24. Timothy Brennan elaborates on the relationship between desire and national narrativity in "The National Longing for Form," in *Nation and Narration*, ed. Homi Bhabha (New York: Routledge, 1990), 44–70. For a book-length monograph that builds Hayden White's theory of narrative into a persuasive account of contemporary literature, see Jay Clayton, *The Pleasures of Babel: Contemporary American Literature and Theory* (New York: Oxford University Press, 1993).
2. The text of Clinton's address is reprinted in "Nominee Clinton Describes Vision of New Covenant" (July 18, 1992), *Congressional Quarterly*, 2128–30.
3. Kevin W. Dean has published a useful discussion of the fundamentalist assumptions embedded in Clinton's covenantal rhetoric in "Bill Clinton's 'New Covenant': Re-Visioning an Old Vision," *National Forensic Journal* 10 (Fall 1992): 101–10.
4. Clinton's efforts to produce his "Third Way" by constructing a homology between extremists on the right and the left resurfaced during Hillary Clinton's recent presidential campaign. Clinton described the "radicalization" of the caucus states by left-wing activists as largely responsible for Barack Obama's having soundly defeated Hillary Clinton in the majority of the caucuses. For an example of what religious fundamentalists thought of Clinton's New Covenant, consider the following description of it from the "William Jefferson Clinton Memorial Library" at http://www.clintonmemoriallibrary.com/clint_spirit.html: "Finally, liberals had found a leader who was willing to create a Gospel that not only allows them to continue their chosen pursuits, but actually encourages them. Clinton's 'New Covenant' gives a seal of approval to varieties of self-indulgence that a few short years ago would have earned universal rebuke. Clinton brought with him to Washington a cadre of God-hating activists, Socialists, population control earth worshippers, homosexuals, radical feminists, pro-abortionists, labor union bosses, big-union enemies of Christian education, civil-rights extremists who still demand Affirmative Action and Busing, 'children's rights' advocates, the media and Hollywood 'cultural elite's' and the like.

They were people with an agenda and a vision. 'They exchanged the truth of God for a lie, and worshipped and served created things rather than the Creator' [Romans 1:25]."

5. In "The New Revolutionaries," *New York Review of Books* 42, no. 13 (20 July 1995), Gary Wills describes the silent majority as a constituency held together by a complex of ideas that he finds continuous with the cold war mentality: "For decades the American people were spied on and encouraged to suspect others while submitting to suspicion themselves. Industry 'blacklists' outran governmental scrutiny. War level secrecy reduced governmental accountability and citizen participation in government" (54).

6. Lee Quinby, *Anti-Apocalypse: Exercises in Genealogical Criticism* (Minneapolis: University of Minnesota Press, 1994), xvi.

7. In a work that has influenced my understanding of American apocalypse, the Girardian critic Gil Bailie has defined the apocalypse as a myth that "camouflages the (state's) violence in ways that make it seem valiant and divinely ordained" for those who have benefited from it. Gil Bailie, *Violence Unveiled: Humanity at the Crossroads* (New York: Crossroad, 1995), 27.

8. Douglas Robinson, *American Apocalypses: Images of the End of the World in American Literature* (Baltimore: Johns Hopkins University Press, 1985), 27.

9. The History Place Great Speeches Collection: George Washington Prevents the Revolt of His Officers on March 15, 1783, http://www.historyplace .com/speeches/washington.htm.

10. Alan Nadel, *Television in Black-and-White America: Race and National Identity* (Lawrence: University Press of Kansas, 2005), 43.

11. The Australian critic Jon Stratton has described the cold war deployment of the mythos of the American apocalypse and the American frontier to incorporate "developing" third world countries within U.S. providential history as a national fantasy. Stratton diagnoses U.S. imperialism as itself a symptom of a national identity crisis. The Anglo-Irish inhabitants of this former settler colony in the Anglo-American Empire compulsively reenacted, Stratton explains, imperialist adventures in order to work through their shared condition of displacement. This transference enabled the United States to "transpose the experience of its identity crisis as a settler colony of displaced people from a relation with the indigenous people of the country—that it aggressively misnamed as Indians—with the diversity of the non-western world." See "The Beast of the Apocalypse: The Postcolonial Experience of the United States," *New Formations* 21 (1994): 35–63.

12. See Renata Salecl's discussion of the fantasy structure of war in *Spoils of Freedom*, 15–19.

13. My understanding of the significance of the events at Waco and Oklahoma City draws upon the work of Stuart A. Wright, *Armageddon in Waco: Critical Perspectives on the Branch Davidian Conflict* (Chicago: University of Chicago Press, 1995) and Marita Sturken, *Tourists of History: Memory, Kitsch, and Consumerism from Oklahoma City to Ground Zero* (Durham: Duke University Press, 2007).

14. *New York Times*, April 30, 1995.

15. Gary Wills, in "New Revolutionaries," has described the reasoning of the militia as homologous with the reason and violence of the National Security State. For both security formations "A peace would have to be a war called peace . . . with substitute peacetime activities replicating those of war" (54).

16. Judith Butler's important work on injurious speech acts can be found in *Excitable Speech: A Politics of the Performative* (New York: Routledge, 1997). I discuss the significance of what she calls sovereign speech acts and how hate speech emulates the sovereign violence of the state's speech acts in "Regulating Multi-Adhoccerists, Fish's Rules," *Critical Inquiry* 23 (1997): 396–418.

17. Rastko Mocnik, "Ideology and Fantasy," in *The Althusserian Legacy*, ed. E. Ann Kaplan and Michael Sprinker (New York: Verso, 1993), 148–49.

18. Ibid., 145.

19. Quoted by Lewis Lapham in "Seen but Not Heard: The Message of the Oklahoma Bombing," *Harper's* 291, no. 1742 (July 1995), 31.

20. For spectacular elaborations of these mortalizing fantasies, see the Web site Fight 4 Truth at http://fight4truth.com/concentrationcamps.htm: "Why are we all in denial over these possibilities? Didn't we hear about prison camps in Germany, and even in the United States during World War II? Japanese individuals were rounded up and placed in determent camps during the duration of the War. Where was their freedom? You don't think it could happen to you? Obviously those rounded up and killed didn't think it could happen to them either. How could decent people have witnessed such atrocities and still said nothing? Are we going to do the same here as they cart off one by one those individuals who are taking a stand for the rights of the citizens as they expose the truth happening behind the scenes? Are we all going to sit there and wonder what happened to this country of ours? Where did we go wrong? How could we let it happen?"

21. Zygmunt Bauman, *Modernity and the Holocaust* (Ithaca: Cornell University Press, 1989). This fantasy is significant for its interidentification of the callers with the disposable populations previously confined to the always already surpassed category of symbolic mortality. The enslavement fantasy is elaborated most fully in Andrew MacDonald's 1978 novel *The Turner Diaries* (Memphis: National Vanguard Books, 1978).

22. Edith Wyschogrod, *Spirit in Ashes: Hegel, Heidegger, and Man-Made Mass Death* (New Haven: Yale University Press, 1985), 14–15. On the emergence of the historical fact as traumatic matter, voided of the historical witness that it also solicits, see Cathy Caruth's "An Interview with Robert Jay Lifton," in *Trauma: Explorations in Memory* (Baltimore: Johns Hopkins University Press, 1995), 128–50.

23. For the classic discussion of the ideological operation of interpellation, see Louis Althusser, "Ideology and the Ideological State Apparatuses (Notes towards an Investigation)," in *Lenin and Philosophy and Other Essays*, trans. Ben Brewster (New York: Monthly Review Press, 1971), 145.

24. In "Seen but Not Heard," 29–37, Lewis H. Lapham explains these incompatible rationalities. In 1993, attorney Linda Thompson of the American Justice Foundation articulated her own theory of the relationship between Waco and the Oklahoma City bombing when she produced and distributed a video entitled *WACO: The Big Lie*. This document's footage supported several troubling allegations about the government's responsibility for the catastrophe. But her subsequent claims that Waco was only one element in a vast U.N. conspiracy that included tanks and various unmarked military vehicles nationwide and that the BATF killed its own agents, several of whom had been Secret Service bodyguards for President Bill Clinton, have both been thoroughly discredited. For a brilliant discussion of the paradoxes that ensue at moments when a liberal democracy confronts the rights claims of previously disenfranchised cultural groups, see Elizabeth Povinelli, *The Cunning of Recognition: Indigenous Alterties and the Making of Australian Multiculturalism* (Durham: Duke University Press, 2002), esp. 1–34.

25. President Clinton, quoted by Lapham in "Seen but Not Heard," 32.

26. For a cogent account of the political rationale for this linkage, see Lapham, "Seen but Not Heard."

27. President Clinton, quoted by Lapham in "Seen but Not Heard," 35.

3. A National Rite of Passage

1. "Tocqueville and the Mullah," *New Republic* 333, no. 4 (2 February 1998): 7. All quotations from this editorial can be found on this page.

2. Apropos of the imaginary geography that undergirded this dual containment policy, Edward Said has observed: "It can be argued that Islam (in the shape of the Muslim populations of North Africa, Turkey, and Indian subcontinent) is now the primary form in which the Third World presents itself to Europe.... and the North-South divide, in the European context, has been largely inscribed onto a pre-existing Christian-Muslim division." *Orientalism* (London: Routledge, Kegan and Paul, 1978), 97. Following its exclusion from the precincts of western civilization, "Islam," as Aziz Al-Azmeh has observed "appears indifferently among other things to name history, indicate a religion, ghettoize a community, describe a 'culture,' explain a despicable exoticism, and fully specify a political program." *Islams and Modernities* (London: Verso, 1993), 24.

3. Khatami more specifically said: "Policies pursued by American politicians outside the United States over the past half a century, since World War II, are incompatible with the American civilization founded on democracy, freedom and human dignity." "Tocqueville and the Mullah," 7.

4. See Benjamin Barber, *Jihad vs. McWorld: How the Planet Is both Falling Apart and Coming Together and What This Means for Democracy* (New York: Random House, 1995) for an example of this construction of the United States and the Islamic Republic as utterly opposed political formations. In positioning Iran within the dual containment policy, Barber enlisted the following orientalist

fantasy: "The apparent truth, which speaks to the paradox at the core of this book, is that tendencies of both Jihad *and* McWorld are at work, both visible sometimes in the same country at the very same instant. Iranian zealots keep one ear to the mullahs urging holy war and the other to Rupert Murdoch's Star television beaming in *Dynasty, Donahue,* and the *Simpsons* from hovering satellites" (5). Except for the fact that President Khatami was probably watching C-Span's *Traveling Tocqueville's America* rather than Rupert Murdoch's *Dynasty,* Barber's fantasy bears a family resemblance to the editorial perspective of the *New Republic.* His account of the official reaction of the Islamic state to Murdoch's Star TV describes what the editors of the *New Republic* might have expected to hear from President Khatami. About satellite programs being beamed into Teheran, Barber quotes an unidentified official of the "Iranian Ministry of Culture and Islamic Guidance" as having declared, "These programs, prepared by international imperialism, are part of an extensive plot to wipe out our religious and sacred values" (207).

5. Bobby Sayyid has described this process whereby Islam is correlated with the negation of civil society with remarkable cogency: "Muslims who use Islamic metaphors draw our attention to the fact that there is another way of doing politics which does not seem to rest upon the dominant language games of the last two hundred years. One of the main reasons why 'Islamic Fundamentalism' causes so much disquiet is because it seems to suggest that we may have confused the globalization of a political tradition with its universalization. By rejecting the dominant political discourses, 'Islamic Fundamentalists' make it difficult for us to describe them, since many of our theoretical tools are bound up with this dominant political tradition." "Sign O'Times: Kaffirs and Infidels Fighting the Ninth Crusade," in *The Making of Political Identities,* ed. Ernesto Laclau (New York: Verso, 1994), 265.

6. Claude Lefort quoted this passage in *Democracy and Political Theory* (Cambridge: Polity Press, 1988), 166.

7. See Hage, *White Nation,* 67–70.

8. Slavoj Žižek, "Eastern Europe's Republics of Gilead," *New Left Review* 183 (September/October 1990), 51–52.

9. Useful accounts of the history of Tocqueville's reception can be found in A. Eisenstadt, ed., *Reconsidering Tocqueville's Democracy in America* (New Brunswick: Rutgers University Press, 1988); Seymour Drescher, *Dilemmas of Democracy: Tocqueville and Modernization* (Pittsburgh: University of Pittsburgh Press, 1968); Marvin Zetterbaum, *Tocqueville and the Problem of Democracy* (Stanford: Stanford University Press, 1967); Timothy Brennan, *At Home in the World: Cosmopolitanism Now* (Cambridge: Harvard University Press, 1997); Louis Hartz, *Liberal Tradition in America* ; Robert A. Nisbet, *The Sociological Tradition* (New York: Basic Books, 1966); and Larry Siedentop, *Tocqueville* (Oxford: Oxford University Press, 1994).

10. Slightly different genealogies of the discourse of U.S. exceptionalism can be found in Seymour Martin Lipset, *American Exceptionalism: A Double-Edged Sword* (New York: W. W. Norton, 1997) and Shafer, *Is America Different.*

11. See Helga Geyer-Ryan, "Imagining Identity: Space, Gender, Nation," in *Vision in Context: Historical and Contemporary Perspectives on Sight*, ed. Teresa Brennan and Martin Jay (New York: Routledge, 1996), 121–22. Donatella Mazzolena has specified the ways in which the imaginary nation functions as a bodily ego. As the site of collective identification, the nation "is in some way, a lived space," she points out, "the totality of those who produce and live a collective construction constitute a collective anthropoid body, which maintains in some way an identity as a 'subject.'" When collectively incorporated this imaginary national body is inhabited and practiced as an American way of life. Its claims on the inner lives of the subjects through which it is reproduced relies, Mazzolena argues, on the fact that in the national imaginary "we find the primary pulsations—Eros and Thanatos—that cannot be contained in the web of any structure or story. The articulations of these impulses are always twofold: there is a need to return to a space which is a container of life, which can metabolize death itself (living)—then there is the need to symbolize, to deflect outward the death instinct (constructing). We could perhaps say that constructing insofar as it is a symbolizing activity, arises from the dwelling of the instincts because of the 'primary paranoia' which attempt to redeem the overwhelming relationship with one's own overshadowing other figure." Donatella Mazzolena, "The City and the Imaginary," *New Formations* 21 (1990): 92–93. While they refer it to the dual containment policy, the anxiety Khatami's interview aroused in the editors might be understood as having derived primarily from the threat it posed to the nation as their imaginary bodily double. More than simply declining to play the assigned role of national menace, Khatami had challenged the East–West divide as well as the geopolitical logic of mutual exclusion that supported the U.S. national identity. Against official representations of Iran as the signifier of civil violence, Khatami refused to acknowledge any recognizable distinction between the two national orders. His rhetoric supplanted representations of Islam as dramatically opposed to American religions with the pronouncement that it bore similarities to the Puritanism of the early settlers.

12. In the editorial he contributed to "The Nation" section of the July 22, 1997, issue of *Time* magazine entitled "Civic Engagement in America Isn't Disappearing but Reinventing Itself," the columnist Richard Stengel has also observed a pathological tendency particularly evident within smaller embattled communities that choose to break apart from larger social aggregations and form internally cohesive groups. After observing that the Southern Poverty Law Center has tracked some eight hundred militia and patriot groups and that many of them have formed in the past few years, Stengel concludes that Tocqueville would not have been surprised to learn that America leads the world in militia movements. "The recently arrested Viper militia in Arizona fits Tocqueville's description of a classic American association" (33), Stengel notes apropos of this pathology. Like the civic associations that Tocqueville established as a model of democratic self-governance, the militia movement organizes groups of like-minded neighbors who gather together for the purpose of planning violent

assaults either upon the government or upon other groups and individuals who happen not to be of the same mind.

13. In his response to the *New Republic* editors, Khatami was reacting to a systematic effort by the post–cold war state to substitute Khomeini's religious nationalism for the imperial Soviet as representative, in the wake of the cold war, of the fundamentalist threat to the national security. This substitution links Islam with religious nationalist movements that emerged throughout the United States after the cold war. See Mark Juergensmeyer, *The New Cold War: Religious Nationalism Confronts the Secular State* (Berkeley: University of California Press, 1993), 11–45.

14. See Arthur M. Schlesinger Jr., *The Disuniting of America: Reflections on a Multi-Cultural Society* (Knoxville: Whittle Direct Books, 1991); Newt Gingrich, *To Renew America* (New York: HarperCollins, 1995); Robert Bellah, "Civil Religion in America," *Daedalus* 96, no. 1 (Winter 1967): 1–21; Lipset, *American Exceptionalism*; Anne Norton, "Engendering Another American Identity," and William E. Connolly, "Democracy and Territoriality," both in *Rhetorical Republic: Governing Representations in American Politics*, ed. Frederick M. Dolan, and Thomas L. Dumm (Amherst: University of Massachusetts Press, 1993), 124–42 and 249–74; Michael J. Shapiro, "Introduction," and David Campbell, "Political Prosaics, Transversal Politics, and the Anarchical World," both in *Challenging Boundaries*, ed. Michael Shapiro and Hayward R. Alker (Minnesota: University of Minnesota Press, 1996), xv–xxiii and 7–32. In its November 13, 1995, issue, *The Weekly Standard* reported finding forty-seven separate references to *Democracy in America* in the congressional record of the 104th Congress, including Clinton's citation of Alexis de Tocqueville in the State of the Union address of January 24, 1995, and House Speaker Newt Gingrich's citation of him in the opening session of the 104th Congress, January 4, 1995. See http://theweeklystandard.com, November 1995. The editors added that Tocqueville was frequently misquoted.

15. In *The Meaning of Democracy and the Vulnerability of Democracies* (Ann Arbor: University of Michigan Press, 1997), Vincent Ostrom has discerned civic associations as the core value of the Tocqueville project: "It is within families and other institutional arrangements characteristic of neighborhood, village and community life that citizenship is learned and practiced for most people most of the time. The first order of priority in learning the craft of citizenship as applied to public affairs needs to focus on how to cope with problems in the context of family, neighborhood, village and community" (x).

16. Alexis de Tocqueville, "Author's Preface to the Twelfth Edition," *Democracy in America*, trans. George W. Lawrence, ed. J. P. Mayer (Garden City: Doubleday, 1969), xiv.

17. Thomas L. Dumm, *Democracy and Punishment: Disciplinary Origins of the United States* (Madison: University of Wisconsin Press, 1987).

18. In *Politics and Remembrance: Republican Themes in Machiavelli, Burke and Tocqueville* (Princeton: Princeton University Press, 1985), 189–93, Bruce

James Smith argues persuasively the proposition that Tocqueville's reading of "democratic values" constituted a cover for aristocratic sentiments. "He understood the distemper of the aristocratic affections, that its origin lay in a great sense of loss. He, too, had drunk from the bitter cup of revolution" that could only be abated by giving up the rage for the great memory of aristocracy that democracy afforded. *Democracy in America*, in Smith's reading, had gratified Tocqueville's aspiration to efface the memory of the revolution from the French past.

19. Blandine Kriegel cites George Lefebvre as the source of this quote in *The State and the Rule of Law* (Princeton: Princeton University Press, 1995), 157.

20. See Lefort, *Democracy and Political Theory* , 180.

21. In *Headless History: Nineteenth-Century French Historiography of the French Revolution* (Ithaca: Cornell University Press, 1990), Linda Orr has remarked incisively concerning Tocqueville's politics of displacement, "It would be easy to say that the 'only essential difference' between the 'then' (Old Regime) and 'now' (Empire) of the text is the Revolution—and this would be true except that the Revolution would be seen as an imperceptible step toward the Empire or the displacement between two historical objects (Old Regime and Empire) that are almost identical" (100). Whereas Orr concentrates her analysis in *The Old Regime and the French Revolution*, I would argue that *Democracy in America* did the work of displacing the difference between the Old Regime and Empire, thereby rendering the two events all but indistinguishable.

22. Lefort, *Democracy and Political Theory*, 167.

23. Neil Hertz, *The End of the Line: Essays on Psychoanalysis and the Sublime* (New York: Columbia University Press), 174.

24. See Jacques Rancière, "Discovering New Worlds: Politics of Travel and Metaphors of Space," in *Traveller's Tales: Narratives of Home and Displacement*, ed. Jon Bird et al. (London: Routledge, 1994), 35.

25. See ibid., 33.

26. See ibid., 36

27. In *Radical Renewal: The Politics of Ideas in Modern America* (New York: Pantheon, 1988), Norman Birnbaum has remarked that "De Tocqueville wrote about a preindustrial society: the recurrence of his thought may suggest something else than a commendable desire to go to the historical roots of our political culture. The nation has changed immensely since de Tocqueville's visit. The French thinker, a recalcitrant liberal (in the European sense) with deep doubts about democracy," may have served to legitimate ambivalence about democracy. "He, or his ideas have also served to avert our gaze from problems presented by industrialization, by immigration, by the end of slavery and by empire" (66).

28. See Patricia Yaeger, *The Geography of Identity* (Ann Arbor: University of Michigan Press, 1996), 28–29.

29. See Lisa Lowe, *Critical Terrains: French and British Orientalisms* (Ithaca: Cornell University Press, 1991), 31.

30. See Michel de Certeau, *The Practice of Everyday Life* (Berkeley: University of California Press, 1988), 123.

31. See Chantal Mouffe, "For a Politics of Nomadic Identity," in Bird et al., *Traveller's Tales*, 105–13, for an illuminating discussion of this dynamic.

4. Patriot Acts

1. Quoted in Michael Rogin, *Independence Day, or, How I Learned to Stop Worrying and Love the Enola Gay* (London: BFI, 1998), 36.

2. Ibid., 52.

3. Richard Rorty, *Achieving Our Country: Leftist Thought in Twentieth-Century America* (Cambridge: Harvard University Press, 1998), 38. All further page citations will appear in the body of the text.

4. Rachel Aberly and Suzanne Fritz, *The Patriot: The Official Companion* (London: Carlton, 2000), 28.

5. In *America Right or Wrong: An Anatomy of American Nationalism* (New York: Oxford University Press, 2004), Anatol Lieven has formulated the role the South and the West have played in the propagation of what he calls the American Credo. In Lieven's estimation these territories constitute the antithesis to the nation's official self-representations. These geographical sites bear the memories of the frontier violence and the plantation slavery that the Northeastern elite disavowed. But according to Lieven, the inhabitants of the South and West nevertheless harbor the values that in fact resulted in the settling of the landmass. Lieven also suggests that this antithesis constitutes the spectral support for the nation's official self-representations. In the 1947 election campaign, Harry Truman drew on the sentiments behind this representation when he observed that the Republican Party and the business elite "treat the South and West as colonies to be exploited commercially and held down politically" (quoted in ibid., 98). *The Patriot* converted what Anatol Lieven called the American Antithesis into the national thesis, and it elevated the "homelands" of the South and the West into the representatives of the national geography. For a fine account of the southernification of America, see Michael Lind, *Made in Texas: George W. Bush and the Southern Takeover of American Politics* (New York: Basic Books, 2003).

6. Aberly and Fritz, *The Patriot*, 34.

7. Jacques Derrida has spelled out the criteria for law's inability to legitimate itself with the following description of its double bind: "On the one hand, it appears *easier* to criticize the violence that founds since it cannot be justified by any preexisting legality and so appears savage. But on the other hand ... it is *more difficult*, more illegitimate to criticize this same founding violence since one cannot summon it to appear before the institution of any preexisting law: it does not recognize existing law in the moment that it founds another." *Acts of Religion*, ed. and with an Introduction by Gil Anidjar (London: Routledge, 2002), 274.

8. Walter Benjamin, "Critique of Violence," in *Walter Benjamin's Selected Writings*, vol. 1: *1913–1926*, ed. M. Bullock and M. W. Jennings (Cambridge, Mass.: Belknap Press of Harvard University, 1996), 295.

9. The event in the film that sutured both of these correlations to a master discourse of apocalyptic nationalism was Colonel Tavington's giving the order to set ablaze a church building in Pembroke, South Carolina, where the town's women, children, and civilian noncombatants had assembled in an effort to obtain temporary shelter from the violence. The conflagration of the church at Pembroke did not merely recall the image of the Branch Davidian compound after it was set ablaze in Waco, Texas. This apocalyptic event also recalls the scene of retributive violence acted out by members of the Michigan Militia in Oklahoma City. The latter event also secured the equivalence *The Patriot* adduces between British terrorists and government agents.

10. Derrida, *Acts of Religion*, 273. This ghost also bears a family resemblance to what George Lipsitz has described as the possessive investment of whiteness. His rage is now justified in advance; he carries the flag as the ghost of the son. But the values are not the grand ideological values of freedom and equality. The uncanny violence that would guarantee the security of his home also would transform his home into the equivalent of a militarized zone.

11. The fact that the film was released at the very moment in which the presidential candidates, John McCain and George W. Bush were engaged in a controversy over the political implications of Confederate flag waving atop the state house in Charlestown, South Carolina, also strongly challenged the accuracy of the distinction that Rorty adduced between spectatorial and real "or electoral" politics.

12. For an illuminating analysis of the religion of the Lost Cause with great relevance to this discussion, see Charles Reagan Wilson, "The Religion of the Lost Cause," in *Myth and Southern History*, ed. Patrick Gerster and Nicholas Cords (Urbana: University of Illinois Press, 1989), 169–90.

13. The film would thereby seem to up the ante of Lieven's argument in *America Right or Wrong*. In Lieven's estimation, the South constitutes the antithesis to the nation's official self-representations. But Emmerich's film has turned the South into the representative national geography.

5. From Virgin Land to Ground Zero

1. Henry Nash Smith, *Virgin Land: The American West in Symbols and Myth* (Cambridge, Mass.: Harvard University Press, 1950), supplied an insight into the mobilizing effects of these collective representations on the U.S. populations throughout history when he observed: "These illustrations point to the conclusion that history cannot happen—that is, men cannot engage in purposive group behavior—without images which simultaneously express collective desires and impulses and impose coherence on the infinitely varied data of experience. These images are never, of course, exact reproductions of the physical and social environment. They cannot motivate and direct action unless they are drastic simplifications" (ix). But the historian William H. McNeill provided the most cogent description of the role myths played in the articulation of state governance policies in an article that he published in *Foreign Affairs* 61 (1981):

1–13 entitled "The Care and Repair of Public Myth." In that article, McNeill argued the indispensable role that myths and symbols played in the manufacturing of the public's consent for domestic and foreign policy. And he admonished revisionist scholars for the propagation of their demythologizing proclivities.

2. Richard Slotkin, "Myth and the Production of History," in *Ideology and Classic American Literature*, ed. Sacvan Bercovitch and Myra Jehlen (New York: Cambridge University Press, 1986), 70.

3. President Bush, September 20, 2001, address to the nation.

4. I first began to think of the biopolitical settlement that the Bush administration had constructed out of the relay of signifiers it installed in between 9/11 and the Homeland Security State while I listened to Amy Kaplan deliver a talk at the Dartmouth American Studies Institute in June of 2002 in which she ruminated over the connotations of the terms "Ground Zero," "Homeland," and "Guantánamo Bay." Amy Kaplan has since published those remarks as "Homeland Insecurities: Reflections on Language and Space," *Radical History Review* 85 (Winter 2003): 82–93. My indebtedness to as well as my divergences from Kaplan's meditation can be discerned from a reading of that article.

5. When George W. Bush observed that "Americans have known wars, but for the past 136 years they have been wars on foreign soil," he referenced the conclusion of the Civil War in 1865 as the historical benchmark for the figure of 136 years. But the last occasion on which the country was subject to "foreign attack" was the War of 1812 that took place 189 years earlier. In recalling the Civil War rather than the War of 1812 as the historical precedent for 9/11, Bush also wanted to invoke the South as the symbolic geography that he wished primarily to represent in his "crusade" against world evil.

6. R. W. B. Lewis, *The American Adam: Innocence, Tragedy and Tradition in the Nineteenth Century* (Chicago: University of Chicago Press, 1955); Perry Miller, *Errand into the Wilderness* (Cambridge, Mass.: Belknap Press of Harvard University, 1956); H. N. Smith, *Virgin Land*; Leo Marx, *The Machine in the Garden: Technology and the Pastoral Ideal in America* (London: Oxford University Press, 1964).

7. Virginia Carmichael has supplied Kenneth Burke's notion of a justifying myth with the interpretation that I just cited in *Framing History: The Rosenberg Story and the Cold War* (Minneapolis: University of Minnesota Press, 1993), 7.

8. Robyn Wiegman and I have elaborated upon the Myth and Symbol school as an aesthetic ideology of the centralizing postwar state in the "Introduction" to *Futures of American Studies* (Durham: Duke University Press, 2002). Although I have replicated some of the major claims of that essay, a more nuanced discussion of this dynamic can be found on pages 16–21 of that "Introduction."

9. Hellmann, *American Myth and the Legacy of Vietnam*, x.

10. David Noble, *The Death of the Nation: American Culture and the End of Exceptionalism* (Minneapolis: University of Minnesota Press, 2002), has recently described the formation of the field as a more or less conscious effort to construct an imaginary relation to postwar realities. "The first students of F. O.

Matthiessen and Perry Miller at Harvard—Henry Nash Smith, R. W. B. Lewis and Leo Marx—had the terrifying experience in the 1940's of having their narrative of an 'American' civilization separate from Europe suddenly change from reality to myth. They could not imagine, however, writing about the role of the United States in the universal marketplace.... They chose ... to spend their scholarly energy and love on the narrative of the separation of the 'American' nation from the time when progress resulted in the 'West.' ... These men preferred to return imaginatively to the crisis of Frederick Jackson Turner in the 1880's and 1890's rather than to admit that the national landscape had been displaced by an international capitalist marketplace in the 1940's" (17).

11. My understanding of the fantasy structure of war draws upon Renata Salecl's discussion of this topic in *Spoils of Freedom*, especially 15–19.

12. Alan Wolfe, "Anti-American Studies," *New Republic*, 10 February 2003, 25.

13. My discussion of the biopolitical settlement as well as my understanding of the state of emergency and the space of the exception is indebted to Giorgio Agamben's remarkable discussion of the relationship between forms of life and biopolitics in *Means without End: Notes on Politics* (Minneapolis: University of Minnesota Press, 2000).

14. Amy Kaplan, "Manifest Domesticity," in Pease and Wiegman, *Futures of American Studies*, 581–82.

15. The United States displayed its mastery of the art of imperial governance through the construction of highly contradictory domains of jurisdiction wherein ad hoc exemptions from the law on the basis of race and cultural difference resulted in the construction of exceptional spaces for exceptional peoples like those included within the phrase "domestic dependent nations" invented by Justice Marshall in *Worcester v. Georgia* (1831), and in the production of the stateless and kinless peoples who were brought into existence by Justice Taney's notion of "natal alienation" in *Dred Scott v. Sandford* (1856). When Justice Marshall described native tribes as "domestic dependent nations" voided of the right to the lands that they neither colonized nor cultivated, he intended that their condition of dependency be understood as the consequence of their lands having formerly been targeted for expropriation by European empires. This benchmark decision, which turned native peoples into surrogates for the European imperial powers to which the United States had positioned itself in opposition, became one of the defining principles of the U.S. imperial state. The trope of Manifest Destiny justified the state's policies of Indian removal by representing them as alternatives to European strategies of imperial colonization. After they were represented as the bearers of properties of alien imperial powers, Indians could not be nationalized. They were instead converted into racialized aliens.

16. In *The Terror Dream: Fear and Fantasy in Post-9/11 America* (New York: Metropolitan, 2007), Susan Faludi has written about the effects of this regression to the mentality of the colonial frontier as a spectacular regression to the era of Westward expansion. "We reacted to our trauma, in other words, not by interrogating but by cocooning ourselves in the celluloid chrysalis of the baby

boom's childhood. In the male version of that reverie, some nameless reflex had returned us to that 1950s badlands where conquest and triumph played and replayed in an infinite loop.... From deep within that dream world, our commander in chief issued remarks like 'We'll smoke him out' and 'Wanted: Dead or Alive,' our political candidates proved their double-barreled worthiness for post-9/11 office by brandishing guns on the campaign trail, our journalists cast city firefighters as tall-in-the-saddle cowboys patrolling a Wild West stage set, and our pundits proclaimed our nation's ability to vanquish 'barbarians' in a faraway land they dubbed 'Indian Country.' The retreat into a fantasized yesteryear was pervasive, from the morning of the televised attack (ABC news anchor Peter Jennings called the national electronic enclave 'the equivalent to a campfire in the days as the wagon trains were making their way westward') to the first post-9/11 supper at Camp David (the war cabinet was served a 'Wild West menu' of buffalo meat), to our invasion of Iraq (which tank crews from the Sixty-fourth Armor Regiment inaugurated with a 'Seminole Indian war dance') to our ongoing prosecution of the war on terror (which *Wall Street Journal* editor Max Boot equated with the small-scale 'savage wars' waged in the republic's earliest days and which *Atlantic Monthly* correspondent Robert Kaplan hailed as 'back to the days of fighting the Indians' and 'really about taming the frontier')" (4–5).

17. Agamben examines the transformation of politics into biopolitics through a reconsideration of Foucault's account of this mutation in the essay "Form-of-life," in *Means without End*, 3–14. See Agamben's discussion of *homo sacer* in ibid., 3–9.

18. This formulation derives from Agamben's discussion of the State of Exception in "What Is a Camp?" in *Means without End*, 43.

19. Agamben describes the prefigurations of the detainees in the Nazi camps with great eloquence in *Means without End*: "Inasmuch as its inhabitants have been stripped of every political status and reduced completely to naked life, the camp is also the most absolute biopolitical space that has ever been realized— a space in which power confronts nothing other than pure biological life without any mediation" (40).

20. My understanding of the empty or singular universal draws upon Slavoj Žižek's discussion of this concept in *The Ticklish Subject: The Absent Center of Political Ontology* (New York: Routledge, 1999), 187–239.

21. Jacques Rancière elaborates upon the importance of the phrase "the part of no part" to political contestations in *Disagreement: Politics and Philosophy* (Minneapolis: University of Minnesota Press, 1999), 1–60.

6. Antigone's Kin

1. Arif Dirlik discusses this process with great acuity in *Global Modernity: Modernity in the Age of Global Capitalism* (Boulder: Paradigm, 2007), 10–25.

2. The standard of acceptability for what counts as cruel, inhuman, and degrading treatment changes in response to changing circumstances. The structure of debate invoked a series of clauses from international treaties and agree-

ments to which the United States had been a signatory that valorized the violation of bodily rights negatively. Article 5 of the Universal Declaration of Human Rights reads: "No one shall be subjected to torture or to cruel, inhuman or degrading treatment or punishment." The 1984 Convention against Torture and Other Cruel, Inhuman or Degrading Treatment or Punishment defines torture as "any act by which severe pain or suffering, whether physical or mental, is intentionally inflicted on another person for such purposes as obtaining from him or a third person information or a confession." The 1984 Convention seemed to address the emergency state justification head on when it further declared that "No exceptional circumstances whatsoever, whether a state of war or a threat of war, internal political instability or any other public emergency, may be invoked as a justification of torture."

3. Susan Sontag, "Regarding the Torture of Others," *New York Times Magazine*, 23 May 2004. See http://donswaim.com/nytimes.sontag.html, 2.

4. *The Abu Ghraib Investigations: The Official Reports of the Independent Panel on the Shocking Prisoner Abuse in Iraq*, ed. Steven Strasser (New York: Public Affairs, 2004), designated as "Detainee Number 15." "These photographs were taken between 2145 and 2345 on 4 November 2003. Detainee-15 described a female making him stand on the box, telling him if he fell off he would be electrocuted, and a 'tall black man' as putting the wires on his fingers and penis" (132).

5. Sontag, "Regarding the Torture of Others," http://donswaim.com/nytimes.sontag.html.

6. In his lecture Tom Mitchell also proposed an imperial theme linking the historical occasion for both figures (MACS Symposium, Dartmouth College, July 21, 2009).

7. A photograph of this piece of Iraqi street art can be found in *Abu Ghraib: The Politics of Torture* (Berkeley: North Atlantic, 2004), 143.

8. In his essay "The Logic of Torture," in *Torture and Truth in America: Abu Ghraib and the War on Terror* (New York: New York Review of Books, 2004), 18, Mark Danner reports that in addition to the week-long course on Iraqi history, the Marine Corps distributed to its troops a pamphlet that spelled out the following codification of prohibited behaviors: 1. Do not shame or humiliate a man in public. Shaming a man will cause him and his family to be anti-Coalition. 2. The most important qualifier for shame is for a third party to witness the act. If you must do something likely to cause shame, remove the person from the view of others. 3. Shame is given by placing a hood over a detainee's head. Avoid this practice. 4. Placing a detainee on the ground or putting a foot on him implies you are God. This is one of the worst things you can do. The manual also explained that Arabs consider the following things unclean: 1. Feet or soles of feet. 2. Using the bathroom around others. Unlike marines who are used to open-air toilets, Arab men will not shower/use the bathroom together.

9. In his talk, Mitchell mentioned that Berkeley artist Guy Colwell reconfigured several of the Abu Ghraib photographs to reveal their resemblance to gay and lesbian liberationist practices. Barbara Ehrenreich discussed the ways

in which the photographs of Lynnde England disfigured feminist prerogatives in "Feminism's Assumptions Upended," in *Abu Ghraib: The Politics of Torture*, 65–70.

10. Gayatri Chakravorty Spivak, "Terror: A Speech after 9/11," *boundary 2* 31, no. 2 (Summer 2004), 91.

11. I am indebted to Tony Bogues for this insight into the relationship between liberation in the first world as a technology of oppression in another culture. This seems to me the crucial way in which Enlightenment ideals get linked to imperialism, which imposes those ideals as the rule of law.

12. Amy Goodman frequently brought Iraq veterans who expressed criticism of the U.S. war effort onto her *Democracy Now* television program. She reflects on the history of the gathering opposition to the war in Amy Goodman and David Goodman, *Static: Government Liars, Media Cheerleaders, and the People Who Fight Back* (New York: Hyperion, 2006).

13. Amy Goodman provides a fine account of the political significance of Cindy Sheehan's public drama that bears on this discussion in Goodman and Goodman, *Static*.

14. For an example of the kind of censorship directed against Cindy Sheehan, see *Letters to Cindy Sheehan: Messages to the Left on America's Noble Cause in Iraq*, by http://www.TownForumPress.com.

15. Amy Goodman devotes several chapters to these structures of censorship in Goodman and Goodman, *Static*.

16. Accounts of the change in the public attitude toward the war can be found in ibid.

17. See Cindy Sheehan, *Not One More Mother's Child* (Kihei, Hawaii: Koa Books, 2005), 71.

18. See ibid., 71–72.

19. Susan Faludi has correlated what I am calling the maternal imago of the state with what she has dubbed the mythical figure of the security mom who "seemed to have a life beyond the reality—in fact, independent of reality." To Faludi, the security mom was a character "crucial to the restoration of that larger American myth of invulnerability, and documenting her existence mattered less than mobilizing her image in our dream life." Faludi, *Terror Dream*, 162.

20. For the role played by the foreclosure of the maternal bond in the formation of the state, see Luce Irigaray, *This Sex Which Is Not One*, trans. Catherine Porter with Carolyn Burke (Ithaca, N.Y.: Cornell University Press, 1985). Throughout this account of kinship and Antigone's performance of an alternative I have drawn upon Judith Butler, *Antigone's Claim: Kinship Between Life and Death* (New York: Columbia University Press, 2000).

21. For a brilliant analysis of the relationship between this emotional compact and the state after 9/11, see Lauren Berlant, "The Epistemology of State Emotion," in *Dissent in Dangerous Times*, ed. Austin Sarat (Ann Arbor: University of Michigan Press, 2006), 46–78.

22. I am indebted to Renata Salecl, *Spoils of Freedom* , 32–37, for my understanding of founding words.

23. Slavoj Žižek explains Lacan's notion of "traversing the fantasy" in *Ticklish Subject*, 265–69.

24. Žižek elaborates on this notion in his engagement with Judith Butler's notion of passionate attachments in ibid., 247–300.

25. See ibid., 235.

26. See ibid., 182–200.

27. See ibid., 145 for a meditation on subjectivization to the Thing.

28. I have already mentioned Susan Faludi's account in *Terror Dream* of the return of this mythological figure. President Bush also officially recognized a group called Gold Star Mothers comprised of women who had lost sons in the Iraq War.

29. This line of speculation draws upon Judith Butler's discussion of Antigone and the law in *Antigone's Claim*, 2–27.

30. Ibid., 30–58.

31. Amy Goodman spells out some of the Bush administration's actions against Sheehan in Goodman and Goodman, *Static*. Also see John Nichols's essay from *The Nation*, 17 August 2005, and Arianna Huffington's August 13, 2005, post in Huffington Post. Both are archived at http://www.commondreams.org.

32. I drew these statistics from http://www.commondreams.org, August 15, 2005.

33. Benjamin, "Critique of Violence," 283. I am indebted to Giorgio Agamben, *State of Exception*, 51–57, for my understanding of the debate between Schmitt and Benjamin. See also Schmitt, *Concept of the Political*.

34. Benjamin, "Critique of Violence," 291.

35. "Theses on the Philosophy of History," in Walter Benjamin, *Illuminations*, ed. and with an introduction by Hannah Arendt, trans. Harry Zohn (New York: Schocken Books, 1988), 263.

36. Ibid., 261.

37. Ibid., 267.

38. Antonio Negri, *Insurgencies: Constituent Power and the Modern State*, trans. Maurizia Boscagli (Minneapolis: University of Minnesota Press, 2000), 21.

39. See Barack Obama, *The Audacity of Hope: Thoughts on Reclaiming the American Dream* (New York: Crown, 2006), 295.

40. As if inspired to add to the series, Slavoj Žižek, *Violence: Six Sideways Reflections* (New York: Picador, 2008), has drawn parallels between the looting after Katrina hit on August 29, 2005, and the aftermath of the shelling of Kabul and Baghdad. He arrived at these associations after he watched the TV reporters compare events in New Orleans to images from third world cities descending into chaos during a civil war (Kabul, Baghdad, Somalia, Liberia...)—and this accounts for the true surprise of the New Orleans eclipse: "What we were used to seeing happening THERE was now taking place HERE" (93–94).

41. Barack Obama, *Dreams from My Father: A Story of Race and Inheritance* (New York: Times Books, 1995).

Index

Aberly, Rachel, 232n4, 232n6
Abu Ghraib, 37, 184–92, 194, 196, 237n4, 237n9
Adams, David Keith, 216n9
Afghanistan, 171–72
Agamben, Georgio, 184, 218n22, 235n13, 236nn17–19, 239n33
Al-Azmeh, Aziz, 227n2
Alexander, J. Robert, 217n10
Althusser, Louis, 88, 226n23
American exceptionalism, 70; and the American Revolution, 77; in American studies, 11–13, 162–66; and apocalyptic imagination, 78; history of, 7–10, 23–26; Janus face of, 140–41; as political doctrine, 11–13; as primal scene, 14–20; and Puritans, 76–77; shifts of meaning, 8–9. *See also* state fantasy
Ames, Aldrich, 94
Anderson, Benedict, 126
Ashcroft, John, 130, 151, 177

Bailie, Gil, 225n7
Barber, Benjamin, 227n4
Baudrillard, Jean, 222n3
Bauman, Zygmunt, 90–91, 216n6, 226n21
Bell, Daniel, 11, 217n13
Bellah, Robert, 230n14
Benjamin, Walter, 38, 138, 206–7, 232n8, 239nn33–35
Berlant, Lauren, 220–21n30, 238n21
Birnbaum, Norman, 231n27
Bogues, Tony, 238n11
Boot, Max, 235–36n16
Brennan, Timothy, 224n1, 228n9
Burke, Kenneth, 164, 234n7
Burns, Ken, 73
Bush, George H. W., 37, 50, 223n15; and New World Order, 4, 36, 40–44, 68–69, 154; and Persian Gulf War, 46–48
Bush, George W., 180–83, 184, 190, 200–201, 233n11, 234n3, 234n5, 239n28; as Creon, 37, 198–99;

241

Donald E. Pease is professor of English and Avalon Foundation Chair
of the Humanities at Dartmouth College.